Lecture Notes in Computer

Commenced Publication in 1973
Founding and Former Series Editors:
Gerhard Goos, Juris Hartmanis, and Jan van Lee... .. ..

Mercedes G. Merayo
Edgardo Montes de Oca (Eds.)

Testing Software and Systems

26th IFIP WG 6.1 International Conference, ICTSS 2014
Madrid, Spain, September 23-25, 2014
Proceedings

 Springer

Volume Editors

Mercedes G. Merayo
Universidad Complutense de Madrid
Facultad de Informática
Dpto Sistems Informáticos y Computación
Prof. Jose García Santesmases s/n
28040 Madrid, Spain
E-mail: mgmerayo@fdi.ucm.es

Edgardo Montes de Oca
Montimage
39 rue Bobillot
75013 Paris, France
E-mail: edgardo.montesdeoca@montimage.com

ISSN 0302-9743   e-ISSN 1611-3349
ISBN 978-3-662-44856-4   e-ISBN 978-3-662-44857-1
DOI 10.1007/978-3-662-44857-1
Springer Heidelberg New York Dordrecht London

Library of Congress Control Number: 2014948209

LNCS Sublibrary: SL 2 – Programming and Software Engineering

Typesetting: Camera-ready by author, data conversion by Scientific Publishing Services, Chennai, India

Printed on acid-free paper

Springer is part of Springer Science+Business Media (www.springer.com)

Preface

This volume contains the proceedings of the 26th IFIP International Conference on Testing Software and Systems, ICTSS 2014. The conference was held in Madrid, Spain, during September 23–25, 2014. The purpose of the ICTSS conference is to bring together researchers, developers, testers, and users from industry to review, discuss, and learn about new approaches, concepts, theories, methodologies, tools, and experiences in the field of testing of software and systems.

We received 36 submissions. After a careful reviewing process, the Program Committee accepted 11 regular papers and 6 short papers. Therefore, the acceptance rate of the conference stayed close to 47%. The conference program was enriched by the keynotes of Franz Wotawa, on "On the boundary between testing and fault localization", and Salvador Ignacio Folgado Bellido, on "Advanced solutions for automation of functional test".

Several people contributed to the success of ICTSS 2014. We are grateful to the Steering Committee for its support. Its chair, Professor Rob Hierons, deserves a special mention for his guidance and valuable advice. We would like to thank the general chair Manuel Núñez, the Program Committee, and the additional reviewers, for their work on selecting the papers. The process of reviewing and selecting papers was significantly simplified through using EasyChair. Finally, the proceedings have been published through Springer-Verlag and we are grateful for the assistance provided by Alfred Hofmann and Anna Kramer.

On behalf of the ICTSS organizers, we welcome all attendants to the conference and hope that you find the conference's program useful, interesting, and challenging.

September 2014

Mercedes G. Merayo
Edgardo Montes de Oca

Organization

Program Committee

Rui Abreu	University of Porto, Portugal
Bernhard K. Aichernig	TU Graz, Austria
Fevzi Belli	University Paderborn and Izmir Institute of Technology, Turkey
Gregor Bochmann	University of Ottawa, Canada
Ana Cavalli	Institut Mines-Telecom/Telecom SudParis, France
Byoungju Choi	Ewha Womans University, Korea
Khaled El-Fakih	American University of Sharjah, UAE
Mercedes G. Merayo	Universidad Complutense de Madrid, Spain
Angelo Gargantini	University of Bergamo, Italy
Vahid Garousi	Atilim University, Turkey University of Calgary, Canada
Wolfgang Grieskamp	Google, USA
Klaus Havelund	Jet Propulsion Laboratory, California Institute of Technology, USA
Rob Hierons	Brunel University, UK
Teruo Higashino	Osaka University, Japan
Dieter Hogrefe	University of Göttingen, Germany
Guy-Vincent Jourdan	University of Ottawa, Canada
Thierry Jéron	Inria Rennes - Bretagne Atlantique, France
Ferhat Khendek	Concordia University, Canada
Moez Krichen	REDCAD Research Unit, Tunisia
Pascale Le Gall	Ecole Centrale Paris, France
Bruno Legeard	Smartesting & Université de Franche-Comté, France
Hareton Leung	Hong Kong Polytechnic University, China
Keqin Li	SAP Product Security Research, France
Wissam Mallouli	Montimage, France
Karl Meinke	Royal Institute of Technology (KTH) Stockholm, Sweden
Zoltan Micskei	Budapest University of Technology and Economics, Hungary
Edgardo Montes de Oca	Montimage, France
Jan Peleska	University of Bremen, Germany
Alexandre Petrenko	CRIM, Canada
Andrea Polini	University of Camerino, Italy
Ina Schieferdecker	FU Berlin/Fraunhofer FOKUS, Germany
Holger Schlingloff	Fraunhofer FOKUS, Germany

Kenji Suzuki	Kennisbron Co., Ltd, Japan
Jan Tretmans	TNO - Embedded Systems Innovation, The Netherlands
Andreas Ulrich	Siemens AG, Germany
Hasan Ural	University of Ottawa, Canada
Margus Veanes	Microsoft Research, USA
Cesar Viho	IRISA/University of Rennes 1, France
Tanja E.J. Vos	Universidad Politecnica de Valencia, Spain
Bachar Wehbi	Montimage, France
Hüsnü Yenigün	Sabanci University, Turkey
Nina Yevtushenko	Tomsk State University, Russia
Cemal Yilmaz	Sabanci University, Turkey

Additional Reviewers

Chai, Ming
Gromov, Maxim
Hafaiedh, Khaled B.
Kondratyeva, Olga
Kushik, Natalia
La, Vinh Hoa

Lackner, Hartmut
Mirtaheri, Seyed M.
Nuñez, Manuel
Rivera, Diego
Schwarzl, Christian
Turker, Uraz Cengiz

Invited Talk
(Abstracts)

On the Boundary between Testing and Fault Localization

Franz Wotawa

Graz University of Technology

Abstract. Debugging comprises the activities of fault detection, localization, and correction, which we usually consider to be carried out separately during program development. In testing and here in particular automated test case generation, the question is more on how to generate effective tests that most likely reveal bugs instead of how such tests might help to locate and fix a bug once revealed. In this talk I discuss the relationship between testing and fault localization. Besides giving an introduction into the current state of the art in debugging, I introduce a method for computing tests in order to facilitate debugging. The key idea behind the method is to construct test cases that allow distinguishing bug candidates. In the talk I introduce the basic ideas, empirical results obtained, and focus also on current research questions that has to be tackled in order to further increase automation in fault localization and correction.

Advanced Solutions for Automation of Functional Test

Salvador Ignacio Folgado Bellido

Bull Spain S.A.

Abstract. It is common knowledge that the most efficient solution to obtain high quality systems is to perform test automation. However, does not it sound like unfinished business, unresolved? Is it a utopia to achieve a high degree of test automation? Are we creating a new problem of developing and maintaining evidence? What actual the coverage that we have or that we can get? And what about mobile devices, smartphone, tablets? 80% of organizations attempting to address automation of functional tests fail. The main reason is that the acquisition of a test automation tool does not solve the problem (actually, it generates a new one!). This objective must be addressed based on a sustainable strategy that addresses the reality of the organization (changing their requirements, more frequent deployments, business oriented). This talk discusses Bullšs approach on how to carry out automation of functional tests, based on the following principles: reusability, consistency and productivity. I will present data and results of projects (case studies) in order to draw the best strategic approach to functional test automation and also will address the future of testing related to new technologies and platforms.

Table of Contents

Testing Methodologies

A Framework for Genetic Test-Case Generation for WS-BPEL
Compositions.. 1
Antonia Estero-Botaro, Antonio García-Domínguez,
Juan José Domínguez-Jiménez,
Francisco Palomo-Lozano, and Inmaculada Medina-Bulo

Evaluating Normalization Functions with Search Algorithms for Solving
OCL Constraints.. 17
Shaukat Ali and Tao Yue

Lookahead-Based Approaches for Minimizing Adaptive Distinguishing
Sequences... 32
Uraz Cengiz Türker, Tonguç Ünlüyurt, and Hüsnü Yenigün

Plan It! Automated Security Testing Based on Planning 48
Franz Wotawa and Josip Bozic

Minimum Number of Test Paths for Prime Path and Other Structural
Coverage Criteria 63
Anurag Dwarakanath and Aruna Jankiti

Tools and Frameworks

An Approach to Derive Usage Models Variants for Model-Based
Testing 80
Hamza Samih, Hélène Le Guen, Ralf Bogusch, Mathieu Acher, and
Benoit Baudry

AUTSEG: Automatic Test Set Generator for Embedded Reactive
Systems 97
Mariem Abdelmoula, Daniel Gaffe, and Michel Auguin

Well-Defined Coverage Metrics for the Glass Box Test 113
Rainer Schmidberger

Industrial Experiences

Cutting Time-to-Market by Adopting Automated Regression Testing
in a Simulated Environment 129
Manuel Palmieri, Antonio Cicchetti, and Anders Öberg

Testing Robotized Paint System Using Constraint Programming:
An Industrial Case Study   145
   Morten Mossige, Arnaud Gotlieb, and Hein Meling

What Characterizes a Good Software Tester? – A Survey in Four
Norwegian Companies   161
   Anca Deak

Short Contributions

A Customizable Monitoring Infrastructure for Hardware/Software
Embedded Systems.   173
   Martial Chabot and Laurence Pierre

Towards Testing Self-organizing, Adaptive Systems   180
   Benedikt Eberhardinger, Hella Seebach, Alexander Knapp, and
   Wolfgang Reif

Design of Prioritized N-Wise Testing   186
   Eun-Hye Choi, Takashi Kitamura, Cyrille Artho, and Yutaka Oiwa

Change Detection System for the Maintenance of Automated Testing . . .   192
   Miroslav Bures

On Code Coverage of Extended FSM Based Test Suites:
An Initial Assessment   198
   Khaled El-Fakih, Tariq Salameh, and Nina Yevtushenko

Search-Based Testing for Embedded Telecom Software with Complex
Input Structures   205
   Kivanc Doganay, Sigrid Eldh, Wasif Afzal, and Markus Bohlin

Author Index   211

A Framework for Genetic Test-Case Generation for WS-BPEL Compositions

Antonia Estero-Botaro, Antonio García-Domínguez,
Juan José Domínguez-Jiménez, Francisco Palomo-Lozano,
and Inmaculada Medina-Bulo

Departamento de Ingeniería Informática, Universidad de Cádiz,
C/Chile 1, 11002, Cádiz, España
{antonia.estero,antonio.garciadominguez}@uca.es
{juanjose.dominguez,francisco.palomo,inmaculada.medina}@uca.es

Abstract. Search-based testing generates test cases by encoding an adequacy criterion as the fitness function that drives a search-based optimization algorithm. Genetic algorithms have been successfully applied in search-based testing: while most of them use adequacy criteria based on the structure of the program, some try to maximize the mutation score of the test suite.

This work presents a genetic algorithm for generating a test suite for mutation testing. The algorithm adopts several features from existing bacteriological algorithms, using single test cases as individuals and keeping generated individuals in a memory. The algorithm can optionally use automated seeding when producing the first population, by taking into account interesting constants in the source code.

We have implemented this algorithm in a framework and we have applied it to a WS-BPEL composition, measuring to which extent the genetic algorithm improves the initial random test suite. We compare our genetic algorithm, with and without automated seeding, to random testing.

1 Introduction

Search-based testing [10] consists of generating test data according to a certain adequacy criterion, by encoding it as the fitness function that drives a search-based optimization algorithm. Evolutionary testing is a field of search-based testing that uses evolutionary algorithms to guide the search. The global searches performed by these algorithms are usually, but not always, implemented as genetic algorithms (GAs) [9,11].

Using GAs for generating test data dates back to the work by Xanthakis et al. [22]. Since then, various alternative approaches for generating test data have been proposed, both using GAs and other evolutionary techniques. Mantere and Alander [13] published a review of the works that applied evolutionary algorithms to software testing at the time.

M.G. Merayo and E. Montes de Oca (Eds.): ICTSS 2014, LNCS 8763, pp. 1–16, 2014.
© IFIP International Federation for Information Processing 2014

Search-based testing has been mostly used for structural test data generation, with branch coverage as the most common adequacy criterion. The survey by McMinn [15] classified evolutionary algorithms for structural test data generation by the type of information used by the fitness function.

Mutation testing [19] is a testing technique injecting simple faults in the program under test through the use of *mutation operators*. As a result, we obtain *mutants*: variants of the original program. The original program and its mutants are executed on a given test-suite. When the output of a mutant for a test-case does not agree with the output of the original program for the same test-case, the mutant has been *killed* by that test-case and, so, it is *dead*. This means that the test-case has served a purpose: detecting the fault that is present in the mutant. If the output is always the same as the original program for every test case in the test-suite, then the mutant remains *alive*. When this is always the case, regardless the input, the mutant is said to be *equivalent* to the original program.

Mutation testing uses the *mutation score* to measure the quality of the test-suite. The mutation score is the ratio of the number of mutants killed by the test-suite to the number of non-equivalent mutants. Obtaining test-suites with mutation scores in the 50%–70% range can be relatively easy, but increasing these scores to the 90%–100% can be very hard. For this reason, developing new techniques for generating test-suites is currently a very active field of study [4].

Several evolutionary approaches for generating test data for mutation testing already exist. Baudry et al. [4] compared genetic and bacteriological algorithms for generating test data for a mutation testing system. Likewise, May et al. [14] compared genetic and immunological algorithms for the same purpose. In both cases, the alternative worked better than the GA.

This work presents an evolutionary technique for test-case generation using a GA for a mutation testing system. Our GA adopts some features from the bacteriological algorithm proposed by Baudry et al. We built a framework to apply it to WS-BPEL (Web Service Business Process Execution Language [18]) compositions. WS-BPEL was targeted because testing service-oriented software is not an easy task, and this language is an OASIS standard and an industrial-strength alternative in its field. WS-BPEL compositions may build new WS from other WS from all around the world, while using unconventional and advanced programming concepts as well. As the relevance and economic impact of service compositions grow, the need for efficient and effective testing techniques for this kind of software increases.

This work is structured as follows. Section 2 introduces the WS-BPEL language and the basic concepts behind GAs. Section 3 discusses related work. Section 4 describes the overall design of the GA for generating test-suites. Section 5 describes how the GA can be applied to WS-BPEL compositions and shows the results obtained by the GA generating tests for a particular WS-BPEL composition. Finally, we present our conclusions and future work in Section 6.

```
<flow> ↩ Structured activity
  <links> ↩ Container
    <link name="checkFlight-To-BookFlight" ↩ Attribute /> ↩ Element
  </links>
  <invoke name="checkFlight" ... > ↩ Basic activity
    <sources> ↩ Container
      <source linkName="checkFlight-To-BookFlight" ↩ Attribute /> ↩ Element
    </sources>
  </invoke>
  <invoke name="checkHotel" ... />
  <invoke name="checkRentCar" ... />
  <invoke name="bookFlight" ... >
    <targets> ↩ Container
      <target linkName="checkFlight-To-BookFlight" /> ↩ Element
    </targets>
  </invoke>
</flow>
```

Fig. 1. WS-BPEL 2.0 activity sample

2 Background

2.1 A Brief Introduction to WS-BPEL

WS-BPEL 2.0 is an OASIS standard [18] and an industrial-strength programming language for WS compositions. WS-BPEL is an XML-based language allows one to specify the behavior of a business process based on its interactions with other WS. The major building blocks of a WS-BPEL process are *activities*. There are two types: basic and structured activities. Basic activities only perform one purpose (receiving a message from a partner, sending a message to a partner, assigning to a variable, etc.). Structured activities define the business logic and may contain other activities. Activities may have both attributes and a set of containers associated to them. Of course, these containers can include elements with their own attributes too. We can illustrate this with the example skeleton in Figure 1.

WS-BPEL provides concurrency and synchronization between activities. An example is the `flow` activity, which launches a set of activities in parallel and allows to specify the synchronization conditions between them. In the aforementioned example we can see a `flow` activity that invokes three WS in parallel: `checkFlight`, `checkHotel`, and `checkRentCar`. Moreover, there is another WS, `bookFlight`, that will be invoked upon `checkFlight` completion. This synchronization between activities is achieved by establishing a `link`, so that the target activity of the link will be eventually executed only after the source activity of the link has been completed.

2.2 Genetic Algorithms

Genetic algorithms [9,11] are probabilistic search techniques based on the theory of evolution and natural selection proposed by Charles Darwin, which Herbert Spencer summarized as "survival of the fittest".

GAs work with a population of solutions, known as *individuals*, and process them in parallel. Throughout successive generations, GAs perform a selection process to improve the population, so they are ideal for optimization purposes. In this sense, GAs favor the best individuals and generate new ones through the recombination and mutation of information from existing ones. The strengths of GAs are their flexibility, simplicity and ability for hybridization. Among their weaknesses are their stochastic and heuristic nature, and the difficulties in handling restrictions.

There is no a single type of GA, but rather several families that mostly differ in how individuals are encoded (binary, floating point, permutation, . . .), and how the population is renewed in each generation. Generational GAs [9] replace the entire population in each generation. However, steady-state or incremental GAs [21] replace only a few (one or two) members of the population in each generation. Finally, in parallel fine-grained GAs [17] the population is distributed into different nodes.

As each individual represents a solution to the problem to be solved, its *fitness* measures the quality of this solution. The average population fitness will be maximized along the different generations produced by the algorithm. The encoding scheme and the individual fitness used are highly dependent on the problem to solve, and they are the only link between the GA and the problem [16].

GAs use two types of operators: selection and reproduction. *Selection operators* select individuals in a population for reproduction attending to the following rule: the higher the fitness of an individual, the higher the probability of being selected. *Reproduction operators* generate the new individuals in the population: *crossover operators* generate two new individuals or offspring, from two preselected individuals, their parents. The offspring inherit part of the information stored in both parents. On the other hand, *mutation operators* aim to alter the information stored in a given individual. The design of these operators heavily depends on the encoding scheme used.

Please, notice that the above mutation operators are related to the GA and are different from those for mutation testing.

3 Related Work

Evolutionary algorithms in general and GAs in particular have been widely used in various fields of software engineering, and especially so in software testing. A large part of the works on search-based testing used structural criteria to generate test cases.

Bottaci [5] was the first to design a fitness function for a GA that generated test data for a mutation testing system. This fitness function is based on the three conditions listed by Offutt [20]: *reachability*, *necessity* and *sufficiency*. Being the first of its kind, it has been used in many works, even with other evolutionary algorithms. As an example, Ayari [3] used it with ant colonies.

Baudry et al. [4] have compared GAs and bacteriological algorithms for generating test cases for a mutation system. The main issues of GAs were slow convergence and the need to apply the mutation genetic operator more often. The main difference between the bacteriological algorithm and the GA is that it stores the best individuals and that it does not use the crossover operator. In addition, individuals now represent individual test cases instead of entire test suites. This alternative approach is shown to converge much faster than the previous one, producing higher mutation scores in less generations.

Our approach is based on a GA that has been modified to obtain some of the advantages of a bacteriological algorithm. The individuals of our GA are individual test cases and both crossovers and mutations are performed. We do not need to use a separate store for the best individuals, as we store all individuals in a memory to preserve the useful information that may reside in individuals with low fitness scores. Our fitness function differs from that in Baudry et al., as it takes into account both the number of mutants killed by the test-case and how many other test cases killed those mutants.

May et al. [14] presented two evolutionary approaches for obtaining test cases for a mutation testing system: one based on an immune approach, and a GA. The algorithm based on the immune approach iteratively evolved a population of antibodies (individual test cases), looking for those that killed at least one mutant not killed by any previous antibody. The selected antibodies were added to the internal set which would become the final output of the process.

4 Approach

We advocate an approach based on a GA whose goal is generating test cases killing the mutants generated from the program under test. Figure 2 illustrates the architecture underlying the test generation procedure. The test-case generator consists of two main components: the preprocessor and the GA.

The preprocessor can produce all the information required by the GA to generate the test cases from the original program, providing the GA with an initial population of randomly generated test cases, completed with some test cases generated by automated seeding. The actual operations run by the preprocessor depend on the particular programming language in which the program under test is written. Please see Section 5.1 for the specific details.

The test cases produced in each generation are executed against all the mutants. The fitness of each test-case is computed by comparing the behavior of each mutant and the original program on it. This guides the search of the GA. As the GA completes its execution, a final test-suite is obtained.

The goal of a test-case generator is producing an optimal test-suite. We propose a GA with a design based on several features of bacteriological algorithms. The individuals of our GA are individual test cases. The GA will gradually improve the initial test-suite, generation by generation, using a memory similar to

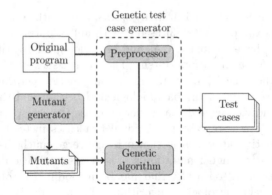

Fig. 2. Architecture of the test-case generator

a *hall of fame*. The memory will store all the test cases produced so far. Therefore, the output of the GA will not be its last generation, but rather all the test cases in the memory. This memory plays the same role as the memory used in the bacteriological algorithm proposed by Baudry et al. [4].

Next, we discuss the particular choices that characterize this GA, paying particular attention to how they contribute to produce good test cases.

Encoding of individuals. Each individual encodes one test-case. As test cases are highly dependent on the program under test, the structure of individuals should be flexible enough to adapt to any program. In order to solve this problem, each individual will contain an array of key-value pairs, where the key is the *type* of a program variable and the *value* is a particular literal of the corresponding type. Figure 3 illustrates how individuals are encoded.

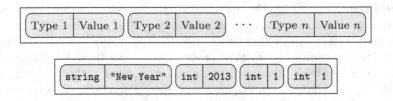

Fig. 3. Encoding of individuals

Fitness of individuals. Individual fitness is a function of the number of mutants killed by the corresponding test-case. However, though tempting, just taking the number of killed mutants per test-case is not an appropriate fitness metric. Let us consider specialized test-cases able to kill just one mutant which can not be killed by any other test-case in the population. A metric based only in the number of kills would assign this important test-cases a low fitness.

For this reason, an additional variable has to be taken into account when assessing the fitness of individuals: the number of test-cases killing the same mutant. This is key in both distinguishing individuals with the same number of kills and being fair in the evaluation of specialized test-cases.

Let M be the set of mutants generated from the original program and T be the set of test-cases in a given population. The fitness function is computed from the *execution matrix*, $E = [e_{ij}]$, where e_{ij} is the result of comparing the execution of the original program versus the execution of mutant $m_j \in M$ on test-case $t_i \in T$: $e_{ij} = 0$ when no difference can be found, while $e_{ij} = 1$ if m_j was killed by t_i. We define the fitness of individual t_i as:

$$f(t_i) = \sum_{j=1}^{|M|} \frac{e_{ij}}{\sum_{k=1}^{|T|} e_{kj}} \qquad (1)$$

Initial Population. We have implemented two ways of generating the initial population at the beginning of the execution of the GA:

1. The initial population corresponds to valid random data.
2. The initial population corresponds to valid random data with additional test-cases where some components are replaced by constants of matching types found in the source code. This approach is similar to those proposed in [1], [2], and [8]. We have named this approach *automated seeding*.

Generations. The test-case generator is based on a generational GA in which the population of the next generation consists of offspring produced from pairs of individuals of the population of the previous generation by the genetic operations of crossover and mutation.

The selection scheme determines the way that individuals are chosen for haploid reproduction, and eventually mutation, depending on their fitness. We select individuals with the roulette wheel method designed by Goldberg [9]. Therefore, we make selection probability proportional to fitness.

Algorithm 1 illustrates how crossover and mutation operators can be applied to generate a pair of *offspring* from the current *population*. We assume that p_c is the crossover probability, that p_m is the probability of mutation, and that *random-uniform*(a, b) produces a random number uniformly distributed in the real interval $[a, b)$. This procedure is iterated until a new population of identical size is reached. New populations will be generated until a given termination condition is met.

In a whole population of size n, crossover contributes a total of np_c individuals. As mutation does not alter the number of individuals at all, $n(1 - p_c)$ selected individuals remain unchanged to maintain the population size constant.

Crossover Operator. The crossover genetic operator exchanges the components of parents to produce two offspring. We use one-point crossover, in which the point is randomly chosen using a uniform distribution. Figure 4 shows how crossover is performed on a pair of individuals.

▶ *Selection with Goldberg's roulette-wheel method.*
parents ← *select-parents*(*population*)
▶ *Crossover with probability* p_c.
if *random-uniform*(0, 1) < p_c **then**
    offspring ← *do-crossover*(*parents*)
else
    offspring ← *parents*
end if
▶ *Mutation with probability* p_m.
if *random-uniform*(0, 1) < p_m **then**
    offspring ← *do-mutation*(*offspring*)
end if
return *offspring*

Algorithm 1. Offspring generation

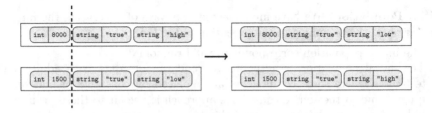

Fig. 4. Application of the crossover operator

Mutation Operator. The mutation genetic operator changes the *value* field of one component in an individual. The actual change will depend on its data type. For instance, a *float* value v is mutated into $\hat{v}$ using the following formula:

$$\hat{v} = v + s \cdot \frac{r}{p_m} \tag{2}$$

where s is randomly chosen between -1 or 1 and r is a parameter which modulates the change of v. For instance, if $r = 1000$, v may be incremented or decremented by up to $1000/p_m$. To summarize: v undergoes a perturbation that may be positive or negative, depending on the value of s. This perturbation is proportional to the inverse of p_m: as mutations become less common, perturbations are larger.

Values of type *string* are mutated by replacing them with a new value.

When mutating *list* values, the operator randomly decides (with equal probabilities) whether to mutate its length or mutate an element picked at random. The length l of the list is mutated into a new length $\hat{l}$ as follows:

$$\hat{l} = random\text{-}uniform(0, 1) \cdot \frac{l}{p_m} \tag{3}$$

Finally, *tuple* values are mutated by picking one of its elements at random, as their lengths are fixed.

Termination. Termination conditions are checked on each generation after computing the fitness of the individuals. Our GA implements four termination conditions that can be combined or used in isolation: maximum number of generations, percentage of mutants killed, stagnation of maximum fitness, and stagnation of average fitness.

5   Application to WS-BPEL

In order to evaluate our approach we have implemented a framework for WS-BPEL compositions. By design, the framework encapsulates all the language-specific (in this case, WS-BPEL-specific) details in a component known as the *Preprocessor*. Mutants are generated, executed, and evaluated using our mutation testing tool for WS-BPEL, MuBPEL [7], which incorporates the mutation operators defined by Estero et al. [6].

5.1   Preprocessor

A test-case for a WS-BPEL composition consists of the messages that need to be exchanged among the various partners in a business process: the client, the composition itself and the external services invoked by the composition. Generating test-cases automatically requires knowing the structure of the messages that constitute these test-cases.

In order to obtain the test-case file used by the GA as the initial population, an *Analyzer* produces a message catalog from the WSDL documents describing the public interfaces of the WS-BPEL composition. The message catalog contains a set of templates that can generate the required messages. Each template declares the variables used in it and their types. From this message catalog, a specification of the test data format is produced. This specification is used by the random test generator in the framework to produce a test data file.

We will use the *LoanApproval* composition [18] to illustrate these steps. This composition simulates a loan-approval service in which customers request a loan of a certain amount. Whether the loan is approved or denied depends on the requested amount and the risk level associated to the customer. Two external WS are used: the assessor service and the approval service. When the requested amount is modest (less than or equal to 10000 monetary units) the assessor WS is invoked to assess the risk presented by the customer. If the risk is low, the loan is immediately approved. In any other case, that is, large loans or high-risk customers, the decision is delegated to the approval WS.

The *LoanApproval* composition uses three WSDL files: one for each of the external WS and another for the composition itself. From these files, the *Analyzer* obtains the message catalogs describing the variables from which the messages exchanged between the composition and its partners can be generated. The *LoanApproval* composition uses a single input variable named *req_ amount* of type *int*. The approval service is invoked by the WS-BPEL composition, and its output is controlled by the Boolean variable *ap_ reply*. The assessor service is also invoked by the composition, and its output variable *as_reply* accepts a *string* value between "high" or "low" which just represents the estimated risk.

Figure 5 shows the test data format specification that was extracted from the message catalog and that will be used to generate the test-cases. It is written in a domain-specific language used by the random test generator in the framework, which can produce files such as the one shown in Figure 6. This file shows seven test cases. Variable *req_amount* is set to 54907 in the first test case, 103324 in the second test-case and so on. Variables *ap_reply* and *as_reply* contain the replies to be sent from the mockups of the approver and the assessor services, respectively, and can take the values "true" or "false" and "high" or "low". The special value "silent" indicates that the mockup will not reply.

```
typedef int      (min = 0, max = 200000)                    Quantity;
typedef string (values = { "true", "false", "silent" }) ApReply;
typedef string (values = { "low",  "high",  "silent" }) AsReply;

Quantity req_amount;
ApReply  ap_reply;
AsReply  as_reply;
```

Fig. 5. Specification of the data used to build messages for the *LoanApproval* composition

```
#set($req_amount = [54907,    103324,   175521,   122707,  160892, 115354, 130785])
#set($ap_reply   = ["false", "silent", "false", "false", "true", "true", "silent"])
#set($as_reply   = ["high",  "silent", "low",   "high",  "low",  "low",  "high"])
```

Fig. 6. Test data file for the *LoanApproval* composition

Figure 7 shows a potential individual for the *LoanApproval* composition. We can see that a test-case for this composition consists of one component of type *int* and two *string* components that correspond to the variables *req_amount*, *ap_reply* and *as_reply* respectively. These were shown in Figure 6 as well.

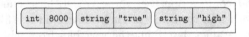

Fig. 7. Individual representing a test-case for the *LoanApproval* composition

5.2   A Case Study: The Loan Approval Composition

In this section, we will conduct several experiments to provide answers to the following research questions:

RQ1. *How much does the GA improve the quality of the initial test suite?* The initial population of the GA is randomly generated. We use three quality metrics to compare the initial population with the test-suite produced by the GA: mutation score, sentence coverage and condition/decision coverage.

RQ2. *Are the improvements just a consequence of the greater size of the final test-suite?* The GA is a test-case generator. As such, the test suite generated can be much greater than the initial test-suite. Thus, it could be more powerful just because of its size. We compare the test suites produced by the GA with randomly generated test-suites of the same size, using the same metrics employed in RQ1.

We will use the *LoanApproval* composition from Section 5.1 to answer the proposed research questions. This composition has 154 LOC, it generates 90 mutants, 2 mutants are invalid, and 9 mutants are equivalent.[1]

We can observe that BPEL compositions tend to be smaller than traditional programs in the sense that they define the logic of the composition of the external WS or partners, while the bulk of the code is in the WS themselves. Therefore, the number of mutants obtained is comparatively much lower than in traditional programming languages.

Next we will describe the experimental procedure used to answer the research questions and summarize the results obtained.

Since the initial population of the GA is randomly generated, results could largely vary from one execution to another. In order to alleviate this, we decided to select as the initial population a good representative of possible initial populations through these steps:

1. Population sizes were defined.
2. Thirty random test-suites were generated, with sizes matching each population size.
3. Test-suites were run against the original composition and their mutants to measure their mutation scores, sentence coverages, and condition/decision coverages.[2]
4. Medians for the quality metrics were computed.
5. A test-suite with median mutation score was selected.

The result of this process is a typical test-suite, which has been generated at random, but it is unbiased. Thus, it is a good candidate for initial population in our experiments.

---

[1] Equivalent mutants have been manually detected by inspecting the source code of surviving mutants.

[2] Sentence and condition/decision coverages have been computed as the percentage of killed mutants from those generated by a sentence coverage mutation operator and a condition/decision mutation operator, respectively.

Regarding population sizes, it is well known that a GA is likely to find better solutions when the population size is greater. But bigger population sizes demand more computational resources to find those solutions. However, Krishnakumar [12] found that a population size of 10 individuals can produce similar convergence rates with a tailored GA.

Since the *LoanApproval* composition produces 90 mutants, a test suite might need up to 90 test-cases to kill them all, though much fewer test cases will usually suffice. For this reason, we defined population sizes in terms of percentages of the total number of mutants. Percentages of 15%, 20%, and 25% were selected as candidate values to produce small populations still having more than 10 individuals.

As to the number of executions, we decided to use 30 executions for each population size. Therefore, 30 different seeds were employed to generate random data for 30 different executions.

Table 1 shows the values of the three metrics for the selected test-suite (the random initial test-suite) and for the final test-suite produced by the GA, with and without automated seeding. These are the medians of all the values produced by the 30 executions for each population size. The configuration parameters for

Table 1. Quality metrics for the initial test-suite (random) and the test-suites generated by the GA. In columns: MS are mutation scores, SC are sentence coverages, and CDC are condition/decision coverages. Coverages are measured as percentages.

Pop. size	RANDOM			GA			GA (AUT. SEEDING)		
	MS	SC	CDC	MS	SC	CDC	MS	SC	CDC
15%	0.72	75.0	75.0	0.96	100.0	100.0	0.99	100.0	100.0
20%	0.72	75.0	75.0	0.96	100.0	100.0	0.99	100.0	100.0
25%	0.72	75.0	75.0	0.96	100.0	100.0	0.99	100.0	100.0

the GA are shown in Table 2. We set p_m to 10%, as it is also suggested by Baudry et al. [4]. In agreement with Baudry's results, it was easy to obtain a mutation score within the 50%–70% range: in this particular case, the mutation score of the initial test-suite was 72%. Even without automated seeding, the three quality metrics have been considerably improved by the GA: mutation score increases from 0.72 to 0.96, and both coverage metrics increases from 75% to 100%. With automated seeding, mutation score further increases to 0.99.

Table 2. Configuration parameters of the GA

Population	p_c	p_m	r
15% 20% 25%	90%	10%	10

Since all the population sizes obtained the same medians in their quality metrics, we compared the results from each of their 30 executions without automated seeding and with automated seeding. The results are shown in Tables 3 and 4, respectively. Without automated seeding, the size that produces the most stable results is 25%. With automated seeding, the size that produces the best results is 20%, reaching 100% mutation score in two executions.

Table 3. Quality metrics obtained by the GA without automated seeding for each population size, grouped by execution results

Population	Seeds	MS	SC (%)	CDC (%)
	2	0.72	75.0	75.0
15%	1	0.90	93.8	100.0
	1	0.95	100.0	100.0
	26	0.96	100.0	100.0
20%	2	0.95	100.0	100.0
	28	0.96	100.0	100.0
25%	30	0.96	100.0	100.0

Table 4. Quality metrics obtained by the GA with automated seeding for each population size, grouped by execution results

Population	Seeds	MS	SC (%)	CDC (%)
15%	7	0.97	100.0	100.0
	23	0.99	100.0	100.0
	3	0.97	100.0	100.0
20%	2	1.00	100.0	100.0
	25	0.99	100.0	100.0
25%	3	0.97	100.0	100.0
	27	0.99	100.0	100.0

As the GA generates test-suites much bigger than the initial test-suites, the next step is comparing random generation of bigger test-suites with the results produced by our GA, with and without automated seeding. For a 20% population size, the GA executed a median of 156 distinct test-cases without automated seeding, and a median of 153 different test-cases with automated seeding.

Table 5 compares the median values of metrics corresponding to 30 random test-suites, with 156 test-cases each, with those produced by both variants of our GA. Results indicate that the metrics for random test-suites were as good as those for the GA without automated seeding.

This can be explained by the fact that small compositions usually have few execution paths and, thus, random test-suites of considerable size are likely to produce high sentence and condition/decision coverages. Moreover, at the same time, those compositions tend to generate a small number of mutants. As a consequence, their mutants might be mostly killed by a random test-suite of even modest size and high mutation scores can be expected.

This is the case, with the *LoanApproval* composition, which in fact has few mutants and execution paths. However, the GA with automated seeding obtained better mutation score (0.99) than the random test-suite (0.96).

Table 5. Results produced by random test generation and the two versions of our GA

	Random	GA	GA (autom. seeding)
Size test-suite	156	156	153
MS	0.96	0.96	0.99
SC (%)	100.0	100.0	100.0
CDC (%)	100.0	100.0	100.0

From these results, we can now answer the two research questions that were posed at the beginning of this section for the *LoanApproval* composition.

RQ1. *How much does the GA improve the quality of the initial test suite?* The test-suite generated by our GA improves the initial test-suite with respect to all the quality metrics measured (mutation score, sentence coverage, and condition/decision coverage). Without automated seeding, the GA increases the mutation score from 0.72 to 0.96. Sentence coverage and condition/decision coverage increase from 75% to 100%. With automated seeding, the mutation score further increases to 0.99.

RQ2. *Are the improvements just a consequence of the greater size of the final test-suite?* Once we extend the initial test-suite with sufficient random test-cases to match the size of the final test-suite, the GA shows no difference when automated seeding is disabled. However, with automated seeding, the GA obtains a higher mutation score: 0.99 instead of 0.96.

6 Conclusions and Future Work

We have presented a GA for generating test-cases for a mutation testing system. The initial population can be generated in two ways. The first way simply generates all individuals at random. The second way mixes in test-cases which are derived from the constants present in the source code of the program. Our GA also adopts several features of the bacteriological algorithms proposed for test-case generation by Baudry et al. [4].

We have implemented both approaches in a framework which generates test-cases for WS-BPEL compositions. The GA was applied to a standard WS-BPEL composition. We compared the quality of the initial random test-suite against the test-suites produced by the GA. Test-suite quality was measured using mutation score, sentence coverage and condition/decision coverage. It is shown that, for this composition, the median of the quality metric values across 30 executions improves, both with and without automated seeding.

The quality of the test-suites generated by the GA has been also compared to the quality of random test-suites of the same size. In this case, random testing produces the same results as using the GA without automated seeding. However, the GA with automated seeding produces slightly better results. This has been traced to the fact that the composition under study is small and have few execution paths. Therefore, random test-suites of considerable size are likely to produce high sentence and condition/decision coverages. At the same time, its number of mutants is modest and they can be killed by a random test suite. Consequently, random test-suites enjoy higher mutation scores than usual and the margin of improvement for the GA, which starts from an initial population of random test-cases, gets drastically reduced.

These preliminary results are promising, but we acknowledge that one of the limitations of the present study is that it has only been applied to a single WS-BPEL composition so far. Future work will be devoted to validate our results with a number of increasingly complex WS-BPEL compositions. The main hindrance here is the absence of a standard set of WS-BPEL compositions suitable for functional testing.

Another limitation of the current study is that we have mainly concentrated in assessing the impact of the population size. Other configuration parameters, for which reasonable values were used, might be adjusted and hopefully improve our results. Further research and extensive experimentation could lead to better combinations of parameters for generating test-suites.

Acknowledgments. This work was funded by the Spanish Ministry of Science and Innovation under the National Program for Research, Development and Innovation, project MoDSOA (TIN2011-27242).

References

1. Alshahwan, N., Harman, M.: Automated web application testing using search based software engineering. In: 26th IEEE/ACM International Conference on Automated Software Engineering, pp. 3–12 (2011)
2. Alshraideh, M., Bottaci, L.: Search-based software test data generation for string data using program-specific search operators. Softw. Test. Verif. Reliab. 16(3), 175–203 (2006)
3. Ayari, K., Bouktif, S., Antoniol, G.: Automatic mutation test input data generation via ant colony. In: 9th Conference on Genetic and Evolutionary Computation, pp. 1074–1081. ACM (2007)

4. Baudry, B., Fleurey, F., Jézéquel, J.M., Le Traon, Y.: From genetic to bacteriological algorithms for mutation-based testing. Soft. Test. Verif. Reliab. 15(2), 73–96 (2005)
5. Bottaci, L.: A genetic algorithm fitness function for mutation testing. In: 23rd International Conference on Software Engineering using Metaheuristic Inovative Algorithms, pp. 3–7 (2001)
6. Estero-Botaro, A., Palomo-Lozano, F., Medina-Bulo, I.: Mutation operators for WS-BPEL 2.0. In: ICSSEA 2008: 21th International Conference on Software & Systems Engineering and their Applications (2008)
7. Estero-Botaro, A., Palomo-Lozano, F., Medina-Bulo, I., Domníguez-Jiménez, J.J., García-Domnguez, A.: Quality metrics for mutation testing with applications to WS-BPEL compositions. Software Testing, Verification and Reliability (2014), http://dx.doi.org/10.1002/stvr.1528
8. Fraser, G., Arcuri, A.: The seed is strong: Seeding strategies in search-based software testing. In: IEEE Fifth International Conference on Software Testing, Verification and Validation, pp. 121–130 (2012)
9. Goldberg, D.E.: Genetic Algorithms in Search, Optimization and Machine Learning. Addison-Wesley Longman Publishing Co., Inc., Boston (1989)
10. Harman, M., McMinn, P.: A theoretical and empirical study of search-based testing: Local, global, and hybrid search. IEEE Trans. Soft. Eng. 36(2), 226–247 (2010)
11. Holland, J.: Adaptation in Natural and Artificial Systems, 2nd edn. MIT Press (1992)
12. Krishnakumar, K.: Microgenetic algorithms for stationary and nonstationary function optimization. In: Society of Photo-Optical Instrumentation Engineers Conference Series, vol. 1196, pp. 289–296 (1990)
13. Mantere, T., Alander, J.T.: Evolutionary software engineering, a review. Applied Soft Computing 5(3), 315–331 (2005)
14. May, P., Timmis, J., Mander, K.: Immune and evolutionary approaches to software mutation testing. In: de Castro, L.N., Von Zuben, F.J., Knidel, H. (eds.) ICARIS 2007. LNCS, vol. 4628, pp. 336–347. Springer, Heidelberg (2007)
15. McMinn, P.: Search-based software test data generation: A survey. Soft. Test. Verif. Reliab. 14(2), 105–156 (2004)
16. Mitchell, M.: An introduction to genetic algorithms. Massachusetts Institute of Technology (1996)
17. Mühlenbein, H.: Evolution in time and space - the parallel genetic algorithm. In: Foundations of Genetic Algorithms, pp. 316–337. Morgan Kaufmann (1991)
18. OASIS: Web Services Business Process Execution Language 2.0 (2007), http://docs.oasis-open.org/wsbpel/2.0/OS/wsbpel-v2.0-OS.html
19. Offutt, A.J., Untch, R.H.: Mutation 2000: Uniting the Orthogonal. In: Mutation Testing for the New Century, pp. 34–44. Kluwer Academic Publishers (2001)
20. Offutt, J.: Automatic test data generation. Ph.D. thesis, Georgia Institute of Technology, Atlanta, GA, USA (1988)
21. Syswerda, G.: A study of reproduction in generational and steady-state genetic algorithms. In: Foundations of Genetic Algorithms, pp. 94–101. Morgan Kaufmann Publishers (1991)
22. Xanthakis, S., Ellis, C., Skourlas, C., Gall, A.L., Katsikas, S., Karapoulios, K.: Application of genetic algorithms to software testing. In: Proc. of the 5th Int. Conf. on Software Engineering, pp. 625–636 (1992)

Evaluating Normalization Functions with Search Algorithms for Solving OCL Constraints

Shaukat Ali and Tao Yue

Certus Software V&V Center,
Simula Research Laboratory, P.O. Box 134,
Lysaker, Norway
{shaukat,tao}@simula.no

Abstract. The use of search algorithms requires the definition of a fitness function that guides the algorithms to find an optimal solution. The definition of a fitness function may require the use of a normalization function for various purposes such as assigning equal importance to various factors constituting a fitness function and normalizing only one factor of a fitness function to give it less/more importance than the others. In our previous work, we defined various branch distance functions (a commonly used heuristic in the literature at the code-level) corresponding to the constructs defined in the Object Constraint Language (OCL) to solve OCL constraints to generate test data for supporting automated Model-Based Testing (MBT). The definition of several of these distance functions required the use of a normalization function. In this paper, we extend the empirical evaluation reported in one of the works in the literature that compares the impact of using various normalization functions for calculating branch distances at the code-level on the performance of search algorithms.

The empirical evaluation reported in this paper assesses the impact of the commonly used normalization functions for the branch distance calculation of OCL constraints at the model-level. Results show that for one of the newly studied algorithms Harmony Search (HS) and Random Search (RS), the use of the normalization functions has no impact on the performance of the search. However, HS achieved 100% success rates for all the problems, where RS obtained very poor success rates (less than 38%). Based on the results, we conclude that the randomness in creating a solution in search algorithms may mask the impact of using a normalization function.

Keywords: OCL, Search Algorithm, Test data, Model-Based Testing, Empirical evaluation.

1 Introduction

The Object Constraint Language (OCL) is a commonly used language to specify constraints on the Unified Modeling Language (UML) for various applications, such as supporting Model-Based Testing (MBT) [1, 2] and automated code generation [3]. In the context of MBT, a typical purpose of solving constraints is to generate test data for automated generation of executable test scripts from models. In our previous work

M.G. Merayo and E. Montes de Oca (Eds.): ICTSS 2014, LNCS 8763, pp. 17–31, 2014.
© IFIP International Federation for Information Processing 2014

[4], to solve OCL constraints on models for automated test data generation, we defined a set of novel heuristics for various OCL constructs. Some of these heuristics require the use of a normalization function, which is proposed in [4]. In this paper, we empirically evaluate the impact of two commonly used normalization functions in the literature on the performance of various search algorithms for solving OCL constraints for test data generation. The main motivation of this empirical evaluation is to assess if the use of a particular normalization function can improve the performance of solving OCL constraints for test data generation. Studying the impact of the normalization functions on the performance of search algorithms is important since any improvement in the efficiency of test data generation in our application of industrial MBT is appreciated.

Based on the above motivation, we conducted an empirical evaluation to assess the impact of the two commonly used normalization functions reported in [5, 6] on the performance of various search algorithms to solve OCL constraints. The differences of this paper from the one reported in [5, 6] are as follows: 1) We evaluate the use of the normalization functions on heuristics defined on model-level constraints as compared to the code-level branches reported in [5, 6]; 2) We empirically evaluated in total five search algorithms: Genetic Algorithm (GA) and Random Search (RS)— two algorithms that have been evaluated in [5, 6], and the other three algorithms (Alternating Variable Method (AVM), (1+1) Evolutionary Algorithm (EA), and Harmony Search (HS) [7]) which are newly evaluated in this paper.

Based on our empirical evaluation, we observed that the extent of the randomness consideration in generating a solution may mask the effect of using a particular normalization function. For HS and RS, where the extent of the randomness consideration of generating a solution is higher than the other three algorithms we studied, the effect of using a particular normalization function on performance of search is masked. However, HS achieved 100% success rate, whereas RS achieved low success rates (37%). Therefore, HS is recommended for solving OCL constraints when combined with any of the normalization function.

The rest of the paper is organized as follows. Section 2 presents the background necessary to understand the rest of the paper. Section 3 presents our empirical evaluation. Section 4 reports threats to validity of the empirical evaluation. Section 5 provides the related work and Section 6 concludes the paper.

2   Background

In this section, we briefly provide some information required to understand the rest of the paper. Section 2.1 provides a brief introduction to our existing work on test data generation from OCL constraints to provide the context in which the two normalization functions are evaluated. Section 2.2 presents the two commonly used normalization functions in search-based software engineering (SBSE), whereas Section 2.3 provides a brief introduction to Harmony Search (HS) since it is new to SBSE.

2.1   Test Data Generation from OCL Constraints

In our previous work [4], we proposed and assessed novel heuristics for the application of search-based techniques, such as Genetic Algorithms (GAs), (1+1) Evolutionary Algorithm (EA), and Alternating Variable Method (AVM), to generate test data from OCL constraints. A search-based test data generator (EsOCL) was implemented in Java and was evaluated on an industrial case study in addition to the empirical evaluation of each proposed heuristics using several artificial problems.

To guide the search for test data that satisfy OCL constraints, a heuristic tells 'how far' input data are from satisfying the constraint. For example, let us say we want to satisfy the constraint $x=0$, and suppose we have two data inputs: $x1:=5$ and $x2:=1000$. Both inputs $x1$ and $x2$ do not satisfy $x=0$, but $x1$ is heuristically closer to satisfy $x=0$ than $x2$. A search algorithm would use such a heuristic as a fitness function, to reward input data that are closer to satisfy a target constraint.

To generate test data to solve OCL constraints, we used a fitness function that was adapted from work done for code coverage (e.g., for branch coverage in C code [8]). In particular, we used the a fitness function so called branch distance (a function $d()$), as defined in [8]. The function $d()$ returns 0 if the constraint is   solved (an OCL constraint evaluates to *true*), a value k if the constraint evaluates to *undefined* (a special case for OCL that makes it three-valued logic for writing constraints [4]); otherwise a positive value (greater than 0 and less than k) that heuristically estimates how far the constraint was from being evaluated to be *true*. As for any heuristic, there is no guarantee that an optimal solution (e.g., in our case, input data satisfying constraints) will be found in a reasonable period of time. Nevertheless, many successful results have been reported in the literature for solving various software engineering problems by applying heuristic based approaches [9]. In cases where we wanted a constraint to be evaluated to be *false*, we simply negated the constraint and find data for which the negated constraint evaluates to *true*. For example, if we want to prevent firing a guarded transition in a state machine, we can simply negate the guard and find data for the negated guard. We defined various novel heuristics for calculating branch distances for various constructs and operations defined in OCL such as *includes()*, *oclInState()*, and *forAll()* [4] and due to space limitations we cannot provide details about them in this paper. The interested readers may consult the relevant reference [4] for more details.

2.2   Normalization Functions

A normalization function is commonly used in the branch distance calculation (a commonly used heuristic [8]) to normalize a branch distance value within range [0, 1]. The minimum value of the branch distance, i.e., 0 is known; however the maximum value for the branch distance is not known and thus it is important to normalize the branch distance in the range [0, 1].

In SBSE, the following two normalization functions are commonly used:

$$N1(x) = \frac{x}{x+\beta} \tag{1}$$

$$N2(x) = 1 - \alpha^{-x} \quad \dots \tag{2}$$

In the above functions, $\alpha > 1$ and $\beta > 0$ and in the literature a typical value of $\alpha = 1.001$ is used   [5, 6]. Both of the above functions maintain the order of inputs with outputs, i.e., a higher value of input to the normalization functions will output a higher value of the branch distance [5, 6]. Also notice that branch distance values are always greater than or equal to 0, and the minimum value $x=0$ will produce $N1(0) = 0$ and $N2(0) = 0$.

2.3   Harmony Search

Harmony Search (HS) [10] is a meta-heuristic music-inspired algorithm for global optimization.   Music is produced by a group of musicians (variables) together, where each musician produces a note (value) to find a best harmony (global optimal solution). To explain how HS works, considering we have a set of decision variables $V = \{v_1, v_2, .., v_n\}$, HS starts search with *Harmony Memory* (*HM*) consisting of a set of randomly generated solutions (i.e., $HM = \{s_1, s_2, .., s_m\}$) where each s_i consists of randomly generated values for $v_1, v_2, .., v_n$. To create a new solution, each variable in V is set to a value from one of the solutions in *HM* with a probability *Harmony Memory Consideration Rate* (*HMCR*) and an additional modification to the selected value with *Pitch Adjusting Rate* (*PAR*). Otherwise, the variable is set to a random value. This case is referred to as random consideration with a probability of (*1-HMCR*) [10]. If the newly created solution has better fitness than the worst solution in *HM*, then it is replaced with the new solution. The process of creating new solutions continues until the termination criteria are met. On reaching the termination criteria, the solution with the best fitness from *HM* is selected. More details of the algorithm can be found in [10].

3   Empirical Evaluation

In this section, we will provide an empirical evaluation based on various artificial problems (Table 6) to evaluate the two normalization functions (Section 2.2).

3.1   Experiment Design

To empirically evaluate whether the normalization function *N1* really improves the performance of a search algorithm as compared to *N2*, we carefully defined artificial problems to evaluate each heuristic that requires a normalization function. Based on this criterion, we defined eight artificial problems (Table 6). The model we used for the experiment consists of a very simple class diagram with one class X, which has two attributes x and y of type *Integer*. We populated *10* objects of class X. The use of a single class with 10 objects was sufficient to create complex constraints since the overall solution space of each constraint is very small.

In our experiments, we compared four search algorithms: AVM, HS, GA, (1+1) EA, and used RS as a comparison baseline to assess the difficulty of the addressed problems [11]. AVM was selected as a representative of local search algorithms. HS [7] is a music-inspired algorithm, which is not commonly used in SBSE. GA was selected since it is the most commonly used global search algorithm in SBSE [11]. (1+1) EA is simpler than GAs, but in our previous works we found that it can be more effective for software testing problems (e.g., see [4, 12, 13]). For GA, we set the population size to 100 and the crossover rate to 0.75, with a 1.5 bias for rank selection. We use a standard one-point crossover, and mutation of a variable is done with the standard probability $p = 1/n$, where n is the number of variables. For HS, we used the most commonly used parameter settings, which are Harmony Memory Size (HMS) of 5, *HMCR* of 0.9, and *PAR* of 0.4 [10].

In this experiment, we address the following research questions:

RQ1: Is there any impact of using the two normalization functions on the performance of a search algorithm?

RQ2: What are the differences in terms of the performance of the algorithms when using *N1* and *N2*?

To compare the algorithms for *N1* and *N2* (RQ1), we followed the guidelines defined in [11, 14], which recommends a number of statistical procedures to assess randomized test strategies. First, we calculated the success rate for each algorithm, which is defined as the number of times that a solution was found out of the total number of runs (100 in this case). These success rates were then compared using the Fisher Exact test (with a significance level of 0.05), quantifying the effect size using an odds ratio with a 0.5 correction. We chose the Fisher Exact test since for each run of algorithms the result is binary, i.e., either the result is 'found' or 'not found'. This is exactly the condition for which the Fisher's exact test is defined. In addition to statistical significance, we used odds ratio as the results of our experiments are dichotomous. A value greater than 1 means that *N1* has more chance of success as compared to *N2*, whereas a value of 1 means no difference.

When the difference between the success rates of N1 and N2 were not significant for an algorithm, we further compared the number of iterations taken by the algorithm for N1 and N2 to solve the problems. For this purpose, we used Mann-Whitney U-test [10] at a significance level of 0.05. In addition, we report effect size measurements using Vargha and Delaney's Â12 statistics, which is a non-parametric effect size measure. In our context, the value of Â12 tells the probability for N1 to find a solution in less number of iterations than N2. This means that higher the value of Â12 than 0.5, the higher the chance that N1 will take lesser iterations to find a solution than N2. If N1 and N2 are equal then the value of Â12 is 0.5. In Table 1-Table 5, results for Mann-Whitney U-test and Â12 are only shown when the differences are not significant based on success rates. For RQ2, we used the same statistics except that instead of N1 and N2, we compared two algorithms.

Table 1. Results for *N1* vs. *N2* for the Five Algorithms*

Algo	P#	Success Rate				# Iterations		
		S(N1)	S(N2)	OR	p-value	MD	Â12	p-value
AVM	1	0.34	0	104	<0.0001	-	-	-
	2	0.53	0	226	<0.0001	-	-	-
	3	1	0	40401	<0.0001	-	-	-
	4	1	0	40401	<0.0001	-	-	-
	5	1	0	40401	<0.0001	-	-	-
	6	1	1	1	1	-11	0.495	0.98
	7	1	0	40401	<0.0001	-	-	-
	8	1	0	40401	<0.0001	-	-	-
	Avg.	0.859	0.125	-	-	-	-	-
HS	1	1	1	1	1	-114	0.450	0.97
	2	1	1	1	1	-18	0.497	0.71
	3	1	1	1	1	39	0.513	0.99
	4	1	1	1	1	-17	0.495	0.95
	5	1	1	1	1	81	0.498	0.80
	6	1	1	1	1	0	0.5	1
	7	1	1	1	1	37	0.515	0.83
	8	1	1	1	1	218	0.539	0.25
	Avg.	1	1	-	-	-	-	-
1+1(EA)	1	1	0.82	45	<0.0001	-	-	-
	2	1	0.24	628	<0.0001	-	-	-
	3	0.97	0.31	61	<0.0001	-	-	-
	4	1	0.27	537	<0.0001	-	-	-
	5	1	0.22	701	<0.0001	-	-	-
	6	1	1	1	1	0	0.50	1
	7	1	0.39	313	<0.0001	-	-	-
	8	1	0.8	51	<0.0001	-	-	-
	Avg.	0.996	0.506	-	-	-	-	-
RS	1	0	0	-	-	-	-	-
	2	0.44	0.98	0.02	<0.0001	-	-	-
	3	0.29	0.27	1.10	0.87	118	0.567	0.05
	4	0.32	0.39	0.74	0.37	15	0.508	0.79
	5	0	0	-	-	-	-	-
	6	1	1	1	1	0	0.50	1
	7	0.41	0.31	2	0.18	21	0.52	0.82
	8	0	0	1	1	-	-	-
	Avg.	0.308	0.369	-	-	-	-	-
GA	1	1	0.89	26	<0.0001	-	-	-
	2	1	1	1	1	37	0.51	0.92
	3	1	1	1	1	-29	0.48	0.98
	4	1	1	1	1	30	0.50	0.99
	5	0.55	0.14	7	<0.0001	-	-	-
	6	1	1	1	1	0	0.50	1
	7	1	1	1	1	-75	0.48	0.60
	8	1	0.89	26	<0.0001	-	-	-
	Avg.	0.944	0.865	-	-	-	-	-

*S(N1), Success rate with *N1*, OR: Odds Ratio, MD: Mean Difference *(N1-N2)*

3.2   Experiment Execution

We executed the five algorithms 100 times with both *N1* and *N2* for the eight problems. We let the algorithms run up to 20,000 fitness evaluations on each problem and collected data on whether the algorithms found solutions for *N1* and *N2*. We used a PC with Intel Core Duo CPU 2.20 GHz with 4 GB of RAM, running Microsoft Windows 7 operating system for the execution of experiment.

3.3   Experiment Results and Analysis

In this section, we will answer each of our research questions.

RQ1: Is there any impact of using the two normalization functions on the performance of a search algorithm? For AVM, we observed that when using *N2* for all the problems the success rate is 0% (Table 1) except for P6, for which both *N1* and *N2* achieved 100% success rates. For P6, we further compared *N1* and *N2* based on the number of iterations to solve the problem. The results in Table 1 show that *N1* took less number of iterations as *MD* is -11 but no significant difference identified since Â12 value is 0.495 and *p*-value is 0.98.

For HS, there were no significant differences in using *N1* and *N2* in terms of both success rates and number of iterations as all the *p*-values are greater than 0.05.

For (1+1) EA, *N1* is significantly better than *N2* except for P6 in terms of success rates since all *p*-values are less than 0.05 and Odds Ratio (*OR*) values are greater than 1. For P6, there was no significant difference between *N1* and *N2* in terms of number of iterations (*MD*=0, Â12=0.5, and *p*-value=1).

For RS, there was no significant difference between *N1* and *N2* except for P6. Overall success rates are very low, i.e., 31% for *N1* and 37% for *N2*. For P6, both *N1* and *N2* achieved 100% success rates and in terms of the number of iterations there was no significant difference between them.

For GA, for P1, P5, and P8, *N1* is significantly better than *N2* in terms of success rates. For the rest, there was no significant difference between *N1* and *N2* in terms of success rates and the number of iterations.

Based on the above results, we can answer RQ1 as follows: Using *N1* significantly improves the performance of AVM and (1+1) EA. For HS using *N1* or *N2* doesn't have any impact on its performance. For GA, *N1* either improves the effectiveness (3 out of 8 problems) or has no significant difference than *N2*.

We observe that for P6 all the algorithms with both *N1* and *N2* achieved 100% success rates since the problem was the easiest one as it can be seen from the fact even RS has 100% success rate for P6.

RQ2: What are the differences in terms of the performance of the algorithms when using *N1* and *N2*? In this section, we will compare each pair of the algorithms with *N1* and *N2*.

AVM vs HS. When *N1* was applied, HS is significantly better than AVM in terms of success rates for P1 and P2 (Table 2) since the *OR* values are less than 1 and *p*-values are less than 0.05. However, there is no significant difference for the rest of the problems and thus we further compared these two algorithms in terms of the number of iterations (Table 3). Except for P6 and P8, *N1* took significantly less number of iterations as $\hat{A}12$ values are less than 0.5 and *p*-values less than 0.05 (Table 3). For P6, there is no significant difference between the two algorithms and for P8 HS took significantly more iterations than AVM ($\hat{A}12=0.81$ and *p*-value<0.05 as shown in Table 3). For P3, *N1* took lesser number of iterations than *N2*; however the differences are not significant (Table 3). We can observe from Table 4 and Table 5 that for *N2*, HS is significantly better than AVM for all the problems except P6, where there is no significant difference identified between the two algorithms both in terms of success rates and number of iterations.

AVM vs. (1+1) EA. With *N1*, there is no significant difference for all the problems except for P1 and P2, where (1+1) EA is significantly better than AVM in terms of success rates (Table 2). As one can observe from Table 3, there is no significant difference for P3, P6, and P7; For P4 and P5, (1+1) EA took significantly more iterations than AVM; For P8, AVM took significantly more iterations than (1+1) EA. As shown in Table 4 and Table 5, with *N2*, (1+1) EA is significantly better than AVM for all the problems except for P6, where there is no significant difference between them both in terms of success rates and the number of iterations.

AVM vs. RS. With *N1*, except for P2 and P6, AVM is significantly better than RS (Table 2). For P2 and P6, in terms of the number of iterations there is no significant difference between the two algorithms (Table 3). For *N2*, RS achieved significantly higher success rates for P2, P3, P4, and P7, whereas for P1, P5, and P8 both of the algorithms have 0% success rates (Table 4). For P6, there is no significant difference in terms of success rates and number of iterations (Table 4 and Table 5).

AVM vs. GA. With *N1*, for P1, P2, and P5, GA achieved significantly higher success rates than AVM. For the rest, there is no significant difference in terms of success rates (Table 2). For these problems, GA took significantly more iterations than AVM for P4 and P5, whereas for P8 AVM took significantly more iterations than GA (Table 3). There is no significant difference between GA and AVM for P3, P6, and P7 (Table 3). With *N2*, GA achieved significantly higher success rates than AVM except for P6, for which, as for other algorithms, we didn't observe any significant difference in terms of both success rates and the number of iterations (Table 4 and Table 5).

HS vs. (1+1) EA. With *N1*, there is no significant difference in terms of success rates (Table 2). However, for P1, P5, and P8, HS took significantly less iterations than (1+1) EA (Table 3). For P2, P3, P6, and P7, no significant difference was observed between the two algorithms (Table 3). For P4, (1+1) EA took significantly less iterations than HS as shown in Table 3. With $N2$, HS achieved significantly higher success rates for all the problems except for P6 (Table 4 and Table 5).

HS vs. RS. With $N1$, HS achieved significantly higher success rates than RS except for P6 (Table 2). With $N2$, HS obtained significantly higher success rates than RS except for P2 and P6 (Table 4).

HS vs. GA. With $N1$, there is no significant difference between the two algorithms except for P5, where HS achieved significantly higher success rates than GA (Table 2). For the rest of the problems (excluding P5), no significant difference was observed in terms of the number of iterations except for P2 where HS took significantly less number of iterations than GA (Table 3). With $N2$, for P1, P5, and P8, HS achieved significant higher success rates than GA. For the rest of the problems, where there was no significant difference in terms of success rates, we didn't even observe difference in terms of the number of iterations (Table 4 and Table 5).

(1+1) EA vs. RS. With $N1$, (1+1) EA is significantly better than RS except for P6, where there is no significant difference in terms of both success rates and iterations (Table 2 and Table 3). With $N2$ for P1, P5, and P8, (1+1) EA achieved significantly higher success rates than RS. For P2, RS obtained higher success rates than (1+1) EA. For the rest, there is no significant difference in terms of both success rates and the number of iterations (Table 4 and Table 5).

(1+1) EA vs. GA. With $N1$, there is no significant difference for all the problems except for P5, where (1+1) EA achieved significantly higher success rates (Table 2). For P2 and P4, GA took significantly less iterations and vice versa for P1 (Table 3). For the rest of the problems, there is no significant difference as shown in Table 3. With $N2$, for P2, P3, P4, and P7, GA achieved significant higher success rates than (1+1) EA and for the rest of the problems, there is no significant difference in terms of both success rates and the number of iterations (Table 4 and Table 5).

RS vs. GA. With $N1$, GA is significantly better than RS in terms of success rates except for P6 (Table 2 and Table 3). With $N2$, GA is significantly better than RS in terms of success rates except for P2 and P6, where there were no significant differences in terms of success rates and iterations (Table 4 and Table 5).

Overall Conclusion. Based on the results from RQ1 and RQ2, for HS and RS, we observed that there was no significant difference in using any of the two normalization functions. However, for HS, the success rates with $N1$ and $N2$ were both 100%, whereas for RS, the success rates were 31% and 37% respectively. One possible explanation of this phenomenon may be due to the extent of the randomness consideration in both of the algorithms in creating a new solution. In case of RS, solutions are created randomly and thus the effect of the normalization functions on performance is masked since the probability of the randomness for RS is always 1. Similarly for HS, there is always (1- $HMCR$), i.e., 0.1 probability in our context to pick a random value (Section 2.3 and Section 3.3). Considering there are n decision variables ($n=10$ in our case as we discussed in Section 3.1), there is roughly a probability of (1-$HMCR$)^n randomness in a solution, which in our context equals to 0.1^{10} plus randomness due to HMS random solutions in HM. Another possible explanation could be that the excellent performance of HS masked the effect of normalization: it achieved 100% success rates for all the problems with no significant difference in terms of the number of iterations (Table 1). In case of more complicated problems, it might be possible to observe performance difference, when using different normalization functions. We will investigate this in the future with more focused experiments. Similarly for RS, its performance was consistently low for all the problems and thus difference when applying the two normalization functions was not visible.

For (1+1) EA (see [4] for detailed description of how the algorithm works), randomness is only considered in the mutation operator, which mutates each variable in the solution with a probability p. Suppose that we have n variables ($n=10$), then the total amount of randomness is roughly: ($1/n$)^n (0.1^{10} in our case). This value is lower than the one for RS and HS since HS also introduces more randomness because of random solutions in HM (Section 2.3). In case of AVM (see [4] for the detailed description of the algorithm), considering that there are n decision variables, the extent of the randomness consideration in each solution can be roughly calculated as: $\frac{n-1}{n} * \frac{n-2}{n} * \ldots * \frac{1}{n} * p^n$ ($\frac{9!}{10^{10}} * 0.1^{10}$ in our context). This value is again less as compared with the randomness consideration in RS and HS. In summary, RS and HS have stronger randomness consideration than (1+1) EA and AVM, which might explain why HS and RS were not affected when using different normalization functions. However, to further understand this phenomenon, more focused experiments are required to test the algorithms combined with the normalization functions when given various values to parameters (e.g., p). This will be our future work.

As reported in [5, 6] for GA, when using $N1$, it achieved significantly better performance than N2. In our context, we however observed partially consistent results as what was reported in [5, 6]: as for 3 out of 8 problems (Table 1), $N1$ showed significantly better performance than $N2$ and for the rest, no difference was observed. In GA as we discussed in Section 3.1, the probability of randomness is roughly equivalent to p^n due to mutation. Considering $n=10$ in our context, we have a probability of 0.1^{10}. Notice that this is a rough calculation of the probability of randomness since we didn't account for randomness due to crossover. Since this probability is somewhat similar to the probability of randomness in HS, we observed similar results as HS since for 5 problems there was no significant difference, when using any normalization function in case of GA. However the performance of HS is significantly better than GA (Section 3.3). This can be explained based on how the algorithms work as discussed in [15]. The main difference between GA and HS is that HS considers all existing solutions when generating a new solution, while GA considers only two solutions (parents). This feature increases the flexibility of HS and therefore produces better solutions as we observed from our experiment results.

Based on the above discussion, we can conclude that the extent of the consideration of randomness in an algorithm may affect the use of a particular normalization function. This means that higher the randomness consideration in an algorithm in generating new solutions, higher the chance that the performance of the algorithm will not be impacted by the use of any particular normalization function. Based on these observations, we recommend using HS with any of the two normalization functions for solving OCL constraints to support MBT, considering that HS achieved 100% success rates for all the problems and was not affected by the choice of any of the two normalization functions.

4   Threats to Validity

To reduce construct validity threats, we chose an effectiveness measure: the search success rate, which is comparable across all the five search algorithms (AVM, (1+1) EA, HS, GA and RS). Furthermore, we used the same stopping criterion for all the algorithms, i.e., the number of fitness evaluations. This criterion is a comparable measure of efficiency across all the algorithms.

The most probable conclusion validity threat in experiments involving randomized algorithms is due to random variations. To address it, we repeated experiments 100 times to reduce the possibility that results were obtained by chance. Furthermore, we performed Fisher exact tests to compare proportions and determine the statistical significance of the results. We chose this test since it is appropriate for dichotomous data where proportions must be compared [14], thus matching our situation. To determine the practical significance of the results obtained, we measured the effect size using the odds ratio of success rates across the search techniques.

A possible threat to internal validity is that we have experimented with only one configuration setting for the (1+1) EA, AVM, HS and GA parameters. However, these settings are in accordance with the common guidelines in the literature and our previous experience on testing problems. Another threat is the use of fixed values for α and β in the normalization functions. Recall that to deal with this, we used the most commonly used values for α and β reported in the literature.

5   Related Work

To efficiently generate test data for OCL constraints, we previously defined in [4] novel heuristics based on branch distance [8] for various OCL constructs and operations to guide search algorithms including GA, (1+1) EA, and AVM. This is the only work in the literature that explores the use of search algorithms for solving OCL constraints as we comprehensively compared in [4].

Only related work to the empirical evaluation presented in this paper is reported in [5, 6], where the two commonly used normalization functions were studied for the first time. In this paper, we further enhanced the empirical evaluation reported in [5, 6]. The differences of these two works are as follows: 1) The work reported in this paper empirically evaluates the two normalization functions on model-level constraints as opposed to branches in code; 2) This work evaluates three other search algorithms, i.e., (1+1) EA, AVM and HS. The results of the empirical study reported in this paper are partially consistent with the results reported in [5, 6]; however for HS we observed that the choice of a normalization function has no impact on its performance.

6   Conclusion

Model-based testing (MBT) offers an automated and systematic alternative to manual testing and has shown promising results both in industry and academia. MBT requires developing a model of system under test with constraints to support automation of e.g., test data generation. In our previous work, we developed a search-based test generator (EsOCL) from the Object Constraint Language (OCL) to solve constraints on UML state machines to support automated MBT. We defined various heuristics to guide search algorithms to efficiently solve OCL constraints to generate test data. Several of these heuristics required using one of the commonly used normalization functions in the literature. An existing work has evaluated two commonly used normalization functions in search-based software engineering for various search algorithms. In this paper, we further extend this work with more empirical evaluations.

More specifically, in this paper, we reported an empirical evaluation of two commonly used normalization functions in the literature, along with five search algorithms, in the context of solving OCL constraints for supporting automated test data generation at the model level. In contrast, the only related work in the literature evaluates the same normalization functions in the context of program branches at the code-level. In this paper, we evaluated in total five algorithms: Random Search (RS), Genetic Algorithm (GA), (1+1) Evolutionary Algorithm, Alternating Variable Method (AVM) and Harmony Search (HS). We observed that our evaluation results are mostly consistent with what was already reported in the existing work except for HS, for which we observed that the choice of the two normalization functions doesn't affect its performance. We also provided plausible explanation for this observation: the extent of the consideration of randomness in an algorithm might affect the effect of a normalization function on the performance of a search algorithm: higher randomness consideration leads to higher chance that the performance of an algorithm will not be impacted by the use of any particular normalization function. The results also show that HS achieved 100% success rates for all the problems and therefore we recommend HS for solve OCL constraints at the model-level for generating test data, when combined with any of the two normalization functions.

References

1. Utting, M., Legeard, B.: Practical Model-Based Testing: A Tools Approach. Morgan-Kaufmann (2006)
2. Chow, T.S.: Testing Software Design Modeled by Finite-State Machines. IEEE Transactions on Software Engineering 4, 178–187 (1978)

3. Iqbal, M.Z., Arcuri, A., Briand, L.: Environment Modeling with UML/MARTE to Support Black-Box System Testing for Real-Time Embedded Systems: Methodology and Industrial Case Studies. In: ACM/IEEE International Conference on Model Driven Engineering Languages and Systems (MODELS), pp. 286–300. Springer. Heidelberg (Year)

4. Ali, S., Iqbal, M.Z., Arcuri, A., Briand, L.: Generating Test Data from OCL Constraints with Search Techniques. IEEE Transactions on Software Engineering (2013)

5. Arcuri, A.: It Does Matter How You Normalise the Branch Distance in Search Based Software Testing. In: Proceedings of the 2010 Third International Conference on Software Testing, Verification and Validation. IEEE Computer Society (2010)

6. Arcuri, A.: It really does matter how you normalize the branch distance in search-based software testing. Software Testing, Verification and Reliability (2011)

7. Zou, D., Gao, L., Wu, J., Li, S., Li, Y.: A novel global harmony search algorithm for reliability problems. Comput. Ind. Eng. 58, 307–316 (2010)

8. McMinn, P.: Search-based software test data generation: a survey: Research Articles. Softw. Test. Verif. Reliab. 14, 105–156 (2004)

9. Harman, M., Mansouri, A., Zhang, S., Search, Y.: based software engineering: A comprehensive analysis and review of trends techniques and applications. King's College,Technical Report TR-09-03 (2009)

10. Geem, Z.W.: Music-Inspired Harmony Search Algorithm: Theory and Applications. Springer Publishing Company (2009) (Incorporated)

11. Ali, S., Briand, L.C., Hemmati, H., Panesar-Walawege, R.K.: A Systematic Review of the Application and Empirical Investigation of Search-Based Test Case Generation. IEEE Transactions on Software Engineering 99 (2009)

12. Arcuri, A., Iqbal, M.Z., Briand, L.: Black-box system testing of real-time embedded systems using random and search-based testing. In: Petrenko, A., Simão, A., Maldonado, J.C. (eds.) ICTSS 2010. LNCS, vol. 6435, pp. 95–110. Springer, Heidelberg (2010)

13. Fraser, G., Arcuri, A.: Whole Test Suite Generation. IEEE Transactions on Software Engineering (2012)

14. Arcuri, A., Briand., L.: A Practical Guide for Using Statistical Tests to Assess Randomized Algorithms in Software Engineering. In: International Conference on Software Engineering, ICSE (2011)

15. Alia, O.M.D., Mandava, R.: The variants of the harmony search algorithm: an overview. Artif. Intell. Rev. 36, 49–68 (2011)

Appendix A

Table 2. Results for Success Rates for N1 for Each Pair of Algorithms

P#	AVM	HS	1+1(EA)	RS	GA	AVM vs HS OR	AVM vs HS p-value	AVM vs 1+1(EA) OR	AVM vs 1+1(EA) p-value	AVM vs RS OR	AVM vs RS p-value	AVM vs GA OR	AVM vs GA p-value	HS vs 1+1(EA) OR	HS vs 1+1(EA) p-value	HS vs RS OR	HS vs RS p-value	HS vs GA OR	HS vs GA p-value	1+1(EA) vs RS OR	1+1(EA) vs RS p-value	1+1(EA) vs GA OR	1+1(EA) vs GA p-value	RS vs GA OR	RS vs GA p-value
1	0.34	1	1	0	1	0.002	<0.0001	0.002	<0.0001	104	<0.0001	0.002	<0.0001	1	-	40401	<0.0001	1	-	40401	<0.0001	1	-	1	<0.0001
2	0.53	1	1	0.44	1	0.005	<0.0001	0.005	<0.0001	1	0.25	0.005	<0.0001	1	-	255	<0.0001	1	-	255	<0.0001	1	-	1	0.003
3	1	1	0.97	0.29	1	1	-	7	0.24	487	<0.0001	1	-	7	0.24	487	<0.0001	1	-	67	<0.0001	0.13	0.13	0.002	0.002
4	1	1	1	0.32	1	1	-	1	-	423	<0.0001	1	-	1	-	423	<0.0001	1	-	423	<0.0001	1	-	0.002	<0.0001
5	1	1	1	0	0.55	1	-	1	-	40401	<0.0001	164	<0.0001	1	-	40401	<0.0001	164	<0.0001	40401	<0.0001	164	<0.0001	0.004	<0.0001
6	1	1	1	1	1	1	-	1	-	1	-	1	-	1	-	1	-	1	-	1	-	1	-	1	1
7	1	1	1	0.41	1	1	-	1	-	288	<0.0001	1	-	1	-	288	<0.0001	1	-	288	<0.0001	1	-	1	0.003
8	1	1	1	0	1	1	-	1	-	40401	<0.0001	1	-	1	-	40401	<0.0001	1	-	40401	<0.0001	1	-	1	<0.0001
Avg.	0.86	1	0.9963	0.31	0.94	-	-	-	-	-	-	-	-	-	-	-	-	-	-	-	-	-	-	-	-

Table 3. Results for the Number of Iterations for N1 for Each Pair of Algorithms

P#	AVM	HS	1+1(EA)	RS	GA	AVM vs HS A12	AVM vs HS p-value	AVM vs 1+1(EA) A12	AVM vs 1+1(EA) p-value	AVM vs RS A12	AVM vs RS p-value	AVM vs GA A12	AVM vs GA p-value	HS vs 1+1(EA) A12	HS vs 1+1(EA) p-value	HS vs RS A12	HS vs RS p-value	HS vs GA A12	HS vs GA p-value	1+1(EA) vs RS A12	1+1(EA) vs RS p-value	1+1(EA) vs GA A12	1+1(EA) vs GA p-value	RS vs GA A12	RS vs GA p-value
1	0.34	1	1	0	1	-	-	-	-	0.56	-	-	-	0.28	<0.0001	-	-	0.49	0.69	-	-	0.62	<0.0001	-	-
2	0.53	1	1	0.44	1	-	-	-	-	0.56	0.84	-	-	0.57	0.09	-	-	0.42	0.02	-	-	0.4	<0.0001	-	-
3	1	1	0.97	0.29	1	0.45	0.29	0.58	0.27	-	-	0.48	0.56	0.56	0.05	-	-	0.52	0.62	-	-	0.43	0.13	-	-
4	1	1	1	0.32	1	0.24	<0.0001	0.41	0.01	-	-	0.19	<0.0001	0.67	<0.0001	-	-	0.51	0.73	-	-	0.27	<0.0001	-	-
5	1	1	1	0	0.55	0.21	<0.0001	0.32	<0.0001	-	-	0.5	1	0.43	0.03	-	-	0.5	-	-	-	0.5	1	0.5	1
6	1	1	1	1	1	-	<0.0001	0.5	1	0.5	1	0.5	1	0.5	-	0.5	-	0.55	0.23	0.5	1	0.47	0.93	-	-
7	1	1	1	0.41	1	0.4	0.02	0.41	0.1	-	-	0.38	0.18	0.52	0.34	-	-	0.55	0.23	-	-	0.47	0.93	-	-
8	1	1	1	0	1	0.81	<0.0001	0.71	<0.0001	-	-	0.72	<0.0001	0.33	0.001	-	-	0.46	0.63	-	-	0.57	0.005	-	-
Avg.	0.86	1	0.9963	0.31	0.94	-	-	-	-	-	-	-	-	-	-	-	-	-	-	-	-	-	-	-	-

Table 4. Results for Success Rates for N2 for Each Pair of Algorithms

P#	AVM	HS	1+1(EA)	RS	GA
1	0	1	0.82	0	0.89
2	0	1	0.24	0.98	1
3	0	1	0.31	0.27	1
4	0	1	0.27	0.39	1
5	0	1	0.22	0	0.14
6	0	1	1	1	1
7	0	1	0.39	0.31	1
8	0	1	0.8	0	0.89
Avg.	0.13	1	0.50625	0.37	0.87

P#	AVM vs HS A12	p-value	AVM vs 1+1(EA) A12	p-value	AVM vs RS A12	p-value	AVM vs GA A12	p-value	HS vs 1+1(EA) A12	p-value	HS vs RS A12	p-value	HS vs GA A12	p-value	1+1(EA) vs RS A12	p-value	1+1(EA) vs GA A12	p-value	RS vs GA A12	p-value
1	-	-	-	-	-	-	-	-	0.55	0.15	0.49	0.88	0.46	0.23	0.6	-	0.6	0.05	-	0.18
2	-	-	-	-	-	-	-	-	0.6	0.001	-	-	0.88	0.32	-	-	-	-	0.45	-
3	-	-	-	-	-	-	-	-	0.6	0.002	-	-	0.49	-	0.46	0.33	-	-	-	-
4	-	-	-	-	-	-	-	-	0.64	0.001	-	-	0.52	-	0.5	0.76	-	-	-	-
5	-	-	-	-	-	-	-	-	0.45	0.94	-	-	-	-	-	-	0.48	0.48	0.32	0.32
6	1	0.5	1	0.5	1	0.5	1	0.5	0.5	1	0.5	1	0.5	0.93	0.5	1	0.5	1	1	1
7	-	-	-	-	-	-	-	-	0.61	0.01	-	-	0.51	-	0.5	0.73	1	1	-	-
8	-	-	-	-	-	-	-	-	0.54	0.22	-	-	-	-	-	-	0.57	0.11	-	-

Table 5. Results for the Number of Iterations for N2 for Each Pair of Algorithms

P#	AVM	HS	1+1(EA)	RS	GA
1	0	1	0.82	0	0.89
2	0	1	0.24	0.98	1
3	0	1	0.31	0.27	1
4	0	1	0.27	0.39	1
5	0	1	0.22	0	0.14
6	0	1	1	1	1
7	0	1	0.39	0.31	1
8	0	1	0.8	0	0.89
Avg.	0.13	1	0.5063	0.37	0.87

P#	AVM vs HS OR	p-value	AVM vs 1+1(EA) OR	p-value	AVM vs RS OR	p-value	AVM vs GA OR	p-value	HS vs 1+1(EA) OR	p-value	HS vs RS OR	p-value	HS vs GA OR	p-value	1+1(EA) vs RS OR	p-value	1+1(EA) vs GA OR	p-value	RS vs GA OR	p-value
1	1	<0.0001	0.001	<0.0001	1	0.0006	1	0.0006	45	<0.0001	40401	<0.0001	25	<0.0001	896	<0.0001	0.57	0.22	0.0006	<0.0001
2	1	<0.0001	0.01	<0.0001	0.0001	<0.0001	1	<0.0001	627	<0.0001	5	0.49	1	1	1	0.008	1	0.001	0.19	0.49
3	1	<0.0001	0.01	<0.0001	0.01	<0.0001	1	<0.0001	443	<0.0001	537	<0.0001	1	1	1.2	0.64	1	0.002	0.001	<0.0001
4	1	<0.0001	0.01	<0.0001	0.007	<0.0001	1	<0.0001	537	<0.0001	312	<0.0001	1	1	0.58	0.09	1	0.001	0.003	<0.0001
5	1	<0.0001	0.01	<0.0001	1	<0.0001	1	<0.0001	701	<0.0001	40401	<0.0001	1199	<0.0001	57	<0.0001	1.7	0.19	0.02	<0.0001
6	1	1	1	1	1	1	1	1	1	1	1	1	1	1	1	1	1	1	1	1
7	1	<0.0001	0.007	<0.0001	0.01	<0.0001	1	<0.0001	312	<0.0001	443	<0.0001	1	1	1.4	0.29	1	0.003	0.002	<0.0001
8	1	<0.0001	0.001	<0.0001	1	0.0006	1	0.0006	51	<0.0001	40401	<0.0001	25	<0.0001	789	<0.0001	0.5	0.11	0.0006	<0.0001

Table 6. Artificial Problems Used in the Experiment

P#	Example
1	let c = Set(0,1,2,3) in X.allInstances() → select(b|b.y>0 and b.y<5) → size()>=5 and X.allInstances() → select(b|b.y>0 and b.y<5) → collect(b|b.y) → excludesAll(c)
2	X.allInstances() → select(b|b.y > 90) → size() > 4 and X.allInstances() → select(b|b.y > 90) → exists(b|b.y=92)
3	X.allInstances() → select(b|b.y > 90) → size() > 4 and X.allInstances() → select(b|b.y > 90) → isUnique(b|b.y)
4	X.allInstances() → select(b|b.y > 90) → size() > 4 and X.allInstances() → select(b|b.y > 90) → one(b|b.y=95)
5	X.allInstances() → select(b|b.y>0) → size()>6
6	X.allInstances() → select(b|b.y>0) → size()>=1
7	X.allInstances() → select(b|b.y > 90) → size() > 4 and X.allInstances() → select(b|b.y=92) → size() <> 0
8	X.allInstances() → select(b|b.y=0) → size() = 5

Lookahead-Based Approaches for Minimizing Adaptive Distinguishing Sequences

Uraz Cengiz Türker, Tonguç Ünlüyurt, and Hüsnü Yenigün

Sabanci University, Orhanli, Tuzla, 34956, Istanbul, TURKEY
{urazc,tonguc,yenigun}@sabanciuniv.edu

Abstract. For Finite State Machine (FSM) based testing, it has been shown that the use of shorter Adaptive Distinguishing Sequences (ADS) yields shorter test sequences. It is also known, on the other hand, that constructing a minimum cost ADS is an NP-hard problem and it is NP-hard to approximate. In this paper, we introduce a lookahead-based greedy algorithm to construct reduced ADSs for FSMs. The greedy algorithm inspects a search space to make a decision. The size of the search space is adjustable, allowing a trade-off between the quality and the computation time. We analyse the performance of the approach on randomly generated FSMs by comparing the ADSs constructed by our algorithm with the ADSs that are computed by the existing algorithms.

Keywords: Finite State Machines, Adaptive Distinguishing Sequences, greedy algorithms.

1 Introduction

Finite State Machines (FSMs) have been used to model reactive systems [1–6]. A number of techniques, which operate on FSM models of such systems, automatically generate test sequences [1, 7–14]. In order to reduce the cost of testing, shorter test sequences are preferrable and there is an increasing number of studies in the literature in this direction [13, 15–19].

State identification sequences [8, 9, 20] play a central role in the design of these test sequences and a large portion of these test sequences consists of state identification sequences. Many techniques for constructing test sequences use *Distinguishing Sequences* (DSs) as state identification sequences. There exist polynomial time algorithms that generate test sequences when a DS is given. Moreover, the length of the test sequence is relatively short when designed with a DS [15, 16, 21–23][1].

A distinguishing sequence can be preset or adaptive. If the input sequence is known before the experiment, then it is a *Preset Distinguishing Sequence* (PDS). If the input symbol to be applied is decided after observing the response of the FSM to the previous input, then it is an *Adaptive Distinguishing Sequence* (also

---

[1] Although the upper bound on PDS length is exponential, test generation takes polynomial time if there is a known PDS.

M.G. Merayo and E. Montes de Oca (Eds.): ICTSS 2014, LNCS 8763, pp. 32–47, 2014.

known as a *Distinguishing Set*) [21]. Therefore an ADS is essentially a decision tree. The internal nodes of the tree are labeled by input symbols, the edges are labeled by output symbols where the edges emanating from a common node have different labels, and the leaves are labeled by states.

Using an ADS rather than a PDS is advantageous due to the following. Lee and Yannakakis show that checking the existence and computing a PDS is a PSPACE-complete problem. On the other hand, for a given FSM M with n states and m inputs, the existence of an ADS can be decided in time $O(mn \log n)$, and if exists, an ADS can be constructed in time $O(mn^2)$ by using the algorithm presented by Lee and Yannakakis (which we refer to as *LY Algorithm* in this work) [23].

It was proven by Sokolovskii that if an FSM M has an ADS, then an ADS for M with height no greater than $\pi^2 n^2/12$ exists [24]. Later Lee and Yannakakis reduced this bound to $n(n-1)/2$ and they showed that this bound is tight [23]. Kushik et al. present an algorithm for constructing ADSs for nondeterministic observable FSMs [25]. Since the class of deterministic FSMs is a subclass of nondeterministic observable FSMs, naturally the algorithm can also be used to construct ADS for deterministic FSMs.

Although Lee and Yannakakis have proven a tight upper bound on the height of an ADS, there is no work attempting to construct reduced size ADSs, other than the exponential time exhaustive algorithms [20,26]. Recently in [27], Türker and Yenigün showed the potential enhancements of using reduced cost ADSs on the length of test sequences. They also examined the computational complexity of constructing minimum cost ADSs, where the "cost" of an ADS is defined as (i) the height of the ADS, and (ii) the sum of lengths of all root–to–leaf paths in the ADS (which is called *the external path length* of the ADS). They showed that constructing a minimum ADS with respect to these cost metrics are NP-complete and NP-hard to approximate. Thus, to construct reduced size ADSs, heuristic algorithms are needed.

In this paper we present a lookahead-based method for constructing reduced ADSs. The proposed lookahead search methodology uses a tree structure (called EST) to construct reduced size ADSs. The construction of EST is guided by different heuristics based on the objective, such as minimizing the height or the external path length of the ADS. The EST is potentially an infinite tree but the proposed method constructs and evaluates the EST greedily, limiting the size of the EST. By choosing how far one wants to lookahead during the construction of an ADS, a trade off between the time to construct an ADS and the cost of the ADS is possible. We evaluate the proposed method by performing experimental studies on randomly generated FSMs. The results indicate that the proposed method produces better results than LY algorithm, possibly at the expense of more computation time.

In the rest of this paper we first give the definitions and notation that will be used in this paper. We then present the details of the algorithm to construct reduced ADSs. Finally, we present the results of the experiments, and conclude by some discussions and giving some future directions of research.

2 Preliminaries

2.1 Finite State Machines

An FSM (or a Mealy machine) M is defined by a tuple $M = (S, X, Y, \delta, \lambda)$ where S is a finite set of states, X and Y are finite sets of input and output symbols, $\delta : S \times X \to S$ is the state transition function, and $\lambda : S \times X \to Y$ is the output function. If M is at a state $s \in S$, and if an input $x \in X$ is applied, M moves to the state $s' = \delta(s, x)$ and produces the output $y = \lambda(s, x)$. Note that, since the transitions are defined by a function (rather than a relation), M is *deterministic*. When δ and λ are total functions, M is said to be *completely specified*.

We use juxtaposition to denote concatenation. For example, $w = x_1 x_2 \ldots x_k$, where $x_i \in X$, $1 \le i \le k$, denotes an input sequence. An input/output sequence consists of a sequence of input/output pairs of the form $x_1/y_1 x_2/y_2 \ldots x_m/y_m$. The symbol ϵ is used to denote the empty sequence. The transition function and the output function can be extended to sequences of inputs. By abusing the notation, we will use δ and λ for the extended functions. These extensions are defined as follows (where $x \in X$ and $w \in X^*$): $\delta(s, \epsilon) = s$ and $\delta(s, xw) = \delta(\delta(s, x), w)$; $\lambda(s, \epsilon) = \epsilon$ and $\lambda(s, xw) = \lambda(s, x)\lambda(\delta(s, x), w)$. Two states $s, s' \in S$ are said to be *equivalent* if for all input sequences $w \in X^*$, $\lambda(s, w) = \lambda(s', w)$. Otherwise, if there exists an input sequence $w \in X^*$ such that $\lambda(s, w) \ne \lambda(s', w)$, then s and s' are said to be *distinguishable*. An FSM M is *minimal* if the states of M are pairwise distinguishable. In Figure 1, an example FSM is given which is deterministic, completely specified and minimal.

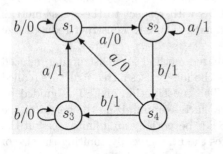

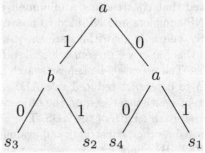

Fig. 1. An example deterministic, completely specified and minimal FSM M

Fig. 2. The ADS $\mathcal{A}$ of FSM M in Figure 1

A subset of states $B \subseteq S$ is called a *block*. We also extend δ and λ to a block as follows: For a block B and an input sequence w, $\delta(B, w) = \{\delta(s, w) \mid s \in B\}$ and $\lambda(B, w) = \{\lambda(s, w) \mid s \in B\}$. An input symbol x is said to be *valid* for a block B, for all $s, s' \in B$ such that $s \ne s'$, $\lambda(s, x) = \lambda(s', x)$ implies $\delta(s, x) \ne \delta(s', x)$. An input sequence w is *valid for* B, if for every prefix vx of w, where $v \in X^*$ and $x \in X$, x is valid for the block $\delta(B, v)$.

2.2   Adaptive Distinguishing Sequence

Definition 1. *An* Adaptive Distinguishing Sequence *of an FSM* $M = (S, X, Y, \delta, \lambda)$ *with n states is a rooted tree* $\mathcal{A}$ *with n leaves such that: (i) Each leaf of* $\mathcal{A}$ *is labeled by a distinct state* $s \in S$. *(ii) Each internal node of* $\mathcal{A}$ *is labeled by an input symbol* $x \in X$. *(iii) Each edge is labeled by an output symbol* $y \in Y$. *(iv) The outgoing edges of an internal node are labeled by distinct output symbols. (v) For a leaf node p labeled by a state* $s \in S$, *if w is the sequence of input symbols that appear in the nodes of the path from the root to p, and v is the sequence of output symbols labeling the edges of the path from root to p, then* $\lambda(s, w) = v$.

An ADS $\mathcal{A}$ defines an adaptive experiment to identify the unknown initial state of an FSM, where the next input to be applied is decided by the input/output sequence observed previously. Let us assume that we are given an FSM M and we want to identify its current unknown state. One starts by applying the input symbol labeling the root of $\mathcal{A}$. We then follow the outgoing branch of the root that is labeled by y where y is the output symbol produced by M as the response to the input applied. This procedure is recursively applied for each subtree reached, until we reach a leaf node. The label of the leaf node gives the initial unknown state. An ADS of the FSM given in Figure 1 is given in Figure 2.

For a given deterministic FSM M, an ADS may or may not exist. One can check if M has an ADS in $O(mn \log n)$ time [23]. In this work, we consider only deterministic, minimal and completely specified FSMs, which are assumptions commonly adapted in the FSM based testing literature. Furthermore, we also consider only FSMs for which an ADS exist.

Let $\mathcal{A}$ be an ADS and p be a node in $\mathcal{A}$. We use *depth* of p to refer to the length of the path from the root of $\mathcal{A}$ to p. The *height* of $\mathcal{A}$ is defined to be the maximum depth of the leaves in $\mathcal{A}$. The *external path length* of $\mathcal{A}$ is the sum of depths of all the leaves in $\mathcal{A}$.

2.3   An Algorithm for Constructing an ADS

The LY algorithm [23] constructs an ADS for an FSM $M = (S, X, Y, \delta, \lambda)$ in two steps. First a tree called *Splitting Tree* (ST) is formed. For any block $B \subseteq S$ such that $|B| > 1$, ST provides a valid input sequence w for B such that $|\lambda(B, w)| > 1$. Hence, w is an input sequence that can partition B into smaller blocks as $B_1, B_2, \ldots, B_{|\lambda(B,w)|}$, where two states $s, s' \in B$ are in the same block B_i iff $\lambda(s, w) = \lambda(s', w)$.

In the second step of LY algorithm, ST is used to construct an ADS $\mathcal{A}$. The construction process explained below does not explicitly form an ADS as given in Definition 1, but it implies the construction of such a tree implicitly. The reader is referred to [23] for more details of the construction.

During the construction of the ADS, each nonleaf node p of $\mathcal{A}$ is labeled by an input sequence and each edge of $\mathcal{A}$ is labeled by an output sequence. Each node p of $\mathcal{A}$ is also associated with a block $\mathcal{C}(p)$ that corresponds to the current set of states. More precisely, if w is the concatenation of the input sequence labels of the nodes from the root to p (excluding the label of p), and v is the concatenation of the output labels of the edges from the root to p, then the block $\mathcal{C}(p)$ is set to $\mathcal{C}(p) = \{\delta(s, w) \mid v = \lambda(s, w), s \in S\}$.

Initially, the root node p of $\mathcal{A}$ is created by setting $\mathcal{C}(p) = S$, where S is the set of all states of M. As long as there is a leaf node p in the (partial) ADS tree constructed so far such that $|\mathcal{C}(p)| > 1$, the tree extended by processing such a node p. First an input sequence w is found from ST such that w is valid for $\mathcal{C}(p)$ and $|\lambda(\mathcal{C}(p), w)| > 1$. Then p is labeled by the input sequence w and a set of children node $p_1, p_2, \ldots, p_k$ of p is created, where a child node p_i is introduced for each possible output sequence $v \in \lambda(\mathcal{C}(p), w)$. The edge from p to p_i is labeled by v and the child p_i is associated with the block $\{\delta(s, w) \mid v = \lambda(s, w), s \in \mathcal{C}(p)\}$.

3   Proposed Algorithm

In this section, we explain the details of the proposed algorithm to construct a reduced ADS for an FSM $M = (S, X, Y, \delta, \lambda)$ which is minimal, deterministic, completely specified and known to have an ADS. Before presenting the details of the actual algorithm we provide some definitions and routines that are going to be used in this section.

For a block B, an input sequence w and an output sequence v, we use the notation $B_{w/v}$ to denote the set $B_{w/v} = \{s \in B \mid \lambda(s, w) = v\}$. In other words, $B_{w/v}$ is the set of states in B that produce the output sequence v when the input sequence w is applied.

In [28], Hennie introduces the use of a tree, called the *successor tree*, for constructing adaptive homing/distinguishing sequences. The successor tree grows exponentially and it possesses information that can be used to find the minimum cost adaptive homing/distinguishing sequences. However since it grows exponentially, it becomes impractical to construct a successor tree to obtain a reduced adaptive homing/distinguishing sequence for large FSMs.

Our method has two phases. In the first phase, a tree called the *Enhanced Successor Tree (EST)* similar to a successor tree is generated. In the second phase, EST is used to construct an ADS.

An EST contains two types of nodes; *input nodes* $\mathcal{I}$ and *output nodes* $\mathcal{O}$. The root and the leaves of an EST are output nodes. Except the leaves, the children of an output node are input nodes, and the children of an input node are output nodes. In other words, on a path from the root to a leaf, one observes a sequence of output and input nodes alternatingly, starting and ending with an output node.

Each input node p is labeled by an input symbol $in(p)$. Similarly, each output node q is labeled by an output symbol $out(q)$, except the root node for which $out(q) = \epsilon$. An output node q is also associated with a block $bl(q)$. For the root node q, $bl(q) = S$. An output node q is a leaf node iff $|bl(q)| = 1$. A non-leaf output node q that is associated with a block $bl(q)$, has a separate input node p as its child for each input symbol x that is valid for $bl(q)$, with $in(p) = x$. An input node p (where $x = in(p)$) with a parent output node q (where $B = bl(q)$), has a separate output node r as its child for each output symbol $y \in \lambda(B, x)$, with $out(r) = y$ and $bl(r) = \delta(B_{x/y}, x)$.

The EST of an FSM M is potentially an infinite tree. Instead of the whole tree, the algorithm constructs a limited size *partial* EST which can be used to construct an ADS. The algorithm uses heuristic approaches to explore the relevant and promising parts of the EST to find a reduced size ADS with respect to different metrics, such as the height and the external path length. The partial EST constructed by the algorithm will be the EST where the tree is pruned at several nodes. For a leaf node q in an EST we have $|bl(q)| = 1$. However, for a leaf node q in a partial EST, it is possible to have $|bl(q)| \geq 1$.

Initially, the algorithm starts with the partial EST consisting of only the root node. In each iteration, an output node q is handled and the partial EST rooted at q is expanded exhaustively upto depth k, where k is a parameter given to the algorithm. Among the children of q, an input node p that seems to be the best (according to the objective and the heuristic being used) is selected, and the search continues recursively under the subtrees rooted at the children of p.

During the construction of the partial EST T, some nodes are marked as the nodes to be used for ADS construction later. Namely, a set of output nodes L and a set of input nodes I are marked. Each output node $q \in L$ has the property that $|bl(q)| = 1$ and it corresponds to a leaf node in the ADS that will be constructed later. Also the nodes in I will be corresponding to the non–leaf nodes of the ADS. The algorithm constructing a partial EST is given in Algorithm 1.

Algorithm 1. Construct a partial EST for M

Input: FSM $M = (S, X, Y, \delta, \lambda)$, $k \in \mathbb{Z}_{\geq 1}$
Output: A partial EST T, a set of leaves L, and a set of input nodes I
begin

1     $L \leftarrow \emptyset$, $I \leftarrow \emptyset$
2   Construct an output node q_0 with $bl(q_0) = S$, $out(q_0) = \epsilon$
3   Initialize T to be a tree consisting of the root q_0 only
4     $Q \leftarrow \{q_0\}$ // Q is the set of output nodes yet to be processed
5   **while** $Q \neq \emptyset$ **do**
6   Pick an output node $q \in Q$ to process
7        $Q \leftarrow Q \setminus \{q\}$
8   ExpandEST(q,k) // expand subtree under q exhaustively upto a certain depth
9   Choose a child node p of q // based on the objective and the heuristic used
10       $I \leftarrow I \cup \{p\}$ // The input node p will be used for the ADS
11   **foreach** child r of p **do**
           if $|bl(r)| > 1$ **then**
12 | $Q \leftarrow Q \cup \{r\}$ // not a singleton yet, needs to be processed
           else
13            $L \leftarrow L \cup \{r\}$ // reached a singleton block

---

The procedure "ExpandEST(q, k)", constructs the partial EST rooted at the node q exhaustively upto the given depth k. If in this partial subtree, for every leaf node r, we have $|bl(q)| = |bl(r)|$ (which means the block $bl(q)$ could not be divided into smaller blocks by using input sequences of length upto k that are valid for $bl(q)$), the procedure increases the depth of the subtree rooted at q until it encounters a level at which there exists a leaf node r with $|bl(r)| < |bl(q)|$. This is always possible since the FSM M has an ADS.

At line 9 of Algorithm 1, a child node p of q is chosen heuristically. This choice is based on the scores of the nodes which are calculated by processing the nodes in the subtree rooted at q in a bottom–up manner. First the scores of the leaves in this subtree are computed. This is followed by the score evaluation of the internal nodes in the subtree. The score of a non–leaf node depends on the scores of its children. The score of a node reflects the potential size of the ADS that will be eventually formed if that node is decided to be used in the ADS to be formed.

When the score of an output node q is computed based on the scores of its children, since we have the control over the input to be chosen, the child node of q having the minimum score is chosen. However, when the score of an input node p is computed based on the scores of its children, since we do not have the control of the output to be produced, we prepare for the worst and use the maximum score of the children of p. A similar approach is in fact also suggested by Hennie (see Chapter 3 of [28]). The process of calculating the scores of the nodes depends on the heuristic used. The details are given in Section 3.1.

Before presenting the algorithm to construct an ADS, we will give some properties of the nodes L and I marked by Algorithm 1. For an output node q, consider the path from the root of T to q (including q). Let w and v be the concatenation of input symbols and output symbols on this path, respectively. We use below the notation $io(q)$ to refer to the input/output sequence w/v.

Proposition 1. *Let q be an output node in T and let $io(q) = w/v$. Then we have $bl(q) = \delta(S_{w/v}, w)$.*

Proof. The proof is trivial by using induction on the depth of q.   □

Proposition 2. $|L| + \sum_{q \in Q} |bl(q)| = |S|$ *is an invariant of Algorithm 1 before and after every iteration the while loop.*

Proof. Before the first iteration, $|L| = 0$ and Q only has the root node q_0 for which we have $bl(q_0) = S$. In an iteration of the algorithm, an output node q is removed from Q and a child (input) node p of q is selected. It is sufficient to observe two facts. First, each state $s \in bl(q)$ is represented by a state $s' \in bl(q')$ where q' is a child of p, $s' = \delta(s, in(p))$ and $out(q') = \lambda(s, in(p))$. Second, no two states $s_1, s_2 \in bl(q)$ can be represented by the same state s' in the same child q', since $in(p)$ is a valid input for the states in $bl(q)$. Therefore, when we consider all children q' of p, we have $\sum_{q'} |bl(q')| = |bl(q)|$. Those children q' of p with $|bl(q')| = 1$ are included in L, and those children q' of p with $|bl(q')| > 1$ are included in Q. Hence the result follows.   □

Proposition 2 implies the following result, since when Algorithm 1 terminates we have $Q = \emptyset$.

Corollary 1. *When Algorithm 1 terminates, $|L| = |S|$.*

Proposition 3. *Let q be an output node in T with $|bl(q)| = 1$, and let $w/v = io(q)$. There exists a unique state $s \in S$ such that $\lambda(s, w) = v$.*

Proof. Suppose s and s' are two distinct states such that $\lambda(s, w) = \lambda(s', w) = v$. By Proposition 1, we would then have $\delta(s, w)$ and $\delta(s', w)$ in $bl(q)$. Since $|bl(q)| = 1$, this implies $\delta(s, w) = \delta(s', w)$. This is not possible since at each step a valid input is applied, therefore no two states can be merged into a single state.   □

Algorithm 2 describes how an ADS can be constructed based on the partial EST T, the set of marked nodes L and I in T by Algorithm 1. Note that at line 6 of Algorithm 2, $S_{w/v}$ is claimed to be a singleton, which is guaranteed by Proposition 3. In order to show that $\mathcal{A}$ which is generated by Algorithm 2 is an ADS, we also prove the following.

Proposition 4. *The leaves of $\mathcal{A}$ constructed by Algorithm 2 is labeled by distinct states.*

Proof. Assume that there are two leaf nodes q'_1 and q'_2 in $\mathcal{A}$ such that they are both labeled by the same state s. Let q_1 and q_2 be the leaf (output) nodes in T that correspond to q'_1 and q'_2. Let w_1/v_1 and w_2/v_2 be the input/output sequences $io(q_1)$ and $io(q_2)$. In this case, we would have $\lambda(s, w_1) = v_1$ and $\lambda(s, w_2) = v_2$. However, this is not possible since M is deterministic.   □

Theorem 1. *$\mathcal{A}$ constructed by Algorithm 2 is an ADS.*

Proof. $\mathcal{A}$ has $n = |S|$ leaves as implied by Corollary 1. We will argue that $\mathcal{A}$ satisfies the conditions of Definition 1. Condition (i) is satisfied as shown by Proposition 4. Condition (ii) and Condition (iii) are easily satisfied due to the construction in Algorithm 2. Condition (iv) is satisfied due to the fact that in T, for an input node p, each child q of p has a distinct output symbol $out(q)$. Lines 5–8 of Algorithm 2, assign the label of leaves in such a way that Condition (v) is satisfied (see Proposition 3).   □

3.1   Heuristics

We use different heuristic approaches to minimize the size of ADSs with respect to two different metrics, which are minimizing the height and minimizing the external path length of the ADS.

As mentioned above, the score of a node q in the partial EST constructed so far is an estimation of the size of the ADS that will be formed by using a child of q in ADS. Let $d(q)$ be the depth of q in the partial EST and $v(q)$ be the score of q. We also keep track of another information, $z(q)$. It is the number of singleton output nodes in the winner subtrees under q in the current partial EST, and used to break the ties as explained below.

Let us consider a leaf node q, where $|bl(q)| = 1$. This is in fact a leaf node also in the complete EST. For such leaf nodes, we set $v(q) = d(q)$ and $z(q) = 1$. However, for a leaf node q in the current partial EST with $|bl(q)| > 1$, we set $z(q) = 0$. Although q is currently a leaf node in the partial EST, if we were to expand q, there will appear a subtree under q. In order to take into account the

Algorithm 2. Construct an ADS

Input: The partial EST T, the set of marked nodes L and I by Algorithm 1
Output: An ADS $\mathcal{A}$
begin

    // Construct and label the internal nodes of $\mathcal{A}$

1   **foreach** node $p \in I$ **do**
2   Construct an internal node p' in $\mathcal{A}$
3   Label p' by $in(p)$

    // Construct and label the leaf nodes of $\mathcal{A}$

4   **foreach** node $q \in L$ **do**
5   Let $w/v = io(q)$
6   Let s be the state such that $\{s\} = S_{w/v}$
7   Construct a leaf node q' in $\mathcal{A}$
8   Label q' by s

    // Construct the edges to the leaves

9   **foreach** leaf node $q' \in \mathcal{A}$ **do**
10   Let q be the corresponding node of q' in T
11   Let p be the parent of q in T
12   Let p' be the corresponding node of p in $\mathcal{A}$
13   Insert an edge between p' and q' with the label $out(q)$

    // Construct the remaining edges

14   **foreach** internal node $p' \in \mathcal{A}$ **do**
15   Let p be the corresponding node of p' in T
16   **if** p *has a grandparent in* T **then**
              // except the root of $\mathcal{A}$
17   Let q be the parent of p in T
18   Let r be the parent of q in T
19   Let r' be the corresponding node of p in $\mathcal{A}$
20   Insert an edge between p' and r' with the label $out(q)$

---

size of the subtree rooted at q (without actually constructing this subtree), we need to estimate the size of the subtree under q. Note that $bl(q)$ is the set of states yet to be distinguished from each other.

We consider two different metrics as the size of an ADS: height or external path length. Depending on the objective, we estimate the size of the subtree that would appear under a (yet to be processed) output node q in different ways. While minimizing for height, we use two different heuristic functions $\mathcal{H}_U : \mathcal{O} \to \mathbb{R}^+$ and $\mathcal{H}_{LY} : \mathcal{O} \to \mathbb{R}^+$. Similarly, while optimizing for external path length, we use heuristic functions $\mathcal{L}_U : \mathcal{O} \to \mathbb{R}^+$ and $\mathcal{L}_{LY} : \mathcal{O} \to \mathbb{R}^+$.

For an FSM with n states the height of an ADS is bounded above by $n(n-1)/2$ [23]. We use this bound for heuristic functions $\mathcal{H}_U$ and $\mathcal{L}_U$ in the following way. The score of node q with respect to function $\mathcal{H}_U$ is given as

$$\mathcal{H}_U(q) = d(q) + |bl(q)|(|bl(q)| - 1)/2$$

where $d(q)$ is the depth of q. On the other hand, function $\mathcal{L}_U$ multiplies the number of states with the expected height of the subtree to approximate the expected external path length. That is

$$\mathcal{L}_U(q) = (d(q) + |bl(q)|(|bl(q)| - 1)/2)|bl(q)|$$

As another estimation method for the size of the subtree to appear under an output node q, one can use LY algorithm to construct an ADS for the states in $bl(q)$. The heuristic functions $\mathcal{H}_{LY}$ and $\mathcal{L}_{LY}$ use this idea. Let A' be the ADS computed by LY algorithm for the states in $bl(q)$, and let $h(A')$ and $l(A')$ be the height and the external path length of A'. Then the heuristic functions $\mathcal{H}_{LY}$ and $\mathcal{L}_{LY}$ are defined as

$$\mathcal{H}_{LY}(q) = d(q) + h(A')$$
$$\mathcal{L}_{LY}(q) = d(q)|bl(q)| + l(A')$$

At line 9 of Algorithm 1, for the output node q being processed in that iteration, an input node p which is a child of q is chosen. Let T' refer to the subtree rooted at q in the partial EST at this point. While choosing the child input node p to be used, the scores of the nodes in T' are calculated in a bottom up manner. First, for each (current) leaf node q' (which is an output node) in T', $v(q')$ is assigned by using one of the heuristic functions ($\mathcal{H}_U(q')$ or $\mathcal{H}_{LY}(q')$ for height optimization, and $\mathcal{L}_U(q')$ or $\mathcal{L}_{LY}(q')$ for external path length optimization) and $z(q')$ is assigned. The score of the remaining nodes in T' are based on the scores of its children and are calculated as follows.

When minimizing for height, for an input node p', $v(p')$ is set to the maximum score of its children and $z(p')$ is set to the sum of singleton scores of its children. For an output node q', $v(q')$ is set to the minimum score of its children, and $z(q')$ is set to the $z(.)$ value of the winner child. When minimizing for external path length, for an input node p', $v(p')$ and $z(p')$ is set to the sum of the scores of its children. For an output node q' on the other hand, $v(q')$ is set to the minimum score of its children and $z(q')$ is set to the $z(.)$ value of the winner child. Note that, there may be ties during this process when we attempt to take minimum or maximum. Among the nodes achieving the same minimum/maximum, the tie is first tried to be broken by maximizing the number of singleton values ($z(.)$). If there is still a tie, this is broken randomly.

4   Experiments

We generated two test suites, TS1 and TS2. In each test suite, we have 6 classes of FSMs. Each class contains 100 FSMs. Thus the number of FSMs used in these experiments is $600(\text{TS1}) + 600(\text{TS2}) = 1200$. In TS1, the state and input/output alphabet cardinalities of the classes are $(30, 4/4)$, $(30, 8/8)$, $(30, 16/16)$, $(60, 4/4)$, $(60, 8/8)$ and $(60, 16/16)$. TS1 is used to see the effect of the changes in the input/output alphabet cardinalities. For these experiments, the value of the lookahead parameter k is set to 1.

In order to see the effect of the changes in the number of states and the value of the lookahead parameter k, we use the FSMs in TS2. In TS2, the input/output alphabet cardinalities are fixed to $(2/2)$ and the state cardinalities of the classes are $\{25, 30, \ldots, 50\}$. For these experiments, the value of k varies between 1 and 3. Note that while computing an ADS for an FSM M, our heuristic reduces to the brute–force approach when k is greater than or equal to the height of the minimum ADS of M. Hence for such FSMs, our heuristic actually gives exact results. In order to see the effect of the parameter k, we need to have FSMs such that the height of the minimum ADS is larger than the maximum k value used in the experiments. Note that, even for the smallest number of states used in TS2 ($n = 25$), the height of the minimum ADS cannot be smaller than $\log_2 25 > 4$.

4.1 FSM Generation

We randomly generated FSMs using the tool utilised in [15, 29]. To construct an FSM M, first, for each input x and state s we randomly assign the values of $\delta(s, x)$ and $\lambda(s, x)$. If M is strongly connected[2], is minimal, and has an ADS[3], M is included into the test suite. Otherwise, it is discarded. We use Intel Xeon E5-1650 @3.2-GHZ CPU with 16 GB RAM to carry out these tests. We implemented proposed algorithm, LY algorithm and the brute-force algorithm using C++ and compiled them using Microsoft Visual Studio .Net 2012 under 64 bit Windows 7 operating system.

4.2 Evaluation

In order to evaluate the relative performance of different approaches, we compute the ADSs using the proposed algorithm with heuristic functions $\mathcal{H}_U, \mathcal{L}_U, \mathcal{H}_{LY}$ and $\mathcal{L}_{LY}$. Also for each FSM we compute an ADS by using LY and brute–force algorithms. The brute–force algorithm (BF) is described in [26]. BF algorithm constructs EST to a depth that is sufficient to form an ADS. Therefore it is an exponential time algorithm.

In the following sections we present the results of our experimental study. We explain below the measures that we use to compare the relative performance of the algorithms. Here, A refers to the heuristics used (i.e. A is one of $\mathcal{H}_U, \mathcal{L}_U, \mathcal{H}_{LY}$ and $\mathcal{L}_{LY}$). We use $size$ to refer to the height or the external path length, depending on the objective of the minimization. For example, for a given FSM M, if we are considering heights, $size(\mathcal{H}_{LY}(M))$ is the height of the ADS computed by $\mathcal{H}_{LY}$, $size(LY(M))$ is the height of the ADS computed by LY algorithm, and $size(BF(M))$ is the height of the ADS computed by BF algorithm. In this case, $\mathcal{G}_1(\mathcal{H}_{LY}, M)$ gives the percentage decrease in the height of the ADS computed by $\mathcal{H}_{LY}$ compared to the height of the ADS computed by LY algorithm. Therefore, higher $\mathcal{G}_1$ values indicate a better performance of the heuristics over LY algorithm.

Similarly, $\mathcal{G}_2(\mathcal{H}_{LY}, M)$ gives the percentage decrease in the height of the ADS constructed by BF algorithm compared to the height of the ADS constructed by $\mathcal{H}_{LY}$. Therefore, lower $\mathcal{G}_2$ values indicate a better performance of the heuristics, approaching to the optimal values computed by BF algorithm.

Finally, $time(LY(M))$ and $time(A(M))$ are used to denote the time required to compute an ADS by LY and a heuristics, respectively. Although, we compare

---

[2] M is strongly connected if for any pair (s, s') of states of M, there exists an input sequence w such that $\delta(s, w) = s'$.

[3] Existence check for an ADS can be performed in $O(mn \log n)$ time [23].

the height and external path length performance with respect to BF, we only compare the time performance of our heuristics with respect to LY algorithm. This is because, for large FSMs, the exponential BF algorithm will take too much time and will be impractical.

$$\mathcal{G}_1(A, M) = \frac{size(LY(M)) - size(A(M))}{size(LY(M))} \times 100$$

$$\mathcal{G}_2(A, M) = \frac{size(A(M)) - size(BF(M))}{size(A(M))} \times 100$$

$$\mathcal{T}(A, M) = \frac{time(LY(M)) - time(A(M))}{time(LY(M))} \times 100$$

A positive $\mathcal{T}$ value for a heuristic means that the heuristic computes an ADS faster than LY algorithm. Hence higher $\mathcal{T}$ values are better.

4.3 Results

The Effect of the Value of the Lookahead Parameter k. We discuss the effect of the lookahead distance, i.e. the value of the parameter k used in Algorithm 1, by using the experimental results given in Table 1. As expected, higher values of k yield a better performance since the heuristics look further into the EST tree to be generated. The results of the measure $\mathcal{G}_1$ is directly proportional, and the results of the measure $\mathcal{G}_2$ are inversely proportional to k. That is, as the value of parameter k increases, regardless to the heuristic function used, the algorithm produces cheaper ADSs than the LY algorithm. Moreover the results suggest that the difference between the ADS costs constructed by the proposed heuristics and the BF algorithm reduces as k increases. However, the time needed to compute ADSs increases with the values of k. Therefore these experiments reveal that increasing the value of k, improves the quality of the results at the expense of increased running times.

The Effect of the Number of States. Again using the results given in Table 1, we see that the results of the measure $\mathcal{G}_1$ increase with the number of states, especially for higher values of k regardless to the heuristic function used. Therefore we deduce that the performance of all heuristic functions (compared to the performance of LY algorithm) increases as the number of states increases. Note that as the number of states increases, the height and the external path length of optimal ADSs also increase. For such ADSs, our lookahead algorithms start to perform even better compared to LY algorithm, since for such ADSs the information provided by the lookahead algorithms becomes more effective in guiding the search.

On the other hand, the results of the measure $\mathcal{G}_2$ also increase with the number of states. This implies that as the number of states increases the costs of the ADSs computed by proposed heuristics diverge from the costs of optimal ADSs computed by the BF. This is also expected, since for a constant k value, as the height of minimum ADSs increases (which is the case when the number of states increases), the effectiveness of looking k steps ahead reduces.

In terms of measure $\mathcal{T}$, we surprisingly see that, heuristics using approximation (i.e. $\mathcal{H}_U$ and $\mathcal{L}_U$) are faster than LY algorithm. Importantly, the values of measure $\mathcal{T}$ are directly proportional to the number of states for $\mathcal{H}_U$ and $\mathcal{L}_U$. Note that, FSMs in TS2 has two input symbols only. Therefore, $\mathcal{H}_U$ and $\mathcal{L}_U$ have to consider only two different input symbols. As the number of input symbols increase, $\mathcal{H}_U$ and $\mathcal{L}_U$ will start to get slower, as also supported by our discussion given below for the effect of the number of input/output symbols on the performance of the heuristics.

The heuristic functions that use LY algorithm (i.e. $\mathcal{H}_{LY}$ and $\mathcal{L}_{LY}$) are the slowest approaches and the values of the measure $\mathcal{T}$ are indirectly proportional to the number of states. This is quite expected, since these heuristics already use LY algorithm many times during their execution.

The Effect of the Size of the Input/Output Alphabet. In order to see the effect of the size of the input/output alphabet, we performed experiments using FSMs in TS1 and by setting $k = 1$. The results of the experiments are given in Table 2. We observe that as the input/output alphabet cardinalities increase, the performance of the heuristics improve with respect to both $\mathcal{G}_1$ and $\mathcal{G}_2$ measures. The reason for this performance increase is that, when there are more input symbols, the search space of our heuristics also increases, which allow heuristics to pick a better option. However, this comes with the cost of increased running time, as the $\mathcal{T}$ measure rows in Table 2 display.

The Effect of the Heuristic Used. $\mathcal{L}_U$ and $\mathcal{H}_U$ are better in their time performances over $\mathcal{L}_{LY}$ and $\mathcal{H}_{LY}$. For both height and external path length minimization, the heuristics based on approximation (i.e. $\mathcal{H}_U$ and $\mathcal{L}_U$) show a similar performance to the other heuristics based on LY algorithm (i.e. $\mathcal{H}_{LY}$ and $\mathcal{L}_{LY}$), regardless of the number of states and the value of k.

Based on these results, the heuristics $\mathcal{H}_U$ and $\mathcal{L}_U$ can be preferred over the heuristics $\mathcal{H}_{LY}$ and $\mathcal{L}_{LY}$.

5   Discussions and Conclusions

In this paper we propose a lookahead-based algorithm for constructing reduced cost ADSs. Since an ADS is a tree, we consider the height and the sum of all paths from the root to the leaves (external path length) as the cost of an ADS. The proposed method uses a tree (called EST) to lookahead while constructing an ADS. The construction of the tree is flexible and allows a trade of between the cost of the ADS and the time required to construct the ADS by changing the value of the lookahead parameter. Based on the objective of the minimization (height or external path length), the proposed algorithm uses different heuristic functions.

Table 1. Comparison of ADS costs and computation times of algorithms with respect to differing state cardinalities and lookahead paramater values (k).

Measure	k	n = 25	30	35	40	45	50
$G_1(\mathcal{L}_U, M)$	1	5.654	3.420	5.879	4.987	6.925	5.244
	2	6.417	6.353	6.102	6.417	7.058	9.131
	3	8.027	8.025	8.009	8.457	7.713	10.650
$G_1(\mathcal{L}_{LY}, M)$	1	6.994	7.105	7.288	7.310	6.896	8.019
	2	7.745	7.812	7.806	8.039	7.497	10.712
	3	7.848	8.240	8.235	8.515	7.880	10.243
$G_1(\mathcal{H}_U, M)$	1	10.503	14.092	13.069	10.327	11.268	9.730
	2	11.883	11.434	9.9852	12.227	10.384	14.554
	3	13.339	15.580	16.412	16.022	15.467	18.889
$G_1(\mathcal{H}_{LY}, M)$	1	11.162	14.541	14.951	14.934	14.410	17.751
	2	13.676	16.246	17.764	17.283	16.457	20.605
	3	13.968	16.955	18.760	17.874	17.341	21.439
$G_2(\mathcal{L}_U, M)$	1	3.338	3.874	2.716	3.883	1.472	6.794
	2	1.883	2.259	2.577	2.587	1.331	2.639
	3	0.249	0.520	0.537	0.433	0.585	0.971
$G_2(\mathcal{L}_{LY}, M)$	1	1.352	1.491	1.320	1.668	1.464	3.68
	2	0.560	0.742	0.764	0.884	0.822	0.937
	3	0.446	0.282	0.300	0.368	0.413	0.355
$G_2(\mathcal{H}_U, M)$	1	3.545	3.783	6.823	8.764	6.911	8.975
	2	2.797	1.053	4.766	6.794	5.634	8.538
	3	1.587	1.746	2.841	3.102	2.238	3.672
$G_2(\mathcal{H}_{LY}, M)$	1	3.262	3.020	4.405	4.241	3.441	5.138
	2	0.511	1.014	1.408	1.607	1.238	1.790
	3	0.219	0.176	0.297	0.959	0.190	0.817
$\mathcal{T}(\mathcal{L}_U, M)$	1	55.213	41.567	50.706	55.688	63.942	63.141
	2	43.112	35.449	26.101	47.613	49.851	55.000
	3	27.234	21.862	12.617	21.916	36.237	37.500
$\mathcal{T}(\mathcal{L}_{LY}, M)$	1	-51.1112	-80.335	-105.958	-99.978	-105.833	-103.653
	2	-107.422	-128.748	-192.155	-158.952	-161.000	-175.598
	3	-140.556	-208.307	-234.701	-271.012	-255.302	-264.040
$\mathcal{T}(\mathcal{H}_U, M)$	1	57.112	54.123	58.620	50.334	61.622	64.624
	2	42.887	40.777	37.077	45.467	54.385	53.400
	3	21.775	36.451	12.093	32.654	29.290	28.232
$\mathcal{T}(\mathcal{H}_{LY}, M)$	1	-65.332	-91.334	-122.624	-99.458	-103.152	-120.690
	2	-102.962	-148.223	-166.762	-175.744	-165.978	-188.476
	3	-156.223	-212.169	-232.074	-269.048	-239.374	-268.426

Table 2. Comparison of ADS costs and computation times of algorithms with respect to differing input output alphabet cardinalities.

Measure	i/o	n = 30	60
$G_1(\mathcal{L}_U, M)$	4/4	6.821	6.367
	8/8	8.300	9.967
	16/16	12.408	11.174
$G_1(\mathcal{L}_{LY}, M)$	4/4	5.839	7.920
	8/8	8.811	9.536
	16/16	12.467	10.842
$G_1(\mathcal{H}_U, M)$	4/4	10.150	9.561
	8/8	16.466	21.250
	16/16	23.166	34.666
$G_1(\mathcal{H}_{LY}, M)$	4/4	17.283	19.895
	8/8	17.300	21.500
	16/16	23.939	35.166
$G_2(\mathcal{L}_U, M)$	4/4	2.204	3.334
	8/8	0.457	0.117
	16/16	0.018	0.041
$G_2(\mathcal{L}_{LY}, M)$	4/4	1.666	1.722
	8/8	1.054	0.491
	16/16	0.413	0.508
$G_2(\mathcal{H}_U, M)$	4/4	2.666	1.600
	8/8	1.110	1.333
	16/16	0.333	0.250
$G_2(\mathcal{H}_{LY}, M)$	4/4	2.750	1.200
	8/8	2.000	0.000
	16/16	0.000	0.666
$\mathcal{T}(\mathcal{L}_U, M)$	4/4	45.234	11.000
	8/8	-12.223	-11.223
	16/16	-24.122	-38.330
$\mathcal{T}(\mathcal{L}_{LY}, M)$	4/4	-34.563	-226.500
	8/8	-145.221	-300.199
	16/16	-167.331	-391.442
$\mathcal{T}(\mathcal{H}_U, M)$	4/4	32.568	10.000
	8/8	-55.332	-131.120
	16/16	-77.127	-167.883
$\mathcal{T}(\mathcal{H}_{LY}, M)$	4/4	-45.223	-204.500
	8/8	-184.331	-315.123
	16/16	-199.221	-412.774

We perform experimental study to evaluate the different heuristics used by the proposed algorithm and compare it to the optimal solutions. The results indicate that the proposed algorithm tends to construct optimum ADSs as we increase the value of the lookahead parameter. This is natural, since as the lookahead parameter value increases, our algorithm approaches to the brute force algorithm, hence the time requirement of our algorithm also increases. However, even with small lookahead parameter values, we efficiently construct ADSs smaller than those constructed by LY algorithm. In some cases, we observe that we can construct smaller ADSs faster than LY algorithm.

As a future work, we are planing to extend the experiments for larger FSMs. Moreover an evaluation is required to see the effect of using reduced ADSs for constructing test sequences. Finally, it would be interesting to extend this work to non-deterministic FSMs.

Acknowledgments. This work is supported by the Scientific and Technological Research Council of Turkey (TÜBİTAK) under Grant #113E292.

References

1. Aho, A.V., Dahbura, A.T., Lee, D., Uyar, M.U.: An optimization technique for protocol conformance test generation based on UIO sequences and rural chinese postman tours. In: Protocol Specification, Testing, and Verification VIII, Atlantic City, pp. 75–86. Elsevier, North-Holland (1988)
2. Alur, R., Cerny, P., Madhusudan, P., Nam, W.: Synthesis of interface specifications for java classes. In: Proceedings of the 32nd ACM SIGPLAN-SIGACT Symposium on Principles of Programming Languages, POPL 2005, pp. 98–109. ACM (2005)
3. Betin-Can, A., Bultan, T.: Verifiable concurrent programming using concurrency controllers. In: Proceedings of the 19th IEEE International Conference on Automated Software Engineering, pp. 248–257. IEEE Computer Society (2004)
4. Chow, T.S.: Testing software design modelled by finite state machines. IEEE Transactions on Software Engineering 4, 178–187 (1978)
5. Pomeranz, I., Reddy, S.M.: Test generation for multiple state-table faults in finite-state machines. IEEE Transactions on Computers 46(7), 783–794 (1997)
6. Whaley, J., Martin, M.C., Lam, M.S.: Automatic extraction of object-oriented component interfaces. SIGSOFT Softw. Eng. Notes 27, 218–228 (2002)
7. Sabnani, K., Dahbura, A.: A protocol test generation procedure. Computer Networks 15(4), 285–297 (1988)
8. Hennie, F.C.: Fault-detecting experiments for sequential circuits. In: Proceedings of Fifth Annual Symposium on Switching Circuit Theory and Logical Design, Princeton, New Jersey, pp. 95–110 (November 1964)
9. Gonenc, G.: A method for the design of fault detection experiments. IEEE Transactions on Computers 19, 551–558 (1970)
10. Vasilevskii, M.P.: Failure diagnosis of automata. Cybernetics and Systems Analysis 9, 653–665 (1973), 10.1007/BF01068590
11. Vuong, S.T., Chan, W.W.L., Ito, M.R.: The UIOv-method for protocol test sequence generation. In: The 2nd International Workshop on Protocol Test Systems, Berlin (1989)

12. Fujiwara, S., Bochmann, G.V., Khendek, F., Amalou, M., Ghedamsi, A.: Test selection based on finite state models. IEEE Transactions on Software Engineering 17(6), 591–603 (1991)
13. Ural, H., Zhu, K.: Optimal length test sequence generation using distinguishing sequences. IEEE/ACM Transactions on Networking 1(3), 358–371 (1993)
14. Petrenko, A., Yevtushenko, N.: Testing from partial deterministic FSM specifications. IEEE Transactions on Computers 54(9), 1154–1165 (2005)
15. Hierons, R.M., Jourdan, G.V., Ural, H., Yenigun, H.: Checking sequence construction using adaptive and preset distinguishing sequences. In: Proceedings of 7th IEEE International Conference on Software Engineering and Formal Methods (SEFM 2009), pp. 157–166. IEEE Computer Society (2009)
16. Hierons, R.M., Ural, H.: Optimizing the length of checking sequences. IEEE Transactions on Computers 55, 618–629 (2006)
17. Hierons, R.M., Ural, H.: Reduced length checking sequences. IEEE Transactions on Computers 51(9), 1111–1117 (2002)
18. Hierons, R.M.: Minimizing the number of resets when testing from a finite state machine. Information Processing Letters 90(6), 287–292 (2004)
19. Ural, H., Wu, X., Zhang, F.: On minimizing the lengths of checking sequences. IEEE Transactions on Computers 46(1), 93–99 (1997)
20. Kohavi, Z.: Switching and Finite State Automata Theory. McGraw-Hill, New York (1978)
21. Boute, R.T.: Distinguishing sets for optimal state identification in checking experiments. IEEE Trans. Comput. 23, 874–877 (1974)
22. Jourdan, G.V., Ural, H., Yenigun, H., Zhang, J.: Lower bounds on lengths of checking sequences. Formal Aspects of Computing 22(6), 667–679 (2010)
23. Lee, D., Yannakakis, M.: Testing finite-state machines: State identification and verification. IEEE Transactions on Computers 43(3), 306–320 (1994)
24. Sokolovskii, M.N.: Diagnostic experiments with automata. Cybernetics and Systems Analysis 7, 988–994 (1971)
25. Kushik, N., El-Fakih, K., Yevtushenko, N.: Adaptive homing and distinguishing experiments for nondeterministic finite state machines. In: Yenigün, H., Yilmaz, C., Ulrich, A. (eds.) ICTSS 2013. LNCS, vol. 8254, pp. 33–48. Springer, Heidelberg (2013)
26. Gill, A.: Introduction to The Theory of Finite State Machines. McGraw-Hill, New York (1962)
27. Türker, U.C., Yenigun, H.: Hardness and inapproximability of minimizing adaptive distinguishing sequences. Formal Methods in System Design 44(3), 264–294 (2014)
28. Hennie, F.C.: Finite-state models for logical machines. Wiley (1968)
29. Gunicen, C., Türker, U.C., Ural, H., Yenigün, H.: Generating preset distinguishing sequences using SAT. In: Gelenbe, E., Lent, R., Sakellari, G. (eds.) Computer and Information Sciences II, pp. 487–493. Springer, London (2012), 10.1007/978-1-4471-2155-8_62.

Plan It! Automated Security Testing Based on Planning

Franz Wotawa and Josip Bozic*

Institute for Software Technology,
Graz University of Technology,
A-8010 Graz, Austria
{wotawa,jbozic}@ist.tugraz.at
http://www.ist.tugraz.at

Abstract. Testing of web applications for common vulnerabilities still represents a major challenge in the area of security testing. The objective here is not necessarily to find new vulnerabilities but to ensure that the web application handles well-known attack patterns in a reliable way. Previously developed methods based on formalizing attack patterns contribute to the underlying challenge. However, the adaptation of the attack models is not easy and requires substantial effort. In order to make modeling easier we suggest representing attacks as a sequence of known actions that have to be carried out in order to be successful. Each action has some pre conditions and some effects. Hence, we are able to represent testing in this context as a planning problem where the goal is to break the application under test. In the paper, we discuss the proposed planning based testing approach, introduce the underlying concepts and definitions, and present some experimental results obtained from an implementation.

Keywords: Model-based testing, planning-problem, security testing, SQL injection, cross-site scripting.

1 Introduction

With the ever growing interconnectivity between systems in our world there is an even stronger growing need for ensuring systems' security in order to prevent unauthorized access or other malicious acts. Vulnerable applications do not only cause costs, they also negatively impact trust in applications and consequently in the companies providing the applications. Consequently preventing vulnerabilities should be a top priority of any provider of systems and services. It is worth noting that from 2010 and 2013 some vulnerabilities like SQL injection and cross-site scripting have belonged to the top three web application security flaws (see OWASP Top 10 from www.owasp.org for more information). More interestingly those two flaws have been under the top 6 from 2004 on, leaving the impression that there has not been enough effort spent in finding well known flaws.

---

* Authors are listed in reverse alphabetical order.

M.G. Merayo and E. Montes de Oca (Eds.): ICTSS 2014, LNCS 8763, pp. 48–62, 2014.
© IFIP International Federation for Information Processing 2014

In our research we focus on the topic of providing methods and techniques for testing web applications with respect to known vulnerabilities. In particular we are interested in automated methods for finding vulnerabilities without or at least with little user interactions. In this paper we introduce a method that is based on planning for computing test cases where a test case is a sequence of interactions with the web application under test. The underlying idea of using planning for test case generation originates from two sources. First, there is already publication available describing testing as a planning problem. Second, and even more important, when having a look of how to break a system, it becomes obvious that providing and executing an attack is nothing else than finding an interaction sequence that finally leads to a situation where we can exploit a vulnerability.

Let us briefly discuss the basic ideas using a variant of cross-site scripting (XSS) on an example used by Hoglund and McGraw [11]. The example makes use of a web application comprising an HTML page, where a user name can be entered, and a server side script handling a request from the HTML page. Communication between a web browser interpreting the HTML page and the server is performed using standard HTTP where sending information to the server is done using the GET message method. Let us now consider the following (partial) HTML page interpreted using the client side browser:

```
<form action=test.cgi method=GET>
User: <input maxlength=10 type=input name=username>
....
</form>
```

From the HTML code an attacker immediately identifies the existence of a script named test.cgi with a parameter username that should be allowed to be of length 10. In order to test whether there is a server side limitation of the parameter the attacker might submit the following request to the server (ignoring the web browser):

```
http://to_server/test.cgi?username=TOO_LONG_FOR_A_USERNAME
```

If this request is does not lead to an appropriate error message coming from the server indicating a far too long user name, the attacker knows at least that it is possible to submit longer strings, which can be used in the next step of the attack, where the attacker tries to execute a cross-site scripting on side of the server by sending the following request:

```
http://to_server/test.cgi?username=../etc/passwd
```

If this request returns the content of the password file, the attacker succeeded. If not, the attacker might try other requests like:

```
http://to_server/test.cgi?username=Mary.log; rm rf /; cat blah
```

where the whole directory structure is going to be removed in case of success, maximizing the potential damage. There are of course many different strings to be used by an attacker. There are also many ways for reactions coming from the server. However, the basic principles are always the same. Every request of an attacker can be seen as potential action having a precondition and an effect. For example, the call `test.cgi?username=TOO_LONG_FOR_A_USERNAME` can be seen as action for testing string boundaries of parameters `bad_bound` with a HTTP address including a server script, the parameter name, and a parameter length as pre-conditions, and the effect that no corresponding error message is returned as effects. The implementation of this action would compose the request string, send it to the server, and parse the return value. The effect of this action can be used by another action, e.g., the action for testing whether access to a password file is possible, and so on.

The contributions of this paper are the following: We present an approach for test case generation and execution in the security domain that is based on planning. We further discuss a first empirical evaluation indicating that the approach has similar capabilities for detecting vulnerabilities of web applications than previous approaches whereas the new approach is easier to adapt and extend.

In the following we discuss our approach. We start with a discussion on related research. Afterwards, we introduce the basic principles of the planning approach to solve security testing based on attacks, and give an algorithm that makes use of a planner for generating test cases, which are executed after generation. We illustrate our approach using a small example, and discuss first empirical results obtained from an implementation. The purpose of the empirical evaluation is to provide evidence that the approach can be used. Hence, we focus on the running time of the algorithm implementation and the capability of revealing the security flaw. Finally, we conclude the paper and discuss future research.

2   Related Work

Planning, i.e., finding actions that lead from an initial state to a goal state, can be considered an old challenge of artificial intelligence. Fikes and Nilsson [7] introduced STRIPS as a planning methodology for solving this challenge, where planning is performed under certain assumptions and where plan generation is separated from its execution. Later Nilsson [15] introduced a planner for solving dynamic real-world problems where plan generation and execution collapses under one framework. There the author introduces the notion of teleo-reactive (T-R) programs, which are artifacts that direct the execution towards a goal by responding to a changing environment according to the perceived sensor data. Teleo-reactive programs might provide a good basis for implementing the behavior of an attacker in the context of security testing. However, in this paper we follow Fikes and Nilssons original work and define attacks as planning problems based on STRIPS planning.

Although, planning is an old artificial intelligence problem, its use for testing is more recent. Howe et al. [12] have been one of the first dealing with the use of planning for test suite generation. Besides the test case generator, the authors compared their test case generator with another technique using a concrete example, i.e., the StorageTek robot tape library command language. Their tool Sleuth made use of the UCPOP 2.0 planner, for plan generation. Howe et al. divided the approach in three parts: problem description generation, plan generation, and transforming the plan into suitable test cases. If a plan was not able to be generated, another initial and goal states were used in order to find a plan fulfilling the final preconditions. Scheetz et al. [16] introduced a very much similar work a plan is derived taking into account initial variable conditions and concrete parameter values.

Froehlich and Link [8] introduced a method to obtain test suites from mapping of UML state charts to a STRIPS planning problem from which plans can be derived using planning tools. The transformation considers the preconditions of transitions. Despite the fact that the whole test suite generation process is automated, the generation of concrete test cases (considering the specification of the system under test) has still to be performed manually.

In [14,13] the authors proposed an automatic contract-based testing strategy, that combines planning and learning for test case generation. The work is based on the programming language Eiffel where pre- and postconditions for methods can be easily specified. Those pre- and postconditions for methods can be directly mapped into a planning problem from which abstract test cases can be extracted. Galler et al. [9] presented similar work. In their paper, the authors discussed an approach called AIana, that is able to transform Design by Contract^{TM} specification for Java classes and methods into a PDDL representation, which then can be used by a planner for generating plans. The generated plan has to be transformed into Java method calls. Random values are generated for primitive type parameters and recursive calls for non-primitive parameters. The authors also provide two case studies for evaluation purposes. Very similar work includes [18], which elaborates a method for using planning for the generation of test cases from visual contracts. The latter are put into a PDDL representation so that the planning tool LAMA is able to produce a plan.

Armando et al. [1] analysed security issues in security protocols using SAT-based model-checking. The authors proposed a method for attacking these protocols using planning. A protocol insecurity problem specifies all execution paths of a protocol, including the possibilities to exploit security leaks, where the entire protocol is depicted by means of a state transition system. The security properties of the protocol are specified using the tool AVISS. The security properties are transformed into an Intermediate Format (IF) and finally, they are read by the model-checker SATMC so that a planning problem can be generated. The problem itself is represented in SAT using Graphplan-based encoding, which is mapped back into a SAT representation in order to produce a solution.

In this paper we follow our previous work [3,4,5] regarding vulnerability testing of web applications against common attacks. In those papers the introduced attack pattern-based testing technique relies on UML state charts representing attack patterns. These attack patterns are executed accordingly to given paths by checking for satisfaction of transition guards in the model. [2] introduced a similar approach. In contrast to these previous papers, we do not use attack pattern models for testing in this paper. For a more general overview about model-based testing and techniques for security testing we refer the interested reader to [19,6] and [17]. However, all of these approaches do not rely on planning for test case generation.

3   The Security Testing via Planning Approach

Planners are commonly used for intelligent agents and autonomous systems in order to generate action sequences that lead a system from the initial state into a defined goal state. Once specified, these plans instruct the system what to do in each step as long as all actions can be undertaken and typically considering that the environment does not change during plan execution. In our security testing approach we use the generated plan for testing web applications with respect to the wel- known vulnerabilities: SQL injection (SQLI), and reflected as well as stored cross-site scripting (XSS). For this purpose we have to specify the test case generation problem as a planning problem. Let us first define the planning problem in the classical way following [7].

Definition 1. *A tuple (I, G, A) is a planning problem, where I is the initial state, G is the goal state, and A is a set of actions, each of them comprising a precondition and an effect (or postcondition). For simplicity we assume that each state is given as a set of (first order logic) predicates that are valid within this state. We also assume that the preconditions and the effects of an action $a \in A$ can be accessed via a function $pre(a)$ and $eff(a)$ respectively.*

An action a can be executed in a state S if and only if its precondition $pre(a)$ is fulfilled in S. If an action a can be executed, then we move to a new state S' comprising all predicates that are in S and do not contradict $eff(a)$ and all predicates of $eff(a)$. In this case we write $S \rightarrow_a S'$.

Definition 2. *A solution to the planning problem (I, G, A) is a sequence of actions $\langle a_1, \ldots, a_n \rangle$ such that $I \rightarrow_{a_1} S_1 \rightarrow_{a_2} \ldots \rightarrow_{a_{n-1}} S_{n-1} \rightarrow_{a_n} G$.*

In classical planning we assume that there is atomic time, i.e., the execution of an action can be done in finite time and no interruption is possible, there are no exogenous events, the action effects are deterministic, and there is omni-science on the part of the agent. In the context of our application all these assumptions are (more or less) fulfilled, when assuming stateless applications. In order to state security testing as a planning problem, we suggest the following representation:

- Each action that can be performed by an attacker has to be modeled as a planning action, considering the preconditions and the potential effects.
- The initial state considers the currently available information of a web application, i.e., the web address, the script to be executed, and the parameter to be used, etc.

– On the other hand, the goal state specifies what to expect from an application in case of a detected vulnerability.

When specifying the security information as a planning problem, the problem of generating tests immediately becomes a planning problem. Every plan is a test case comprising the actions necessary to be carried out in order to detect a vulnerability. This approach is very flexible because it allows for easy adaptation. Every time new information about other attack actions is available, they can be integrated into the set of actions. The plans can be generated once more taking care of the new actions. Moreover, if designed in a good way each action can be used for testing different applications. For this purpose each action definition has to be as general as possible. In this way, also reuse is supported.

In order to implement the proposed approach, we rely on ordinary planner and planning languages. In particular we assume to use the well-known Planning Domain Definition Language (PDDL) in order to specify the corresponding domain, i.e., the actions that are problem independent, and the problem file, i.e., application specific values, the initial state, and the goal state, which are specific to a certain application.

Every action definition in the domain consists of a list of parameters and preconditions as well as the resulting effects. In case the initial values satisfy a specific precondition from some action, this action is put on top of the planner. Because of the execution of the action, its effects might change some values, which may lead to the satisfaction of preconditions from some other action. The action generation continues as long the specified goal is not reached, thus generating a plan. Otherwise the problem is considered improvable.

In order to adapt the planning-problem to security testing, we have to define a specific domain and problem description. Furthermore, we consider a generated plan as one abstract test case. An abstract test case is a test case that cannot directly be executed by the system under test (SUT). This is due to the fact that concrete values are missing or that the abstract actions do not provide any information on how to execute them in the current environment. In order to solve this issue and to come to a concrete test case, we specify for each action a corresponding method in Java. This method implements the interaction with the SUT and makes use of concrete values. In particular, this method contains the source code for communication with the SUT, which includes the generation and if necessary reading (parsing) of HTTP messages as well as detection mechanisms for SQLI and XSS. We handle the message traffic between tester and application using HttpClient[1] and jsoup[2] for parsing of responses. For more information on the entire attack and vulnerability detection mechanisms currently in use, we refer the interested reader to our previous publications [4,5].

In the following we discuss the algorithm **PLAN4SEC** that is for implementing the described approach. **PLAN4SEC** makes use of an ordinary planner. In our implementation we rely on the planning system Metric-FF[3] from [10], which

---

[1] http://hc.apache.org/httpcomponents-client-ga/

[2] http://jsoup.org/

[3] http://fai.cs.uni-saarland.de/hoffmann/metric-ff.html

itself relies on the FF planner[4]. However, our approach is not limited and other planners can be used as well. Algorithm 1 shows the **PLAN4SEC** algorithm.

Algorithm 1. PLAN4SEC – Plan generation and execution algorithm

---

Input: Domain D, problem file P, set of HTTP methods $M = \{m0, \ldots, m_n\}$, set of types $T = \{t0, \ldots, t_n\}$, set of active states $S = \{s0, \ldots, s_n\}$, set of log values $L = \{t, f\}$ and a function J mapping actions defined in D to Java methods.
Output: Set of plans $PL = \{A0, \ldots, A_n\}$ where each $A_i = \{a0, \ldots, a_n\}$

1: $PL = \emptyset$
2: **for** $SELECT\ t \in T,\ m \in M,\ s \in S,\ l \in L$ **do**
3:     $P = \textbf{Compose}(P, t, m, s, l)$ ▷ Initialize the planning problem
4:     $A = \textbf{Planner}(P, D)$ ▷ Generate a plan
5:     $PL = PL \cup \{A\}$
6:     $res(A) = FAIL$
7:     **for** $i = 0$ **to** n **do**   ▷ Execute the plan
8:         **if** $\textbf{Exec}(J(a_i))$ fails **then**
9:             $res(A) = TRUE$
10:            Leave the surrounding for block
11:        **end if**
12:    **end for**
13: **end for**
14: Return (PL, res) as result

PLAN4SEC uses the domain D and the problem file P as inputs. Moreover, other information is used as well, i.e., (1) the type of attack (T), (2) the HTTP method (M) to be used, (3) the currently state of the testing process (S), (4) finally the information whether the user is logged in the application or not (L), which is stored in a set, and (5) a function J mapping actions to their corresponding Java method. The output of **PLAN4SEC** is a set of plans and a function res mapping $PASS$ or $FAIL$ to each plan, where $FAIL$ is assigned if the plan execution reveals a vulnerability, and $PASS$, otherwise.

PLAN4SEC works as follows: First, the set of results is set to empty. Second a new planning problem is generated, which makes use of a specific configuration. For example, we might want to generate a planning problem where the type t is set to **SQLI** or **RXSS** (reflected XSS). In order to generate such a new planning problem, we make use of the method call **Compose**(P, t, m, s, l), which sets the given values of t, m, s and l in the problem file P. Because of the fact that we test all combinations of values in T, M, S, and L, we achieve a large number of planning problem files. Third, a plan for the domain D and the currently instantiated planning problem P is generated. This plan is added to the set of plans. Afterwards, the plan is executed using the **Exec**$(J(a_i))$ call of a corresponding Java method for a specific action in the plan. If the execution

---

[4] http://fai.cs.uni-saarland.de/hoffmann/ff.html

fails, we know that the plan cannot be used for revealing a vulnerability and hence, assign a *PASS*.

Obviously **PLAN4SEC** has to terminate assuming that all called functions terminate. This is due to the fact that all input sets are finite, determining the number of iterations. The algorithm is polynomial in space and time when assuming the execution of external functions in unit time. In the next section we demonstrate our approach making use of a concrete example.

4 Running Example

We demonstrate our approach using the well-known web application DVWA[5]. We explain the plan generation process as well as the execution of plans. As mentioned in the previous section, first we specify the problem and domain files manually, accordingly to our testing purpose and the current SUT. Have a look at the following PDDL description of the problem:

```
(define (problem mbt-problem)
 (:domain mbt)
 (:objects
        x - active
        s - server
        si - status-si
        lo - status-lo
        se - status-se
        type - type
        url - address
        m - method
        a - action
        exp - expect
        un - username
        pw - password
        sqli - sqli
        xssi - xssi
        script - script
        resp - response
 )
 (:init
        (inInitial x)
        (Logged no)
        (not (statusinit two))
        (Type sqli)
        (= (sent se) 0)
        (not (Empty url))
        (GivenSQL sqli)
```

---

[5] http://www.dvwa.co.uk/

```
                (GivenXSS xssi)
                (Method post)
                (Response resp)
                (not (Found exp resp))
                (not (FoundScript script resp))
        )
        (:goal (inFinal x)))
```

Problem description in PDDL

This PDDL description of the problem contains the problem definition, the domain reference, the objects that are used in the domain specification, the initial values, and finally the goal specification. The objects are of certain types, which are set in the domain definition. For the initial values we take various necessary parameters like the type of attack, the used HTTP method, the current position in the execution process, the indicator whether an input for SQLI or XSS is specified etc. into consideration.

When using this PDDL description together with the following partially description of the domain, the planner is able to generate a plan.

```
(define (domain mbt)
  (:requirements :strips :typing :equality :fluents
        :adl)
  (:types active address server status-si status-lo
      status-se type expect result method integer sqli
      xssi response script)
  (:constants init - active no yes - status-lo two -
      status-si sqli rxss sxss - type get post - method)
  (:predicates
        (inInitial ?x)
        (inAddressed ?x)
        (inSentReq ?x)
        (inRecReq ?x)
        (inParse ?x)
        (inSQLI ?x)
        (inRXSS ?x)
        (inSXSS ?x)
        (GivenSQL ?sqli)
        (GivenXSS ?xssi)
        (inFinal ?x)
)
(:functions
        (statusinit ?si - status-si)
        (Method ?m - method)
)

(:action Start
```

```
        :parameters(?x - active ?url - address ?lo -
            status-lo)
        :precondition (and (inInitial ?x)(not   (Empty
            ?url)))
        :effect (and (inAddressed ?x)(not        (
            inInitial ?x))(Logged yes))
)

(:action SendReq
        :parameters(?x - active ?lo - status-lo ?se -
            status-se ?si - status-si)
        :precondition (and (inAddressed ?x)      (Logged
            yes))
        :effect (and (inSentReq ?x)(not          (
            inAddressed ?x))(assign(sent ?se)1)(
            statusinit two)))
)
(:action Finish
        :parameters (?x)
        :precondition (inFound ?x)
        :effect (inFinal ?x))
)
```

Domain description in PDDL

In the domain description at the beginning all possible requirements are listed, in order to allow different planners to use PDDL. Afterwards all object types are initialized whereas the objects themselves are defined in the problem definition. In the PDDL code constants define special values for some of the types. Predicates are logical functions that affect certain objects whereas functions specify entities that can change their value during plan execution. Finally, the actions are constructed with the definition of used parameters within that action, the precondition, and the postcondition. At the beginning of plan generation, the planner will take the initial values and search in the action table for satisfied preconditions. If such an action can be found, it will be added to the current plan. When taking this action, the corresponding effects might change some relation, for example the action *Start* changes the active position from *inInitial* to *inAddressed*. After updating the state, the planner searches for new possible actions to be taken. This process might continue as long as the goal from the problem definition is not reached or the planner notices that it cannot be attained. In the latter case, no plan can be delivered back.

For our running example the following plan can be computed using Metric-FF:

```
0:  START X URL LO
1:  SENDREQ X LO SE SI
2:  RECREQ X SI
3:  PARSE X M USERNAME PASSWORD TYPE
4:  CHOOSERXSS X TYPE
5:  ATTACKRXSS X XSSI M UN PW
6:  PARSERESPXSS X SCRIPT RESP
7:  PARSERESPXSSCHECK X SCRIPT RESP
8:  FINISH X
```

Generated plan

Such a generated plan is read by the parser from JavaFF[6]. Names of the actions are translated into names of the corresponding Java functions. Note in our implementation that the action names and the names of their corresponding Java functions are the same. The Java functions are executed step by step. In addition the Java functions use concrete values for parameters and communication with the web application.

For example, let us assume that we have specified the URL address of the SUT and choose SQLI in the program. In this case we satisfy the initial values $(not(Empty\ url))$ and $(GivenSQL\ sqli)$, $sqli$ being the input string. The object x from the type $active$ is meant to give the current status of the execution, for example $inInitial$ states that the execution has just started. When analysing the action definitions, all preconditions are met in order to satisfy the action $Start$. Now the program runs its corresponding method and then reads the next action, executing its next methods afterwards, thereby manipulating concrete variable by it's own. When picking the action $SendReq$, the program will send a HTTP request with HttpClient to the URL address. But, if the tester has not specified this in the program, a discrepancy emerges between the plan and the program. In that case, the program will not be able to follow the plan until the end and the execution stops immediately, setting the plan execution to $PASS$ because of not reaching a vulnerable state. Otherwise, execution continues until reaching the final action of the plan.

5   Evaluation

In order to provide a first evaluation we tested our planning approach to security testing on several web applications, including DVWA, BodgeIt[7] and NOWASP (Mutillidae)[8]. For the evaluation, we implemented the **PLAN4SEC** algorithm in Java. We used a domain and problem file similar to the ones used in Section 4 but

---

[6] http://www.inf.kcl.ac.uk/staff/andrew/JavaFF/

[7] https://code.google.com/p/bodgeit/

[8] http://sourceforge.net/projects/mutillidae/

extended it substantially. We used in sum 19 action definitions as well as more predicates and initial values. For carrying out the whole evaluation we used three values for the attack type, two for the method, two for the login status and 20 for the current status. The objective of the evaluation was to show the applicability of the approach both in running time as well as the capabilities of detecting vulnerabilities.

DVWA and Mutillidae comprise three difficulty levels, each one of them implementing more sophisticated filtering mechanisms in order to make the application safer against malicious input. Moreover, for every type of attack we used one input string for the concrete test cases. The input string does not cause any harm to the SUT but just indicates whether the application is vulnerable or not. Such an input string in practice might be a good starting point for a potential attacker. For the second application BodgeIt we also make use of one input string. However, this application has no difficulty levels to be set externally.

The obtained results are depicted in Table 1 where for each SUT, the difficulty level (DL), the total time (T) for carrying out the tests, the number of generated plans (#P), the total planning time (planT), the average plan generation time (avgPT), the number of generated actions (#A), the total plan execution time (execT), the average number of generated actions per plan (avgA), and information of how often SQLI, RXSS, and SXSS attacks have been successful, are given. All time values are in second (s).

Table 1. Evaluation Results

SUT	DL	T	#P	planT	avgPT	#A	execT	avgA	SQLI	RXSS	SXSS
DVWA	1	355.10	273	292.06	1.07	972	49.41	3	29	30	30
	2	835.70	273	739.70	2.71	972	57.51	3	29	30	0
BodgeIt	na	357.38	273	308.53	1.13	972	20.99	3	53	18	20
Mutillidae	1	309.56	273	288.44	1.06	972	13.44	3	31	30	25
	2	316.91	273	292.89	1.07	972	13.76	3	31	30	20

When executing **PLAN4SEC** on DVWA and Mutillidae, vulnerability could only be triggered on the first two security levels. In both cases, the third one remains impervious. Because of this reason we did not add a row for the third level of these two applications in Table 1. It is worth noting that stored XSS could not be detected on the second level of DVWA too. This is due to the fact that the used input string was successfully filtered by application. The second application BodgeIt has much more SQLI leaks but seems to be more resistant against XSS. From Table 1 we also see that the time for executing **PLAN4SEC** is acceptable. The approach is performed automatically only requiring the user to specify case specific information, like different URL addresses, and different expected values for SQLI. Beside the small amount of adaptation, no further changes were required. This holds especially for the domain specification, which is the same for all SUTs in this evaluation. Note that the Java methods, which correspond to the actions, have to be slightly changed. The unchanged domain specification is also the reason behind the same number of generated plans for all applications.

The success of the exploitations heavily depends on the used input. Despite the fact that we test the system using different interactions for checking exploits, there is still a need for convert values to be executed. These values have to be adapted (maybe randomly) during execution, which is currently not done. As already said, we used only one type of input string for our evaluation. However, it is worth noting that this is not a principle restriction of the proposed approach.

Because of the relatively high number of potential combination of different input parameters, we received a higher number of plans but also a larger number of successful tests. What might also be interesting is the fact that the average number of actions is rather small. This indicates that the action definitions in the domain specifications use only a small number of preconditions and also originates from the underlying plan generation technique, i.e., Metric-FF. It is also worth mentioning that planning takes much more time than the execution part. Hence, when using the generated test suite for regression testing purposes only the execution time has to be considered, which is the result of the **PLAN4SEC** algorithm.

When we compare this approach and the results given in Table 1 with the results obtained using our previous method relying on models of attack patterns (from [4,5]), we obtain a similar behavior regarding the detection capability for vulnerabilities for the same web applications. Hence, when considering the much more easy adaptation of the model to different SUTs, the planning based approach is indeed an improvement and worth being further investigated.

6   Conclusion and Future Work

In our work we introduce a novel approach to security testing based on planning. In particular we formalize the test case generation problem as a planning problem and make use of an ordinary planner for generating plans that represent abstract test cases. The algorithm described in this paper is meant for security testing of web applications. Besides test case generation the algorithm also allows for automated test execution. In the paper we discuss the underlying method from predefined specifications and explain its realization. A first empirical evaluation using well-known web applications indicates that the approach can be used in practice. The planning time including plan generation and execution is high but acceptable for the application domain. Also, the capabilities of detecting vulnerabilities are in line with other approaches to automated testing of web applications. In contrast to other testing methods the mapping to planning increases reuse of knowledge used for test generation and also makes adaptations to specific languages much easier. In particular, new actions can be added very simple.

However, we have not reached the limitations of the approach. The number of plans to be generated can be much higher when using either more initial values or planners that deliver different plans and not only one. The latter change can be straightforwardly integrated into our algorithm. Even more there is space for improvement when considering the concretization of test cases. Here instead of relying only on one mapping, multiple strings or combination of strings might be used. The idea is to map one abstract test case to many concrete test cases.

Finally, adding more actions of finer granularities in the initial specification might also increase the number of tests and make the approach more effectively in practice. We will tackle these improvements in our future research directions. In particular we are interested in the influence on the certain improvements to the vulnerability detection. Moreover, we want to improve the empirical evaluation and use more different web applications for this purpose.

Acknowledgement. The research presented in the paper has been funded in part by the Austrian Research Promotion Agency (FFG) under grant 832185 (MOdel-Based SEcurity Testing In Practice) and ITEA-2 (DIAMONDS).

References

1. Armando, A., Compagna, L., Ganty, P.: Sat-based model-checking of security protocols using planning graph analysis. In: Araki, K., Gnesi, S., Mandrioli, D. (eds.) FME 2003. LNCS, vol. 2805, pp. 875–893. Springer, Heidelberg (2003)
2. Blome, A., Ochoa, M., Li, K., Peroli, M., Dashti, M.T.: Vera: A flexible model-based vulnerability testing tool. In: Proceedings of the Sixth International Conference on Software Testing, Verification and Validation, ICST 2013 (2013)
3. Bozic, J., Wotawa, F.: Model-based testing - from safety to security. In: Proceedings of the 9th Workshop on Systems Testing and Validation (STV 2012), pp. 9–16 (October 2012)
4. Bozic, J., Wotawa, F.: Xss pattern for attack modeling in testing. In: Proceedings of the 8th International Workshop on Automation of Software Test, AST (2013)
5. Bozic, J., Wotawa, F.: Security testing based on attack patterns. In: Proceedings of the 5th International Workshop on Security Testing, SECTEST 2014 (2014)
6. Busch, M., Chaparadza, R., Dai, Z.R., Hoffmann, A., Lacmene, L., Ngwangwen, T., Ndem, G., Ogawa, H., Serbanescu, D., Schieferdecker, I., Zander-Nowicka, J.: Model transformers for test generation from system models. In: Conquest 2006. Hanser Verlag, Berlin (2006)
7. Fikes, R.E., Nilsson, N.J.: STRIPS: A New Approach to the Application of Theorem Proving to Problem Solving. Artificial Intelligence 2, 189–208 (1971)
8. Fröhlich, P., Link, J.: Automated test case generation from dynamic models. In: Bertino, E. (ed.) ECOOP 2000. LNCS, vol. 1850, pp. 472–491. Springer, Heidelberg (2000)
9. Galler, S.J., Zehentner, C., Wotawa, F.: Aiana: An ai planning system for test data generation. In: 1st Workshop on Testing Object-Oriented Software Systems, pp. 30–37 (2010)
10. Hoffmann, J.: Extending ff to numerical state variables. In: Proceedings of the 15th European Conference on Artificial Intelligence (ECAI 2002), pp. 571–575 (2002)
11. Hoglund, G., McGraw, G.: Exploiting Software: How to Break Code. Addison-Wesley (2004) ISBN: 0-201-78695-8
12. Howe, A.E., von Mayrhauser, A., Mraz, R.T.: Test case generation as an ai planning problem. Automated Software Engineering 4, 77–106 (1997)
13. Leitner, A., Bloem, R.: Automatic testing through planning. Technical report, Technische Universität Graz, Austria (2005)
14. Leitner, A.: Strategies to automatically test eiffel programs. Master's thesis, Technische Universität Graz, Austria (2004)

15. Nilsson, N.J.: Teleo-reactive programs for agent control. Journal of Artificial Intelligence Research 1, 139–158 (1994)
16. Scheetz, M., von Mayrhauser, A., France, R., Dahlman, E., Howe, A.E.: Generating test cases from an oo model with an ai planning system. In: Proceedings of The 10th International Symposium on Software Reliability Engineering, pp. 250–259. IEEE Computer Society, Washington, DC (1999)
17. Schieferdecker, I., Grossmann, J., Schneider, M.: Model-based security testing. In: Proceedings of the Model-Based Testing Workshop at ETAPS 2012, EPTCS, pp. 1–12 (2012)
18. Schnelte, M., Güldali, B.: Test case generation for visual contracts using ai planning. In: Informatik, Beitr.ge der 40. Jahrestagung der Gesellschaft fuer Informatik e.V (GI), pp. 369–374 (2010)
19. Zander, J., Dai, Z.R., Schieferdecker, I., Din, G.: From u2tp models to executable tests with ttcn-3 - an approach to model driven testing. In: Khendek, F., Dssouli, R. (eds.) TestCom 2005. LNCS, vol. 3502, pp. 289–303. Springer, Heidelberg (2005)

Minimum Number of Test Paths for Prime Path and Other Structural Coverage Criteria

Anurag Dwarakanath and Aruna Jankiti

Accenture Technology Labs, Bangalore, India
{anurag.dwarakanath,jankiti.aruna}@accenture.com

Abstract. The software system under test can be modeled as a graph comprising of a set of vertices, V and a set of edges, E. Test Cases are Test Paths over the graph meeting a particular test criterion. In this paper, we present a method to achieve the minimum number of Test Paths needed to cover different structural coverage criteria. Our method can accommodate Prime Path, Edge-Pair, Simple & Complete Round Trip, Edge and Node coverage criteria. Our method obtains the optimal solution by transforming the graph into a flow graph and solving the minimum flow problem. We present an algorithm for the minimum flow problem that matches the best known solution complexity of $O\left(|V|\,|E|\right)$. Our method is evaluated through two sets of tests. In the first, we test against graphs representing actual software. In the second test, we create random graphs of varying complexity. In each test we measure the number of Test Paths, the length of Test Paths, the lower bound on minimum number of Test Paths and the execution time.

Keywords: Model Based Testing, Minimum Number of Test Paths, Prime Path Coverage, Minimum Flow.

1 Introduction

In model based testing, the software artifact describing the system under test (SUT) is abstracted through a model [2]. The model can be created from requirements, design or code [2]. Models are typically represented in the form of a graph, comprising of vertices and edges. Two special vertices are marked, the source vertex, s, and the sink vertex, t. The graph is then used to generate Test Cases. A Test Case consists of a Test Path, Test Data, and Expected Results. The Test Path is a path in the graph from s to t. The number of Test Paths needed to test the SUT is determined by the coverage criterion. For example, Node Coverage implies that the set of Test Paths should collectively visit all vertices in the graph. Similarly, Edge Coverage requires the Test Paths to visit all edges in the graph and Prime Path coverage requires the Test Paths to tour a particular set of paths. Prime Path coverage provides a better quality of coverage as it subsumes Node Coverage and Edge Coverage [2].

Given a particular coverage criterion, it is important to determine a small set of Test Paths which satisfy the criterion. The number and the overall length

M.G. Merayo and E. Montes de Oca (Eds.): ICTSS 2014, LNCS 8763, pp. 63–79, 2014.

of Test Paths directly impacts the amount of time needed to manually execute the test cases. Finding the minimum number of Test Paths needed to satisfy a particular criterion is non-trivial even for the simplest case of node coverage. Using better coverage criterion like Prime Path complicates the problem further since even a small graph can have a large number of Prime Paths [6].

In this paper, we present a method to obtain the optimal solution for the minimum number of Test Paths for different structural coverage criteria. The contribution of our work includes *a)* a generic method for obtaining the minimal number of Test Paths for different structural coverage criteria; *b)* identification of a lower bound on the minimum number which the experimental results show to perform very well; *c)* a new method for computation of minimum number of Test Paths which matches the best known solution complexity.

The identification of the minimum number of Test Paths, although possible in polynomial time, requires a number of graph transformations. We thus test the applicability of our solution against a simple algorithm for Test Path generation. The tests compare the number and length of Test Paths identified and the algorithm execution time. These metrics are compared on a set of manually created graphs representing actual code and a set of randomly generated graphs.

The paper is structured as follows. We present the related work in Section 2. The method of generating the minimum Test Paths is presented in Section 3. We present the experimental results in Section 4 and conclude in Section 5.

2   Related Work

The input for the identification of minimum Test Paths is a directed graph $G_1 = (V_1, E_1)$, where V_1 represents the vertex set and E_1 represents the edge set. G_1 is typically a control flow graph of the SUT. G_1 may contain cycles. V_1 contains the source vertex, s, and the sink vertex, t. s conceptually depicts the point where the execution of a Test Case begins and t denotes the point where the execution ends. The in-degree of s is 0, and the out-degree of t is 0. We focus on the case where $|s| = |t| = 1$. There is no loss in generality since a graph with more than one s or t can be converted to a graph with a single s and a single t, by adding two new vertices, s', t' with edges between s' and every source, and edges between every sink and t'.

A path is a sequence of vertices $v_0, \ldots, v_r$ with a sequence of edges $e_0, \ldots, e_{(r-1)}$, where $e_i = (v_i, v_{(i+1)})$, $v_i \in V_1$, $e_i \in E_1 \forall i$. An $s - t$ path is a path where $v_0 = s$ and $v_r = t$. All Test Paths are thus $s - t$ paths. A path, p is said to visit vertex k (or edge e) if k (or e) is in p. A path p is said to tour (or cover) a path q, if q is a sub-path of p. A path is simple if no vertex is visited more than once with the exception that the first and last nodes may be identical [2]. A Prime Path is a simple path that is not a sub-path of any other simple path [2].

A test requirement is a specific aspect that a Test Path satisfies. TR denotes the set of test requirements. For example, for Prime Path coverage, $TR = $ set of Prime Paths. For Edge Coverage, $TR = $ the set of edges, etc.

A simple solution approach for the generation of Test Paths that cover all Prime Paths has been presented in [2]. The solution 'extends' every Prime Path to visit s and t thus forming a Test Path. The algorithm does not attempt to minimize the number of Test Paths but is extremely fast in execution.

The problem of minimizing Test Paths for Prime Path coverage has been recently studied in [7]. The authors formulate the problem as a variant of the shortest superstring problem, which is NP-complete [7]. The authors then use known approximation algorithms to solve the problem. In our work, we formulate the problem such that the optimal solution is obtained in polynomial time.

While the work in [7] specifically deals with Prime Paths, the problem of minimum Test Path to cover a given set of paths (not necessarily Prime Paths) has been studied earlier in [8]. Here, the given graph, G_1, is transformed into a flow network such that the minimum flow gives the minimum number of Test Paths. The authors use a generic algorithm for minimum flow. One such simple algorithm for minimum flow is the Decreasing Path algorithm [4] which leads to the solution in $O\left(|V|^2 |E|\right)$. However, the methodology in [8] has an inaccuracy which can lead to incorrect results. Consider the graphs in Fig. 1. The Prime Paths of Fig. 1(a) are $\{1, 2, 3\}$ and $\{2, 2\}$. The technique in [8] makes the graph acyclic by introducing a new vertex $2'$ in place of the strongly connected component of $2 - 2$. The minimum flow analysis is then performed on the acyclic graph Fig. 1(b). This results in a minimum number of Test Paths as 1 the path being $1, 2', 3$. Replacing $2'$, we get the path as $1, 2, 2, 3$ to correspond to Fig. 1(a). However, the minimum number of paths to cover the Prime Paths is 2 - $\{1, 2, 3\}$ and $\{1, 2, 2, 3\}$. Our method overcomes this inaccuracy by appropriately handling strongly connected components. Further, our solution of minimum Test Paths is computed in $O\left(|V| |E|\right)$.

Fig. 1. (a) Graph with a cycle (b) reduced to an acyclic graph

The authors of [1] tailor a minimum flow algorithm specifically for minimum Test Paths for node coverage leading to the currently best known solution complexity of $O\left(|V| |E|\right)$. Our algorithm in this paper also achieves this complexity. However, our technique is different and is based on the concept of Decreasing Paths [4]. The concept is similar to that of the Augmenting Path in the Ford-Fulkerson algorithm [5] to find the maximum flow. The Augmenting Path concept is well studied and numerous explanatory material is available. This allows our algorithm based on the Decreasing Path to be easily understood and conceptually simple. Further, our method is generic and handles different coverage criteria including node coverage.

Table 1 summarizes the distinction of our method against related work.

Table 1. Comparison of our solution against related work

Solution	Coverage Criteria	Comments
[2]	Prime Path	Does not attempt to minimize
[1]	Node Coverage	Minimization in $O\left(|V||E|\right)$
[8]	Different structural coverage criteria	In-accuracy in solution. Minimization in $O\left(|V|^2|E|\right)$
[7]	Different structural coverage criteria	Heuristic solution (non-optimal)
Our Work	Different structural coverage criteria	Minimization in $O\left(|V||E|\right)$

Our method to obtain the minimum number of Test Paths is presented below.

3 Generating the Minimum Number of Test Paths

Given a graph $G_1 = (V_1, E_1)$, we need to find the minimum number of Test Paths that cover the set of test requirements TR. We focus for the case of TR = set of Prime Paths of G_1 and cover other coverage criteria in section 3.6. The minimum Test Paths are identified through a series of steps as shown below.

1. First, the set of Prime Paths, P of G_1 is computed. We present a method to obtain the lower bound on the minimum number of Test Paths.
2. G_1 is converted into a transform graph $G_2 = (V_2, E_2)$, where V_2 is the set of Prime Paths, $P = \{p_1, p_2, \ldots, p_n\}$ and $(p_1, p_2) \in E_2$ if a path exists from p_1 to p_2 on G_1 such that the path does not include any other Prime Paths (i.e. other than p_1 and p_2).
3. The transform graph G_2 is made into an acyclic graph, G_3. The work in [8] removed cycles from the original graph, G_1, instead of the transform graph, G_2. This inaccuracy in [8] can lead to incorrect results (refer Fig. 1).
4. G_3 is converted into a flow graph, G_4, with new vertices and edges introduced. Every edge is annotated with lower bounds and capacities of flows. The minimum flow on G_4 is computed through a two-step process. First, G_4 is initialized with a feasible flow. We present a novel initialization algorithm in this paper. Second, the generic Decreasing Path algorithm [4] is used to find the minimum flow. Our initialization algorithm ensures the Decreasing Path algorithm can compute with a complexity of $O\left(|V||E|\right)$.
5. The minimum flow in G_4 is now interpreted as Test Paths in G_1.

We detail each step of the process below. We will also use Fig. 2 as a running example to help explain the algorithms used.

3.1 Generating the Set of Prime Paths

Algorithm 1 generates the set of test requirements TR (Prime Paths in this case). We use known methods ([2] and [3]) to compute the set of Prime Paths.

For the example graph in Fig. 2, there are 10 Prime Paths: $P = \{p_0 = \{s, 1, 3, 4, 5\}, p_1 = \{3, 4, 1, 2, t\}, p_2 = \{5, 4, 1, 2, t\}, p_3 = \{1, 3, 4, 1\}, p_4 = \{s, 1, 2, t\}, p_5 = \{3, 4, 1, 3\}, p_6 = \{5, 4, 1, 3\}, p_7 = \{4, 1, 3, 4\}, p_8 = \{5, 4, 5\}, p_9 = \{4, 5, 4\}\}$.

Algorithm 1. Generating the set of Prime Paths

Input: $G_1 = (V_1, E_1)$, with $\{s, t\} \in V_1$

Output: Set of Prime Paths, $P = \{p_1, p_2, \ldots, p_n\}$

1 initialize $P' = \{p_1, p_2, \ldots, p_n\} = \{e_1, e_2, \ldots, e_n\}, \forall e_i \in E_1$;

2 **while** $p_i \in P' \forall i$ *is not explored* **do**

3   **if** p_i *is not a cycle* **then**

4   **if** p_i *can be extended by edge* $e \in E_1$ **then**

5   **if** e *does not visit a vertex in* p_i **then**

6              $p_i + = e$;

7   **end**

8   **end**

9   **end**

10 **end**

11 sort P' in ascending order of size;

12 **for** $i = \left(|P'| \right)$ **to** 1 **do**

13   **if** p_i *is not a sub-path of any other path in* P **then**

14   add p_i into P;

15   **end**

16 **end**

17 output P;

We define four categories of Prime Paths. $Type\,S$ are those Prime Paths that visit the vertex s. $Type\,T$ are those that visit the vertex t. $Type\,C$ are those Prime Paths that are cycles, and $Type\,P$ are those that are simple paths and do not visit either s or t. In the given example, we have the following cardinality - $|Type\,S| = 2$, $|Type\,T| = 3$, $|Type\,C| = 5$, $|Type\,P| = 1$. These categories hold for other test requirements (i.e. Nodes, Edges, Edge-pair, etc) as well.

Lemma 1. $\max\left(|Type\,S|, |Type\,T| \right)$ *is a lower bound on the minimum number of Test Paths for Prime Path coverage.*

Proof. Consider $P_T = \{p_1, p_2, \ldots, p_n\}$ to be a set of $Type\,T$ Prime Paths. Since each of these Prime Paths visits vertex t, the last node of every Prime Path $p_i \in P_T$ is the vertex t. Now, consider an $s - t$ path that tours p_1. This $s - t$ path cannot tour any other Prime Path of P_T after touring p_1 since the vertex t has an out-degree of 0. Thus, there cannot be any path in the graph where more than 1 Prime Paths of P_T can be toured simultaneously. Therefore, there would be at-least $Type\,T$ $s - t$ paths to cover all Type T Prime Paths. Similarly, there would be atleast $Type\,S$ $s - t$ paths to cover all $Type\,S$ Prime Paths. Thus the number of s-t paths that will cover all Prime Paths will be atleast as much as $\max\left(|Type\,S|, |Type\,T| \right)$. □

The categorization of the Prime Paths can be achieved by checking the first and last vertex of every Prime Path. This can be done in $O\left(|P| \right)$. For the example graph of Fig. 2, the lower bound for the minimum number of Test Paths for Prime Path coverage $= |Type\,T| = 3$.

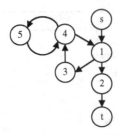

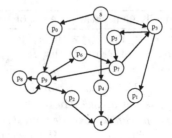

Fig. 2. Example Input Graph, G_1 **Fig. 3.** Transform Graph, G_2 of G_1

3.2   Generating the Transform Graph

The Prime Paths are represented as vertices in a new graph, G_2. Edges are placed between two vertices in G_2 if a path in G_1 can tour the two Prime Paths represented by the vertices. The problem of Prime Path coverage is thus transformed into a problem of node coverage (i.e. we want to identify $s - t$ paths such that all vertices of G_2 are covered). The algorithm for generation of the transform graph is provided below.

Algorithm 2. Generation of the Transform Graph

Input: G_1, P
Output: Transform Graph $G_2 = (V_2, E_2)$
1 create new vertex s, t in V_2; create new vertex v_i in $V_2, \forall i \in P$;
2 **foreach** $p_i \in (P + \{s\})$ **do**
3   **foreach** $p_j \in (P - p_i + \{t\})$ **do**
4          $Path_{ij} = p_i \cup p_j$;
5   **if** $Path_{ij}$ *contains only the prime paths* p_i *and* p_j **then**
6 | add edge (p_i, p_j) into E_2;
7   **end**
8   **end**
9 **end**
10 output $G_2 = (V_2, E_2)$;

The Operator $\cup$ in Step 4 works as follows. Consider the case of $p_i = \{4, 5, 4\}$ and $p_j = \{5, 4, 5\}$, then $p_i \cup p_j = \{4, 5, 4, 5\}$ by observing that the paths p_i and p_j have overlapping vertices. In case of no overlap, $p_i \cup p_j = \{p_i + \{$shortest path from the last node of p_i to the first node of $p_j\} + p_j\}$. Checking for the shortest path in G_1 can be done using breadth first search with a complexity of $O(E_1)$. Checking for the presence of a Prime Path in $Path_{ij}$ (step 5) can be done in $O(|P|)$. Thus, the transform graph can be computed in $O\left(|P|^2 * \max(|P|, |E_1|)\right)$. The transform graph of Fig. 2 is shown in Fig. 3.

An incomparable vertex set, I, is one where for every pair of vertices $v_i, v_j \in I$; v_i does not reach v_j. From Fig. 3, it can be visually seen that the three $Type\ T$

Prime Paths, p_1, p_2, p_4, form an incomparable vertex set, i.e. $I = \{p_1, p_2, p_4\}$. The maximum incomparable vertex set, I_{max} equals the minimum number of Test Paths through Dilworth's theorem for acyclic directed graphs and the proof in [8] for general graphs. From Lemma 1, $|I_{max}| \geq |I|$.

3.3 Removing Cycles

The transform graph, G_2, may have cycles. The minimum flow algorithm works over a directed acyclic graph and thus the cycles need to be removed. We achieve this by replacing a cycle with a new vertex. All incoming edges of any node in the cycle become incoming edges of the new vertex. Similarly, any outgoing edge of any vertex in the cycle become outgoing edges of the new vertex. Algorithm 3 presents the generation of the acyclic transform graph.

Algorithm 3. Reduction of Cycles in Transform Graph

    Input: G_2
    Output: Acyclic Transform Graph $G_3 = (V_3, E_3)$
1 initialize $V_3 = V_2, E_3 = E_2, G_3 = (V_3, E_3)$;
2 **while** G_3 *contains a cycle* **do**
3   let $p_c = \{v_1, v_2, \ldots, v_n, v_1\}$ be a cycle;
4   record vertices $v_i \in V_3$ which have an edge in E_3 with vertices in p_c;
5   remove vertices $\{v_1, v_2, \ldots, v_n\}$ from V_3; create new vertex v_{new} in V_3;
6   **foreach** *vertex* $v_i \in p_c$ **do**
7   **if** v_i *has an edge from vertex* v_k *in* G_2 *where* $v_k \in V_3 - p_c$ **then**
8   remove edge (v_k, v_i) from E_3 & create edge (v_k, v_{new}) in E_3;
9   **end**
10   **if** v_i *has an edge to vertex* v_k *in* G_2 *where* $v_k \in V_3 - p_c$ **then**
11   remove edge (v_i, v_k) from E_3 & create edge (v_{new}, v_k) in E_3;
12   **end**
13   **end**
14 **end**
15 output $G_3 = (V_3, E_3)$;

Algorithm 3 works as follows. For the given transform graph, the cycles are computed using a trivial variant of Algorithm 1. If the graph contains a cycle, any cycle is chosen and reduced to a new vertex. On the resulting graph, the cycles are identified again and the procedure is repeated. The complexity of steps 6 - 13 is $O\left(|V_2|\right)$ by assuming that the chosen cycle visits every vertex. Since, V_2 represents the Prime Paths, this complexity can be written as $O\left(|P|\right)$. If we assume every Prime Path is of *Type C* and reducing one cycle does not impact other Prime Paths, then the complexity of the entire algorithm can be said to be $O\left(|P| * \max\left(|P|, P_c\right)\right)$, where P_c is the complexity of finding a cycle. After removing all the cycles, the acyclic transform graph is shown in Fig. 4.

3.4   Generating the Minimum Flow

The transform graph, G_3, at this stage is a directed acyclic graph. We convert this graph into a flow graph. Each vertex $v_i \in V_3 - \{s, t\}$ is split into two vertices v_i^+, v_i^{++}. Let this new vertex set be represented as V_4. New edges (v_i^+, v_i^{++}) are also added. All incoming edges of v_i are made incoming edges of v_i^+ and all outgoing edges of v_i are made outgoing edges of v_i^{++}. Let this new edge set be represented as E_4. Every edge $(i, j) \in E_4 \,\&\, i, j \in V_4$ is associated with a lower bound (l_{ij}) for a flow and an edge capacity (c_{ij}) as follows:

$$l_{ij} = \begin{cases} 1 & \text{if } (i, j) = (v_i^+, v_i^{++}) \\ 0 & \text{otherwise} \end{cases}$$

$$c_{ij} = \frac{|V_4|}{2} - 1$$

Let the resulting graph be represented as $G_4 = (V_4, E_4, L, C)$, where L is the set of lower bounds and C is the set of capacities. The introduction of new vertices, new edges and the flow requirements are pictorially depicted in Fig.5.

A feasible flow in the flow network is an assignment of a non-negative value, f_{ij} for every edge such that the following conditions hold.

$$f_{ij} \geq l_{ij} \,\&\, f_{ij} \leq c_{ij}, \forall\, (i, j) \in E_4 \,\&\, i, j \in V_4 \qquad (1)$$

$$\sum_i f_{ij} = \sum_j f_{ji}, \forall\, (i, j) \in E_4 \,\&\, i, j \in V_4 - \{s, t\} \qquad (2)$$

The flow of the network, f, is defined as:

$$f = \sum_j f_{sj} = \sum_i f_{it}, \forall\, (i, j) \in E_4 \,\&\, i, j \in V_4 \qquad (3)$$

The minimum flow, f_{min}, is the least amount of feasible flow possible.

A flow in the network G_4 can be mapped to an $s - t$ path in G_1. The flow conditions placed in G_4 ensures the edge (v_i^+, v_i^{++}) is chosen in at-least one flow. Since this corresponds to every vertex $v_i \in V_3 - \{s, t\}$, the minimum flow will ensure every vertex of G_3 is covered. By expanding vertexes placed in lieu of cycles in G_3, every vertex of G_2 is covered. This ensures that every Prime Path of G_1 is toured.

Every edge in G_4 is also annotated with a capacity, c_{ij}, which represents the maximum flow that may be carried on the edge. The capacity is not directly interpretable from the Test Path perspective; however, the minimum flow algorithm requires the specification of a capacity. In the general case of computing

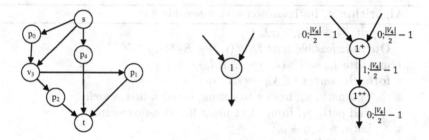

Fig. 4. Creating an acyclic directed graph, **Fig. 5.** Vertex Splitting and flow require-
G_3 from G_2.   ments represented as lower bound; capacity

the minimum flow in a network, the capacity determines if a feasible flow exists.
In our case, we set the capacity in such a way that it guarantees a feasible flow.

Theorem 1. *The capacity on an edge in G_4 can be set as* $\frac{|V_4|}{2} - 1$.

Proof. Consider the graph G_3. The maximum number of $s - t$ paths possible on
G_3 will be $(|V_3| - 2)$. This is because, the maximum will occur when every vertex
of $G_3 - \{s, t\}$ leads to a new $s - t$ path. Now, new vertices have been added in
G_4, but none of the new vertices will contribute to a new path over and above
those that are possible in G_3. Thus, the maximum capacity of every edge in G_4
can be set as $(|V_3| - 2)$. But since $|V_4| = 2 * |V_3| - 2 \Rightarrow (|V_3| - 2) = \frac{|V_4|}{2} - 1$. □

Once the flow graph has been created, we determine the minimum flow through
the technique similar to [4].

The minimum flow algorithm works in two steps, *a)* an initial flow is placed
on the flow graph such that all flow requirements (1 & 2) are met; and *b)* the
minimum flow is computed using the decreasing path algorithm. Using the algorithms for a) and b) as detailed in [4] over the network G_4 provides a method with
a complexity of $O\left(|V_4| |E_4| c_{max}\right)$, where c_{max} represents the maximum value of
the capacity, C. From Theorem 1, $c_{max} = O\left(|V_4|\right)$. Therefore, the complexity of
the method in [4] becomes $O\left(|V_4|^2 |E_4|\right)$. This complexity can be generalized as
$O\left(|V|^2 |E|\right)$. Our work in this paper introduces a novel initialization algorithm
(i.e. aspect a)) such that the complexity of computing the minimum flow using
the standard decreasing path algorithm becomes $O\left(|V_4| |E_4|\right)$. This complexity
can be generalized to $O\left(|V| |E|\right)$.

Initialization with a Feasible Flow. Given the graph $G_4 = (V_4, E_4, L, C)$,
Algorithm 4 places an initial flow such that the flow requirements 1 & 2 are met.

Algorithm 4. Initialization with a feasible flow

    Input: $G_4 = (V_4, E_4, L, C)$
    Output: feasible flow $f_{ij}, \forall\, (i, j) \in E_4 \,\&\, i, j \in V_4$
1 initialize $f_{ij} = 0, \forall\, (i, j) \in E_4 \,\&\, i, j \in V_4$;
2 **foreach** *vertex* $i \in V_4 - \{s, t\}$ **do**
3   find path, p_s, from s to i using breadth-first-search;
4   find path, p_t, from i to t using breadth-first-search;
5   path, $p = p_s + p_t$;
6        $k = \min\{(f_{mn} - l_{mn}), \forall\, (m, n) \in p\}$;
7   **if** $k < 0$ **then**
8   **foreach** *edge* $(m, n) \in p$ **do**
9                $f_{mn}{+} = 1$;
10   **end**
11   **end**
12 **end**

Theorem 2. *Algorithm 4 ensures flow requirements are met.*

Proof. Consider a vertex, i, in G_3. This vertex will now be represented by i^+ and i^{++} in G_4. A path from s to i^{++} will cover the edge (i^+, i^{++}) since i^{++} is reachable only through i^+. Thus, incrementing the flow along the path from s to i^{++} will ensure that the flow condition of $l_{ij} = 1$ for $(i, j) = (i^+, i^{++})$ is met. By checking $\forall i \in V_4$, ensures flow requirement (1) for all edges is met. The increments of the flow is done for every edge of a path from s to t. Consider the vertex i^+ in G_4. Let it have m incoming edges. Since i^+ is created by splitting vertex i, i^+ will have 1 outgoing edge. Let vertex i^+ be part of an $s - t$ path n number of times where $1 \le n \le \frac{|V_4|}{2} - 1$. The m incoming edges will be visited n times with each visit incrementing the flow by 1. Thus the sum of flows on the incoming edges will be n. Similarly, the outgoing edge will be visited n times and will also have a flow of n. Thus, by incrementing the flow of every edge of an $s - t$ path ensures flow requirement (2) is met.   □

Breadth first search has a complexity of $O(|E|)$. Therefore Algorithm 4 has a complexity of $O(|E_4||V_4|)$.

Once an initial flow is placed on the flow graph, the minimum flow is computed using the decreasing path algorithm.

Decreasing Path Algorithm to Find the Minimum Flow. We use the generic Decreasing Path algorithm as detailed in [4]. The algorithm is based on the Augmenting Path concept of the Ford-Fulkerson algorithm [5]. The Decreasing Path concept can be stated as follows. Every edge in G_4 is termed as a forward edge. Let this set be called E_4^f. For every forward edge, a new backward edge is introduced; i.e. a forward edge of the form (i, j), will have a backward edge of the form (j, i). Let this set of backward edges be called E_4^b. For each backward edge, the lower bound, l_{ij}, is set to 0 and the capacity, c_{ij} is set to

$\frac{|V_4|}{2} - 1$. The residual capacity of an edge, $r_{ij}, \forall (i,j) \in E_4^f \cup E_4^b$, is defined as follows:

$$r_{ij} = \begin{cases} f_{ij} - l_{ij} & \text{if } (i,j) \in E_4^f \\ c_{ij} - f_{ij} & \text{if } (i,j) \in E_4^b \end{cases}$$

A decreasing path is a path from s to t where the residual capacity of every edge is greater than 0. If a decreasing path visits a forward edge, then the flow on the edge can be reduced. If on the other hand, the decreasing path visits a backward edge, then the flow on the corresponding forward edge has to be increased. The flow in the graph will be minimum when no more decreasing paths can be found. The minimum flow is the optimal solution as proved in [4].

The algorithm to compute the minimum flow is presented as Algorithm 5.

The complexity of the Decreasing Path algorithm can be determined using the technique in [4]. Each reduction of the flow in the network will need $O(|E_4|)$ because of the path found through breadth first search. Since the maximum flow that may be initialized is $\frac{|V_4|}{2} - 1$ (from Theorem 1), the minimum flow will be found in $O(|V_4||E_4|)$. This can be generalized to $O(|V||E|)$.

Algorithm 5. Decreasing Path Algorithm

    Input: $G_4 = (V_4, E_4, L, C)$, with initial flow
    Output: minimum flow f and flows on G_4
1 **foreach** *edge* $(i,j) \in E_4$ **do**
2   put (i,j) in E_4^f;
3   put (j,i) in E_4^b; $l_{ji} = 0$; $c_{ji} = \frac{|V_4|}{2} - 1$;
4 **end**
5 **while** *path, p, exists from s to t using breadth-first-search such that*
   $r_{mn} > 0, \forall (m,n) \in p$ **do**
6     $r_{min} = \min\{r_{mn}, \forall (m,n) \in p\}$;
7   **foreach** *edge* $(m,n) \in p$ **do**
8   **if** $(m,n) \in E_4^f$ **then**
9           $f_{mn}- = r_{min}$;
10   **else**
11           $f_{mn}+ = r_{min}$;
12   **end**
13        $f_{nm} = f_{mn}$;
14   **end**
15 **end**
16 output $f = \sum_j f_{sj}, G_4$;

The overall complexity of the minimum flow algorithm is the maximum of the complexity between the initialization and the decreasing path algorithm.

$$\text{max (initialization algorithm, decreasing path algorithm)} =$$
$$\text{max} \left(O(|V||E|), O(|V||E|) \right) = O(|V||E|) \quad (4)$$

Thus, the complexity of our method of $O\left(|V||E|\right)$ improves upon the complexity of the generic minimum flow algorithm of $O\left(|V|^2|E|\right)$.

For the running example, the minimum flow is computed as 3 which can be quite clearly observed from Fig. 4. The minimum flow incidentally equals the lower bound for the example.

3.5   Generating the Minimum Test Paths from the Minimum Flow

The minimum number of $s - t$ paths to cover all the Prime Paths is the flow, f, in G_4. The $s - t$ paths in G_4 and the corresponding paths in G_1 are identified using Algorithm 6.

Steps 3 to 7 identify the paths corresponding to the minimum flow in G_3. For the running example, the $path^{G3} = \{s, p_4, t\}, \{s, v_3, p_1, t\}$ and $\{s, p_0, v_3, p_2, t\}$.

Vertices in $path^{G3}$ which represent cycles in G_2 are replaced. In the running example, there are no cycles to be introduced in the first path $\{s, p_4, t\}$. Replacing v_3 in the second path gives $\{s, p_3, p_5, v_2, p_3, p_1, t\}$. Note that although $v3$ represents the cycle - $\{v_2, p_3, p_5, v_2\}$, it is replaced as $\{p_3, p_5, v_2, p_3\}$ such that an edge exists between s and p_3. Step 10 performs this operation. Replacing v_2 gives $\{s, p_3, p_5, p_7, v_1, p_6, p_7, p_3, p_1, t\}$. Replacing v_1 gives the path $\{s, p_3, p_5, p_7, p_9, p_8, p_9, p_6, p_7, p_3, p_1, t\}$. Similarly, after replacing the cycles in the third path, we get $\{s, p_0, p_9, p_8, p_9, p_6, p_7, p_9, p_8, \boldsymbol{p_9}, \boldsymbol{p_3}, p_5, p_7, p_9, p_8, p_9, p_6, \boldsymbol{p_7}, \boldsymbol{p_2}, t\}$.

Note that the vertices p_9 and p_3 in the sub-path $\{p_9, p_3\}$ of the third Test Path are not directly connected in G_2. Similarly, the vertices p_7 and p_2 are not directly connected. This aspect of connectedness is taken care in step 13.

As can be seen from the paths, redundancy exists. For example, the cycle $\{p_9, p_8, p_9\}$ is present 3 times in the third path. We remove this redundancy by replacing such cycles with the first node of the cycle (p_9 in this case) for all occurrences except the first (step 18). Also note that for the cycle $\{p_7, p_9, p_6, p_7\}$ the sub-path $\{p_9, p_6\}$ is occurring more than once. This implies the cycle can be again reduced to the first node of the cycle (step 22). Thus, the set of paths after removing redundancy is $\{s, p_4, t\}, \{s, p_3, p_5, p_7, p_9, p_8, p_9, p_6, p_7, p_3, p_1, t\}, \{s, p_0, p_9, p_2, t\}$.

The last step of the algorithm is to merge the Prime Paths to obtain the $s - t$ paths on G_1. This operation is performed by the operator $\cup$ and is as explained in Section 3.2.

Thus, the minimum $s - t$ paths for the running example needed to cover all Prime Paths are $\{s, 1, 2, t\}, \{s, 1, 3, 4, 1, 3, 4, 5, 4, 5, 4, 1, 3, 4, 1, 2, t\}$ and $\{s, 1, 3, 4, 5, 4, 1, 2, t\}$. Observe that the Test Paths are long in length. The length of the Test Paths are the number of edges and equals 27 in this example.

3.6   Other Coverage Criteria

Our method of identifying the minimum number of Test Paths is generic and can cater to all of the structural coverage criteria of [2] as shown below.

Edge-Pair Coverage Criterion. For the Edge-Pair coverage criterion, the test requirement set, TR, is the set of all paths of length at-most 2. An edge-pair can

---

Algorithm 6. Identifying minimum Test Paths from minimum flow

---

Input: $G_4 = (V_4, E_4, L, C)$, with flow on each edge & minimum flow f
Output: All s-t paths, $path^{G1}$, on G_1 corresponding to the minimum flow

1   Remove all backward edges of G_4. Merge vertices of the form $\{v^+, v^{++}\}$ into
   v. Incoming edges of v = incoming edges of v^+. Outgoing edges of v =
   outgoing edges of v^{++}. Let the resulting graph be G_3;
2   **for** $i = 0$ **to** f **do**
3   remove all edges from G_3 which have flow of 0;
4   find path, $path^{G3}$, from s to t using breadth-first-search;
5   **foreach** $edge(m, n) \in path^{G3}$ **do**
6        $f_{mn} {-}= 1$;
7   **end**
8   **while** $path^{G3}$ *contains a vertex,* v_c^{G3}, *reduced from a cycle,* c **do**
9   Let the cycle be represented as $c = \{v_1^{G2}, v_2^{G2}, \ldots, v_1^{G2}\}$;
10   replace v_c^{G3} with $c = \{v_j^{G2}, v_{j+1}^{G2}, \ldots, v_j^{G2}\}$ where v_{c-1}^{G3} is connected to
        v_j^{G2} through the information recorded in Algorithm 3 Step 4;
11   **end**
12      $path^{G2} = path^{G3}$;
13   ensure an edge exists between every vertex of $path^{G2}$ in G_2;
14 **end**
15 **foreach** $path^{G2}$ **do**
16   **foreach** *cycle,* c' *in* $path^{G2}$ **do**
17   **if** *number of occurrences of* c' *in all paths* $path^{G2} > 1$ **then**
18   except the first instance, replace all other instances of c' in
          $path^{G2}$ with the first vertex of c' ;
19   **end**
20   let $path_{sub} = c'$ −first & last vertices of c';
21   **if** *number of occurrences of* $path_{sub}$ *in all paths* $path^{G2} > 1$ **then**
22   replace c' in $path^{G2}$ with the first vertex of c' ;
23   **end**
24   **end**
25   initialize $path^{G1} = s$;
26   **foreach** *vertex,* $v_i^{G2} \in path^{G2}$ **do**
27        $path^{G1} = path^{G1} \cup$ prime path represented by v_i^{G2};
28   **end**
29      $path^{G1} = path^{G1} \cup t$;
30   Output $path^{G1}$;
31 **end**

---

be represented as a path $\{v_i, v_j, v_k\}$, where (v_i, v_j) & $(v_j, v_k) \in E$. The minimum number of Test Paths such that TR is covered can be obtained directly from our method. Algorithm 1 will have to be modified to generate the set of edge-pairs. Other algorithms can be used exactly as presented. Further, Lemma 1 and the Theorems hold. From Lemma 1, the lower bound on the minimum number of Test Paths would be max($|TypeS|, |TypeT|$), where $Type\,S$ and $Type\,T$ are those test requirements that contain the vertex s and t respectively.

Simple and Complete Round Trip Coverage Criterion. A Round Trip path is a Prime Path of $Type\,C$. The test requirement of the Simple Round Trip coverage criterion contains at least one $Type\,C$ Prime Path which begins and ends for a given vertex. The test requirement for Complete Round Trip coverage criterion contains all $Type\,C$ Prime Paths for a given vertex. Therefore, the Round Trip coverage criteria focuses on a subset of the set of Prime Paths for a given graph. In our formulation, algorithm 1 can be suitably modified to choose the set of Prime Paths needed for the set TR. The minimum number of Test Paths needed for this set of TR is directly obtained by the other algorithms. However, in this case of Round Trip coverage, Lemma 1 will provide a value of 0 as the lower bound since there are no $Type\,S$ or $Type\,T$ test requirements.

Edge Coverage Criterion. To handle Edge Coverage, there would be no need for algorithm 1 as the test requirements are directly available as E. The other algorithms can be used exactly as presented. Algorithm 2 represents every edge as a vertex in the flow network. Algorithm 3 reduces the graph to an acyclic one. The minimum flow computation using algorithms 4 and 5 with algorithm 6 will give the minimum number of Test Paths needed to cover every edge. Lemma 1 will equal the maximum of number of test requirements that contain s or t which in this case is the maximum of the out-degree of s and the in-degree of t.

Node Coverage Criterion. Node Coverage can be handled by using a sub-set of the algorithms in our method. We directly use algorithms 3 to 6 to obtain the minimum number of Test Paths for node coverage. Lemma 1 will equal the maximum of the number of test requirements that contain s or t which in this case will equal 1.

4   Experimental Results

We have evaluated our method through two sets of tests. In the first test we use 18 graphs representing actual open-source software [1] as test inputs. Since these graphs were also used as test inputs in [7], our results can be directly compared with that of [7]. Tables 2 & 3 provides the results of the first test.

   The results show a significant reduction in the number of Test Paths generated over the methods of [2] and [7]. Averaging over the 18 graphs, the number of Test Paths were reduced by 72.9% over the solution of [2]. The reduction varied from a minimum of 16.3% to a maximum of 89.9%. Comparing with [7], the number of Test Paths from our solution reduced by 59.6% on average and varied from a minimum benefit of 0% to a maximum benefit of 91.4%.

---

[1] We thank Nan Li of [7] for sharing the manually created graphs.

Although our solution does not explicitly attempt to minimize the length of the Test Paths, the results show that in many cases, the Test Path length is reduced as well. The average reduction in the Test Path length on the 18 graphs was -9.4% over [2] (i.e. on average, the test path length increased) and 38.5% over [7]. Note that in some cases, the minimization of the number of Test Paths has actually increased the length of the Test Paths.

The identification of the lower bound (Lemma 1) has performed exceedingly well and on average over the 18 graphs, was only 8.2% outside the true value.

The execution time of our method is significant with Algorithm 2 being the most costly. On average, the execution time of our method was 338 times that of [2]. In absolute terms, the average execution time was 3.6 minutes, but varied from a minimum of 5 ms to a maximum of 27.6 minutes.

Table 2. Test Paths & Execution Time (in ms) over graphs representing actual software

Num. of Prime Paths	9	11	27	27	35	38	46	63	69	78 [a]	93 [b]
Num. of Test Paths from Solution in [2]	7	9	14	19	26	22	36	34	49	37	69
Test Paths' Length from Solution in [2]	46	56	200	181	230	210	426	506	544	675	771
Num. of Test Paths from our Solution	5	7	11	14	20	12	17	11	41	18	54
Lower Bound on Num. of Test Paths	5	7	11	14	20	12	8	11	35	18	54
Test Paths' Length from our Solution	33	42	159	133	223	154	294	385	527	764	1043
Execution Time of Solution in [2]	2	2	10	2	7	2	5	14	11	6	15
Execution Time of Algorithm 1	1	1	9	1	6	1	2	12	6	5	12
Execution Time of Algorithm 2	1	1	21	7	36	13	50	153	63	170	150
Execution Time of Algorithm 3	1	1	3	2	5	1	8	19	4	13	22
Execution Time of Algorithm 4 & 5	1	1	2	1	6	1	2	5	6	1	4
Execution Time of Algorithm 6	1	1	11	4	26	7	21	48	23	38	40
Total Execution Time of our Solution	5	5	46	15	79	23	83	237	102	227	228

[a] maps to 71 in results (Table II) of [7] as our solution uses a single source and sink.
[b] similarly maps to 84 in results (Table II) of [7].

In the second test, we created 4391 random graphs of varying complexity as test inputs. The Prime Paths of these graphs varied from 7 to 150. The number of Test Paths, the length of Test Paths and the execution time were recorded averaging over graphs of a particular Prime Path. The execution times were the average of 5 runs over the same graph. The results are shown in Fig. 6. Similar to the first test, we see a significant improvement in terms of number of Test Paths. On average, our method reduced the number of Test Paths by 70.9%. The length of Test Paths were reduced by 2.7% on average. The lower bound was away from the true value by only 0.6% on average. On average, our method took 0.39 seconds to execute which was 105 times the execution time of [2].

Overall, our method of minimizing the number of Test Paths provides good results. To mitigate the concern of the increase in execution time, the quality of the lower bound can be exploited (for example attempting the minimization only when the solution from [2] is over 5 times the lower bound).

Table 3. Test Paths & Execution Time (in ms) over graphs representing actual software

Num. of Prime Paths	98	101	122	170	1074 [2]	1141	1844
Num. of Test Paths from method in [2]	67	60	80	102	933	954	885
Test Paths' length from method in [2]	1096	872	1577	1986	27457	37245	19828
Num. of Test Paths from our Method	41	47	20	42	362	96	102
Lower Bound on Num. of Test Paths	31	47	20	28	362	65	102
Test Paths' Length from our Method	967	1152	1541	1789	34733	37358	21482
Execution Time of Solution in [2]	11	11	14	48	3548	5884	1997
Execution Time of Algorithm 1	9	9	11	26	2376	4454	748
Execution Time of Algorithm 2	306	253	1057	1386	634719	1240553	1315738
Execution Time of Algorithm 3	42	13	79	222	72520	167950	95775
Execution Time of Algorithm 4 & 5	6	4	1	12	137	19	87
Execution Time of Algorithm 6	58	71	230	179	42628	106613	242745
Total Execution Time for our Method	421	350	1378	1825	752380	1519589	1655093

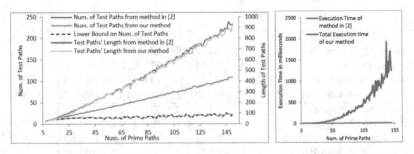

Fig. 6. Test Paths & Execution Time (in ms) over randomly created graphs

5   Conclusion

In this paper, we present a method to achieve the minimum number of Test Paths for Prime Path and other structural coverage criteria. The Prime Path criterion improves the quality of the Test Cases. However, even a small graph can have many Prime Paths and having a less number of Test Paths directly results in time saving over the Test Case execution. Our solution obtains an optimal solution with a time complexity of $O\left(|V||E|\right)$. This matches the best known time complexity till date. We have also presented a lower bound for the minimum number of Test Paths. Experimental results on graphs representing actual software and random graphs shows the superior performance of our method in terms of the number of Test Paths and the quality of the lower bound.

References

1. Aho, A.V., Lee, D.: Efficient algorithms for constructing testing sets, covering paths, and minimum flows. AT&T Bell Laboratories Tech. Memo. CSTR159 (1987)
2. Ammann, P., Offutt, J.: Introduction to software testing. Cambridge University Press (2008)

3. Ammann, P., Offutt, J.: W., X., Li, N.: Coverage computation web applications (2008), http://cs.gmu.edu:8080/offutt/coverage/ (online; accessed April 26, 2014)
4. Ciurea, E., Ciupală, L.: Sequential and parallel algorithms for minimum flows. Journal of Applied Mathematics and Computing 15(1-2), 53–75 (2004)
5. Ford, L., Fulkerson, D.R.: Flows in networks. Princeton University Press (1962)
6. Kaminski, G.K., Praphamontripong, U., Ammann, P., Offutt, J.: An evaluation of the minimal-mumcut logic criterion and prime path coverage. In: Software Engineering Research and Practice, pp. 205–211 (2010)
7. Li, N., Li, F., Offutt, J.: Better algorithms to minimize the cost of test paths. In: 2012 IEEE Fifth International Conference on Software Testing, Verification and Validation (ICST), pp. 280–289. IEEE (2012)
8. Ntafos, S.C., Hakimi, S.L.: On path cover problems in digraphs and applications to program testing. IEEE Transactions on Software Engineering (5), 520–529 (1979)

An Approach to Derive Usage Models Variants for Model-Based Testing

Hamza Samih[1,3], Hélène Le Guen[1], Ralf Bogusch[2],
Mathieu Acher[3], and Benoit Baudry[4]

[1] ALL4TEC, France
{hamza.samih,helene.leguen}@all4tec.net
[2] Airbus Defence and Space, Germany
ralf.bogusch@cassidian.com
[3] University of Rennes 1, IRISA/Inria, France
mathieu.acher@irisa.fr
[4] IRISA/Inria Rennes, France
benoit.baudry@inria.fr

Abstract. Testing techniques in industry are not yet adapted for product line engineering (PLE). In particular, Model-based Testing (MBT), a technique that allows to automatically generate test cases from requirements, lacks support for managing variability (differences) among a set of related product. In this paper, we present an approach to equip usage models, a widely used formalism in MBT, with variability capabilities. Formal correspondences are established between a variability model, a set of functional requirements, and a usage model. An algorithm then exploits the traceability links to automatically derive a usage model variant from a desired set of selected features. The approach is integrated into the professional MBT tool MaTeLo and is currently used in industry.

Keywords: Product Line, Model-based Testing, Usage Model, Usage Model Variant, Orthogonal Variability Model, Requirements.

1 Introduction

Real world success stories of *Product Lines (PLs)* show that the effective management of a large set of products is possible [1, 2]. The factorization and exploitation of common features of the products as well as the handling of their variability is an essential success criteria for this success stories A major challenge in PL engineering is the combinatorial explosion of features, leading to potentially billions of individual products; mastering them it can lead to significant benefits. Yet configuring, deriving, and *testing* a family of products raises new problems [3–5].

Existing V&V approaches (testing, model checking, etc.) usually target validation at the single product level. They mainly consist in validating each product independently from the others and are hardly applicable to a family of products (also called *variants*). This tends to hinder expected benefits of PL engineering

M.G. Merayo and E. Montes de Oca (Eds.): ICTSS 2014, LNCS 8763, pp. 80–96, 2014.
© IFIP International Federation for Information Processing 2014

in terms of reuse, reduction of development cost, and shortening of time-to-market and certification cost. *Model-based Testing (MBT)* has the potential to assist practitioners in building and testing PLs with adequate abstraction and automation. In essence MBT aims at inferring test suites from a test model that is based on the system requirements [6]. A test model can be represented using several formats such as UML state-machines, Markov chains, or a *Usage Model* (see Section 2.2). From a test model, one can define different testing strategies and derive a set of relevant test cases, accordingly to the chosen strategy [7, 8].

Although behavioural MBT is well established for single-system testing, a survey shows insufficient support of PL-based MBT [9]. In particular, usage models (a widely used formalism in MBT) are employed to test only one individual system. We want to go further and equip usage models with *variability* information in order to formally document what can vary in a usage model. For this purpose, features, as end-user visible behaviour of a system, are widely used to distinguish different behaviour variants of a PL. The idea is then to systematize the derivation of usage models variants – each variant being exploited afterwards for generating test cases of a specific product of a PL. Specifically we address the following research questions in this paper: (1) How to infuse variability concerns within a test model and build explicit relationships between a variability model and a usage model? (2) How to extract a valid product-specific test suite from a global usage model, according to a desired set of features (configurations)?

The key idea of our proposal is to establish formal correspondences between features, requirements and a usage model. The relationships are then exploited to automatically synthesize usage model variants. The synthesis algorithm has two major steps. A subset of the requirements is inferred from a specific configuration. A usage model variant is obtained from the set of requirements by pruning unnecessary transitions and correcting probabilities. The paper describes in details the overall testing approach and presents the theoretical foundations. The industrial report of the application of the approach in the aeronautic domain has been published in [10]. To summarize, we make the following contributions:

- We describe a comprehensive approach to relate a variability model, a set of functional requirements, and a usage model. The description of variability is formally defined, non intrusive (separated), and can operate over an existing usage model;
- We develop an algorithm to automatically derive a variant of a usage model from a desired selection of features. We discuss the (polynomial) complexity and the reliability of the algorithm. We integrate the algorithm into the professional MBT tool MaTeLo[1] so that variants of usage models (Markov chains) can be used afterwards to test a system.

The remainder of the paper is organized as follows. Section 2 motivates our work and introduces background information. Section 3 presents our approach to model variability of a usage model. Section 4 describes our algorithm to derive

---

[1] MaTeLo (Markov Test Logic) is a MBT tool developed by ALL4TEC

usage model variants from variability (features) and requirements. Section 5 discusses related work while Section 6 concludes the paper.

2   Background and Example

In this section we present a car dashboard as an example of a product line (PL). The dashboard of a car provides various information such as: vehicle speed, engine speed, engine temperature, fuel level in the tank, oil pressure in the engine and turn indicator. This list may vary depending on the manufacturer, model, version, and the vehicle category. However, certain features of a dashboard are imposed by international standards. In this example of a PL, two kinds of configurations are considered: high-end (HE) and low-end (LE) products, intended for both Europe (EU) and United States (US). We will limit ourselves to some basic features of a dashboard with a couple of variants.

2.1   Overview

In this example we can define 16 valid configurations of the dashboard. In general, testing all variants is impossible due to the resources and time needed, even if the process is automated. The challenge in industry is to optimize the process for PL testing. Nevertheless, deploying a new solution in industry is a decision that needs to be justified by time and cost savings. An important step to improve the adoption of novel PL testing approaches is to propose solutions leveraging already in-use technologies. For instance, MBT is a widely used automated testing solution for embedded systems [6]. In this work we propose to extend MBT to support PL testing in order to derive specific test cases for variants of a PL. We focus on usage models as MBT formalism and choose the MaTeLo tool to develop test models. For PL variability documentation, we use OVM and extend its existing formalization [11].

2.2   The MaTeLo Usage Model

In this work we use MaTeLo usage models which describe the intended behaviour of a system under test (SUT) [12,13]. MaTeLo supports the development of statistical usage based models by using extended Markov chains. Though, MaTeLo usage model is a finite state machines, where the nodes represent the major states of the system and the transitions represent the actions or operations of the SUT. A usage model is built according to textual requirements or existing specification documents of the SUT [14]. The usage model is created with MaTeLo - a MBT solution, that allows automated generation of test cases for complex systems. However, the MaTeLo approach for usage models is based on the traditional approach of MBT, that consider single systems only, whereas for a product line, we should create a model for each variant of the system. In the light of the considerable efforts to build the usage model, the test cases are generated automatically. The usage model [13] is a hierarchical model, it can be composed by multiple extended Markov chains. A chain is a part of the model referenced by a state of another chain at the above level. Each transition has a probability $p_{ss'}(\mathfrak{F})$, which corresponds to the probability of choosing the state s' when the process is in state s for a profile $\mathfrak{F}$. Profiles qualify the usage model to represent how the system will be used statistically. Probabilities are not versus time and do not vary during generation. The usage model provides the stimulation and expected responses of the system which are extracted from the functional requirements and associated thereafter with transitions. We consider a usage model denoted $\mathcal{M}_{\mathcal{T_P}}$ for a single system ($\mathcal{P}$) to be a tuple of the form (S, s_0, s_n, R, T), where:

- S: a finite set of states,
- $s_0 \in S$: unique initial state,
- $s_n \in S$: unique final state,
- R: a set of functional requirements of the SUT,
- T: a set of probabilistic transitions of the form $s \xrightarrow{p_{ss'}, R_{ss'}} s'$, with $s \in S \, / \, s_n$, $s' \in S \, / \, s_0$, $R_{ss'}$ is a set of the requirements associated with $t_{ss'}$, $p_{ss'} \in [0, 1]$ is the probability of choosing state s' from s. The sum of the probabilities associated with the outgoing transitions of state s must be equal to 1.

The initial state and final state are used to define the border of a test case. Loops are allowed in the usage model. All states except the final state s_n have at least one outgoing probabilistic transition. All states except the initial state s_0 have at least one incoming probabilistic transition. A requirement can be associated manually with transitions of the usage model in MaTeLo. Each associated requirement has a role, by default set to *necessary*. It may also have as role *sufficient* or *necessary and sufficient*. For example, the *navigation* requirement r_6 is associated with the action *Start navigation* depicted by the transition t_5 in the usage as shown in Fig. 1.

A generated test case always starts with s_0 and ends with s_n. Test case generation consists of selecting transitions according to their probabilities and the chosen algorithm. The criteria can vary between the random selection or selection of the largest probability of a transition to constitute a valid test case. A requirement is covered, when a sufficient or all the necessary transitions are present in the test case path.

Designing a usage model is not easy and requires a substantial amount of work; all information on the SUT must be integrated, such as stimuli, requirements and usage profiles. Adding a layer of variability to the test model remains tedious and it will be more complicated to track improvements and updates. Consequently, modelling variability separately with a single base model as the Orthogonal Variability Model (OVM), helps to identify inconsistencies and allows reasoning on product lines. We are interested in OVM in order to catch only the variable items and manage system variability in an efficient and consistent way, as well as to avoid a hierarchical arranged set of features.

2.3   Orthogonal Variability Model (OVM)

OVM is a flat model that documents only PL variability [1]. In the OVM model a variation point documents a variable feature. Each instance of a variation point is represented by a feature. A variation point is represented by a triangle and a rectangle depicts a feature.

Each variation point is related to at least one feature and a feature is bound to one variation point. Three types of relationships are possible between variation points and features: *mandatory, optional* and *alternative choices*. A *mandatory* feature is always required in the realization of a new variant. An *optional* feature can be added or not to a variant. A combination of *alternative choice* dependencies allows grouping options; this group of options is associated with a cardinality that defines a minimum number n and a maximum number m of features. The left-hand pane of Fig. 1 depicts the dashboard OVM model.

OVM uses constraints to refine relationships between features and variation points or between both, a constraint can be a *requires* or an *excludes* constraint.

OVM abstract syntax: Metzger et al. [11] have introduced a mathematical formalization for OVM, which describes the basic elements outside the metamodel. We use this formalization to describe the variability model. We consider an OVM denoted $\mathcal{M}_{\mathcal{V}}$ to be a tuple of the form $(VP, V, \mathcal{P}(V), C)$, where:

- $VP(\neq \emptyset)$, is a set of variation points.
- vp, is a variation point, where $vp \in VP$.
- $V(\neq \emptyset)$, is a set of features.
- v, is a feature[2], where $v \in V$.
- $\mathcal{P}(V) = \{V'|V' \subseteq V\}$ power set of any set V, $\mathcal{P}(V)$ is the set of all subsets of V including the empty set and V itself.
- $Req \subseteq (V \times V) \cup (V \times VP) \cup (VP \times VP)$ symbolizes the *required* constraints between V_V, V_VP and VP_VP. *Excl* symbolizes the *excluded* constraints.
- $C = Req \cup Excl$, set of constraints, where $c \in Req$ or $c \in Excl$.

3 Modeling Variability of Usage Models

In this work we adapt MBT such that variant-specific test cases can be generated from derived usage model variants. In order to support PL variability, we extend both the usage model and the OVM semantics.

3.1 Relating Features with Requirements

During the realization of the usage model, the association between requirements and transitions of the model is performed simultaneously. To reconcile the OVM model with the usage model, it is necessary to associate requirements with features. This association is realised by users with MPLM[3] tool implemented to test our approach. During the creation of links between requirements and features, we encounter three different types of requirements:

---

[2] In OVM terminology v is denoted as a "variant". In this paper, we use *feature* (instead of variant) to refer to a discriminant, user-visible characteristic of a system; variant is used for another meaning (see Section 3.3).

[3] MaTeLo Product Line Manager, aims to derive usage models variants for product line testing.

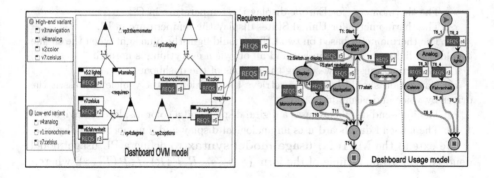

Fig. 1. Reconciliation process of variability model $\mathcal{M}_\mathcal{V}$ with usage model $\mathcal{M}_\mathcal{T}$

- a requirement associated with PL commonalities as r_1. This generic requirement is generally associated only with the transition representing the variation point as vp_3 *thermometer* and not to its features.
- a requirement associated only with one feature as r_6, associated with the v_3 *navigation* feature.
- a requirement associated with a feature that is required by one or more other features. This kind of requirement is addressed specifically in Section 4.2.

We extend the **OVM abstract syntax** introduced in Section 2.3 to reuse it in our contribution to express the requirements-features association. We consider an OVM denoted $\mathcal{M}_\mathcal{V}$ to be a tuple of the form $(VP, V, \mathcal{P}(V), C, \delta)$, where:

- $(VP, V, \mathcal{P}(V), C)$, equivalent to $\mathcal{M}_\mathcal{V}$,
- $\delta : V \nrightarrow \mathcal{P}(R)$ is a partial function, labelling features with requirements.

Thus, thanks to the links made between features and requirements, we can identify transitions related to features.

3.2 The PL Usage Model

In our approach, we suggest to build only one usage model that describe the expected behaviour of features in a PL. That means, the PL usage model will be instantiated differently for each variant. The right-hand pane of Fig. 1 illustrates the dashboard usage model with its sub-chains. The model represents the expected behaviour of the dashboard; stimuli and expected responses are associated with transitions. For example, the thermometer function can reference a sub-chain that represents its behaviour. Test cases may cover an executable path of one or many functionalities of the dashboard. Moreover, the transition t_7 is used to loop back and include new executable paths of others features.

$T = \{t_1, ..., t_{6\_7}, ..., t_{11}\}$ is the set of transitions from $\mathcal{M}_\mathcal{T}$ depicted in right-hand pane of Fig. 1 which are annotated with the following requirements R:

r_1: A sensor located on the engine block or cylinder head provides temperature.

r_2: The thermometer for Europe display the temperature in C°.

r_3: The thermometer for United States display the temperature in F°.

r_4: The thermometer based on two LEDs should light the blue light when the engine is cold, red light when it is too hot and all off when everything is normal.

r_5: The screen must allow setting the options of the dashboard.

r_6: Navigation should be able to retrieve the position of the vehicle and assist the driver by voice and visual indications.

r_7: The high-end dashboard uses a digital display and a color display for navigation.

r_8: The low-end dashboard uses an analogical display and a monochrome display.

We extend the **MaTeLo usage model syntax** to define a PL usage model denoted $\mathcal{M}_\mathcal{T}$ to be a tuple of the form $(S, s_0, s_n, R, \mathcal{P}(R), T, \mathcal{P}(T), \gamma)$, where:

- (S, s_0, s_n, R, T), equivalent to $\mathcal{M}_{\mathcal{T}_\mathcal{P}}$ described in 2.2,
- $\mathcal{P}(R) = \{R'|R' \subseteq R\}$, $\mathcal{P}(R)$ power set of any set of R,
- $\mathcal{P}(T) = \{T'|T' \subseteq T\}$, $\mathcal{P}(T)$ power set of any set of T.
- $\gamma : R \nrightarrow \mathcal{P}(T)$ is a partial function, labelling requirements with transitions.

Those relationships are true only for the PL usage model. To make a valid usage model, we should observe rules presented in Section 2.2. In the following we consider a unique profile $\mathfrak{F}$ associated with the PL usage model. The $\mathfrak{F}$ profile is independent of product variants described in the usage model for multiple variants. It is used to have a valid usage model structure and help the Algorithm 1 to derive variant-specific usage model with their own profile.

Semantics. Each $\mathcal{M}_{\mathcal{T}_\mathcal{P}}$ derived describes the expected behaviour (see Section 2.2) of a usage model variant. The semantics of a $\mathcal{M}_\mathcal{T}$ is thus the union of the behaviours of all valid configurations: $\mathcal{M}_\mathcal{T} = \bigcup_{\mathcal{P} \in \mathbf{P}} [\![\mathcal{M}_{\mathcal{T}_\mathcal{P}}]\!]$.

3.3 Variant Semantics

A variant is a valid configuration composed of a set of features that considers a set of constraints defined in the $\mathcal{M}_\mathcal{V}$. A variant denoted $\mathcal{P}$ is a tuple of the form $(V_\mathcal{P}, R_\mathcal{P}, \mathcal{M}_{\mathcal{T}_\mathcal{P}})$ used to identify $\mathcal{M}_{\mathcal{T}_\mathcal{P}}$ from $\mathcal{M}_\mathcal{T}$, where:

- $V_\mathcal{P}$ set of features that compose $\mathcal{P}$,
- $R_\mathcal{P}$ set of requirements related to $\mathcal{P}$,
- $\mathcal{M}_{\mathcal{T}_\mathcal{P}}$ usage model variant.
- $\mathbf{P} = \{\mathcal{P}_1, ..., \mathcal{P}_n\}$ denotes PL variants.

The proposed formalization allows deriving usage model variants for generation of product-specific test cases.

4 Deriving Usage Model Variants

In this section we present the second part of our contribution. The automated derivation of a usage model variant consists of projecting a set of OVM features composing a valid configuration onto the PL usage model. The bindings between features, PL requirements and the transitions of the PL usage model help to

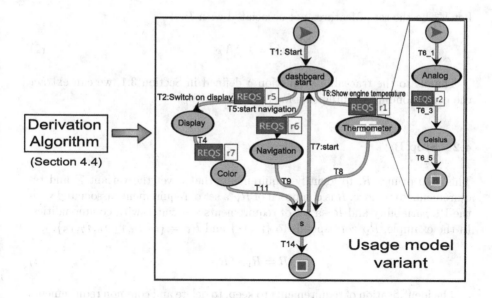

Fig. 2. The derivation process of usage model variants

derive $\mathcal{M}_{\mathcal{T}_{\mathcal{P}}}$ with only the transitions and requirements of variant $\mathcal{P}$. The results of the reconciliation process depicted in Fig. 1 (see items 1, 2 and 3) are taken as input for the derivation process shown in Fig. 2.

In our approach we consider four steps to reach the automated derivation of usage model variants:

Step A Identify and select features that compose the configuration under test and remove features not used or not required.

Step B Extract and classify according to the selected features the requirements to keep and to delete.

Step C Identify and select according to the classified requirements, the transitions to keep and to delete as well as identify incoherent cases.

Step D Derive a usage model variant $\mathcal{M}_{\mathcal{T}_{\mathcal{P}}}$ from $\mathcal{M}_{\mathcal{T}}$ by removing transitions not mapped straightforwardly to the selected variant, while keeping correctness of the derived model as defined in Section 2.2.

For illustration, we use high-end variant $\mathcal{P}_1$ to derive its corresponding usage model variant, rather than low-end variant $\mathcal{P}_2$. As a reminder, $V_{\mathcal{P}_1}$ is equal to $\{v_2, v_3, v_4, v_7\}$, and $V_{\mathcal{P}_2}$ is equal to $\{v_1, v_4, v_7\}$, see left side of Fig. 1.

4.1 Step A

The first step consists of identifying the features that should not be considered for the derived usage model variant. This implies to select all features in the OVM model except the selected features that compose the variant under test.

Let $V_{\bar{\mathcal{P}}}$ be the set of features not associated with $\mathcal{P}$.

$$V_{\bar{\mathcal{P}}} = V \setminus V_{\mathcal{P}} \tag{1}$$

Thanks to the traceability function δ defined in Section 3.1, we can extract the corresponding requirements for both $V_{\mathcal{P}}$ and $V_{\bar{\mathcal{P}}}$.

4.2   Step B

This step prunes R, to identify requirements that cover the variant $\mathcal{P}$ and requirements to remove. R is composed of R_V a set of requirements associated with the PL variability and $R_{\bar{V}}$ a set of requirements associated with commonalities. In the example, $R_{\bar{V}}$ corresponds to $\{r_1, r_5\}$ and $R_V = \{r_2, r_3, r_4, r_6, r_7, r_8\}$.

$$R = R_V \cup R_{\bar{V}} \tag{2}$$

The identification of requirements to keep, to delete and common requirements between both, requires refining R_V, i.e., identifying requirements labelling $V_{\mathcal{P}}$ and $V_{\bar{\mathcal{P}}}$.

$$R_V = R_{V\_\mathcal{P}} \cup R_{V\_\bar{\mathcal{P}}} \tag{3}$$

Where $R_{V\_\mathcal{P}}$ is the set of requirements labelling $V_{\mathcal{P}}$ while $R_{V\_\bar{\mathcal{P}}}$ is the set of requirements labelling $V_{\bar{\mathcal{P}}}$. Nevertheless, some requirements may belong to $R_{V\_\mathcal{P}}$ and at the same time to $R_{V\_\bar{\mathcal{P}}}$. R_{Inter} represents the common requirements between variants, where:

$$R_{Inter} = R_{V\_\mathcal{P}} \cap R_{V\_\bar{\mathcal{P}}} \tag{4}$$

R_{Inter} helps to refine $R_{V\_\mathcal{P}}$ and $R_{V\_\bar{\mathcal{P}}}$ and select accurately the requirements to delete and to keep. Furthermore, R_{Inter} can assist in the detection of the incoherent cases described in 4.3. R_{Inter} of the dashboard example is empty.

$$R_{\|V\_\mathcal{P}\|} = R_{V\_\mathcal{P}} \setminus R_{Inter} \tag{5}$$

$R_{\|V\_\mathcal{P}\|}$, set of requirements labelling only features of the selected variant without common requirements. For $\mathcal{P}_1$, $R_{\|V\_\mathcal{P}_1\|}$ is equal to $\{r_2, r_6, r_7\}$.

$$R_{\|V\_\bar{\mathcal{P}}\|} = R_{V\_\bar{\mathcal{P}}} \setminus R_{Inter} \tag{6}$$

Where $R_{\|V\_\bar{\mathcal{P}}\|}$ is the set of requirements that are not labelling $\mathcal{P}$ features. For $\mathcal{P}_1$, $R_{\|V\_\bar{\mathcal{P}}_1\|}$ is equal to $\{r_3, r_4, r_8\}$.

The objective is to identify R_{Inter}, $R_{\|V\_\mathcal{P}\|}$ and $R_{\|V\_\bar{\mathcal{P}}\|}$ based on $V_{\mathcal{P}}$ and $V_{\bar{\mathcal{P}}}$ as input.

4.3   Step C

We remind that a transition in a usage model can be labelled by several requirements ensured by the traceability function γ. Three subsets of transitions are
identified:

Selection of transitions to be deleted T_D: it consists of selecting each
transition labelled by a requirement of $R_{\|V\_\bar{\mathcal{P}}\|}$ must be removed definitively,
i. e., each transition associated with a subset of requirements R' that satisfies
the following condition should be deleted:

$$R' \subseteq R_{\|V\_\bar{\mathcal{P}}\|} \tag{7}$$

For $\mathcal{P}_1$, T_D is equal to $\{t_3, t_{6\_2}, t_{6\_4}\}$.

Selection of transitions to be kept T_K: it consists of selecting each transition labelled by a requirement of $R_{V\_\mathcal{P}}$ must be kept, i. e., each transition
covering requirements that label features of the selected variant should be kept:

$$R' \subseteq R_{V\_\mathcal{P}} \tag{8}$$

To recap, $R_{V\_\mathcal{P}}$ is the union of $R_{\|V\_\mathcal{P}\|}$ and R_{Inter}. For $\mathcal{P}_1$, T_K is equal to
$\{t_4, t_5, t_{6\_3}\}$. If all transitions of the usage model are selected in T_K, it means
the PL usage model describes only the usage of a system, and it is by no means
a PL usage model. In this case, all transitions will be kept.

Detection of incoherent case $T_{incoherent}$: it consists of identifying all incoherent transitions, i.e. identify the transitions annotated both by a set of re-
quirements to be kept $R_{V\_\mathcal{P}}$ and a set of requirements to be removed $R_{\|V\_\bar{\mathcal{P}}\|}$.
These cases must be detected during the selection and classification of transi-
tions. Incoherent cases are all incoherencies occurred during the construction of
the PL usage model.

The usage model contains transitions not labelled by requirements, but needed
to complete the usage model. Some of these transitions may contain also input
data and expected responses. In some cases, such transitions can be removed if
necessary in order to keep the correctness of the derived usage model variant,
otherwise they will be kept.

$R_{V\_\mathcal{P}}$ and $R_{\|V\_\bar{\mathcal{P}}\|}$ will serve to extract and prune transitions of the usage
model $\mathcal{M}_\mathcal{T}$, corresponding to requirements associated with the variant $\mathcal{P}$. We
use $R_{V\_\mathcal{P}}$, because it represents the specific requirements of variant $\mathcal{P}$ to be
kept.

Table 1, summarizes the classification rules of each transition associated to
one of these subsets of requirements.

4.4   Step D

After pruning transitions, Algorithm 1 proceeds to derive a usage model variant.
This phase consists of deleting all transitions and states that do not correspond
to the variant $\mathcal{P}$. In practice, the generation may result in one of the following

Table 1. Summary for the classification of transitions

$R_{\|V\_\mathcal{P}\|}$	R_{Inter}	$R_{\|V\_\bar{\mathcal{P}}\|}$	
x			$t \in T_K$
x	x		$t \in T_K$
x		x	$t \in T_{incoherent}$
	x		$t \in T_K$
x	x	x	$t \in T_{incoherent}$
	x	x	$t \in T_{incoherent}$
		x	$t \in T_D$

states: a usage model with broken branches, a complete usage model with incorrect profile probabilities. We discuss these cases in the following sections. The expected result of Algorithm 1 is a valid usage model as defined in Section 2.2.

Removal of Transitions. First, the model $\mathcal{M}_{\mathcal{T}_\mathcal{P}}$ is initialized to $\mathcal{M}_\mathcal{T}$. Afterwards, we remove all transitions in T_D from $\mathcal{M}_{\mathcal{T}_\mathcal{P}}$. At this step no incoherent case exists. So, $T_{incoherent}$ is empty. Nevertheless, some inconsistency may appear in the usage model, such as broken branches. To have a valid model, Algorithm 1 is detecting broken branches to be removed. Fig. 3 illustrates the extracted $\mathcal{M}_{\mathcal{T}_\mathcal{P}}$ model with broken branches. For $\mathcal{P}_1$, the broken branches are $\{t_{10}, t_{6\_6}, t_{6\_7}\}$. In the tool implementation, an execution log is intended to help users to identify all deleted transitions and requirements from the PL usage model.

Detection of Broken Branches and Unreachable States Deletion. In the previous step two problems can occur. Firstly, some states can be unreachable

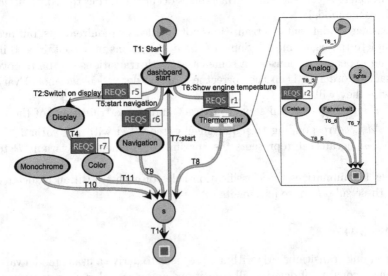

Fig. 3. Usage model of $\mathcal{P}_1$ with its sub-chains

from the initial state s_0 (in case of all incoming states have been removed or they are included in an "island"). Secondly, the situation when it is not possible to reach the final state s_n from another state. So this step consists in detecting all incomplete paths that start in s_0 and where it is not possible to reach s_n.

We denote by $\mathbf{Q}$ the sub-stochastic matrix of size $n + 1$ corresponding to the derived usage model, where:

- $q_{ij} = p_{ij}$, if transition $t_{ij} \in T_K$. p_{ij} is the probability related to t_{ij},
- 0 if $t_{ij} \in T_D$,
- 0 if $i = n$, if it is not possible to reach another state from s_n,
- 0 if $j = 0$, if it is not possible to reach s_0 from another state.

Let $\mathbf{B}$ be the matrix such that $\mathbf{B} = (\mathbf{I} - \mathbf{Q})^{-1}$. The probability to visit s_j when process is in s_i is [15]: $f_{ij} = b_{ij}/b_{jj}$.

State s_i and all incoming and outgoing transitions are removed from the model $\mathcal{M}_{T_p}$ in two specific situations: if $f_{0i} = 0$, in this case s_i is inaccessible, or if $f_{in} = 0$, it is not possible to reach s_n when the process is in state s_i.

After identifying the broken branches, Algorithm 1 proceeds with the suppression of detected unreachable states and the related transitions. However, it is possible that some transitions to be removed belong to the set T_K. This case could result from a bad construction of the PL usage model.

Adjustment of Probabilities. After removing all broken branches from the extracted usage model, we update the associated usage profile. We choose to distribute the probabilities of the removed transitions proportionally on adjacent transitions. This entails applying the following relation: $q_{ij}(\mathfrak{F}) \longleftarrow \frac{q_{ij}}{\sum_{k \in S} p_{ik}}$.

The derived usage model variant for $\mathcal{P}_1$ is depicted in Fig. 2.

4.5   Analysis of Algorithm Complexity and Reliability

Complexity (Algorithm 1). To extract the usage model of variant $\mathcal{P}$, the Step D is based on inputs provided by Step C that involved Step A and Step B. The complexity of the algorithms behind these steps A, B and C are not reported here. We focus only on Algorithm 1 of Step D. The preliminary step of Algorithm 1 consists of seeking all non-reachable states from state s_0 to state s_n. We use matrix to enumerate efficiently all unreachable states in a chain. For this method the worst case is a usage model with a large number of states $(n \times n) \times n$. Therefore the order of complexity is $O(n^3)$, where n is the number of $\mathcal{M}_{T_p}$ states. The second part of Algorithm 1 removes from $\mathcal{M}_{T_p}$ all transitions belonging to unreachable states. Subsequently, Algorithm 1 performs a consistency check of the usage model. The order of complexity is $O(n)$, where n is the number of $\mathcal{M}_{T_p}$ states.

Proof of Algorithm 1. A test case generation is considered as a random walk on a Markov chain until the end state s_n is reached. We are interested in the visiting probability: this probability must be strictly positive from s_0 to every other states of the model and the final state s_n must be accessible from every state of the chain. This visiting probability is calculated on a chain with absorbing state and means the probability to visit a state before absorption.

So we add a new absorbing state in the model and the probability to go from s_n to its new state s_{n+1} is equal to 1. This construction is required, because we consider the probability to reach the final state in case where an incoming transition of this state has been deleted by the previous step of the Algorithm 1.

To calculate the probability of visiting the states before absorption, we remove the line and the column related to this state and we obtain the matrix $\mathbf{Q}$. The matrix $\mathbf{Q}$ has the following form:

$$\mathbf{Q} = \begin{pmatrix} \mathbf{Q'} & \mathbf{q}_n \\ \mathbf{0} & 0 \end{pmatrix} \tag{9}$$

Where the sub-matrix $\mathbf{Q'}$ is the lines and the columns related to states except the final state s_n and $\mathbf{q}_n$ is the vector of the probabilities to go from states $s_0, ..., s_{n-1}$ to the final state s_n.

The inverse matrix $\mathbf{B} = (\mathbf{I} - \mathbf{Q})^{-1}$ always exists, because $\mathbf{Q}$ is a sub-stochastic matrix, i. e., all elements are included between 0 and 1 and the sum of each line

---

Algorithm 1. Derivation of usage model variant

Input: $\mathcal{M}_T$, T_D, T_K, $T_{incoherent}$
Output: $\mathcal{M}_{T_p}$
1. $\mathcal{M}_{T_p} \longleftarrow \mathcal{M}_T$
   {Removal of T_D}
2. remove_transitions($T_D, \mathcal{M}_{T_p}$)
   {Detection of unreachable states in $\mathcal{M}_T$ see Section 4.4 }
3. $S \leftarrow getUnreachableStates(\mathcal{M}_{T_p})$
   {Retrieve all t outgoing and incoming from the state s}
4. **for** s of S **do**
5. $T \longleftarrow s \rightarrow transitions[*]$
6.   **for** t of T **do**
7.   **if** $t \in T_K$ **then**
8. $show\_problems(t)$
9.   **else if** t has DATA **then**
10. $show\_warning(t)$
11.   **end if**
12.   **end for**
13. $remove\_transitions(T, \mathcal{M}_{T_p})$
14. **end for**
    {Removal of all unreachable s}
15. $remove\_states(S, \mathcal{M}_{T_p})$
    {Correct probabilities to get a valid Markov chains see Section 4.4}
16. $Adjust\_probabilities(\mathcal{M}_{T_p})$

---

is inferior or equal to 1. It is possible to denote $\mathbf{B}$ on the following form:

$$\mathbf{B} = \begin{pmatrix} \mathbf{B} & \mathbf{b} \\ \mathbf{0} & 1 \end{pmatrix} \tag{10}$$

Where $\mathbf{b}$ is composed of values equal to 0 or 1. Indeed, as we have considered only one absorbing state, either the process is absorbed by this state or it cannot reach it. Consequently, the states to be removed are identified. If we delete all lines and columns where $b_{0i} = 0$ and $b_{in} = 0$, the visiting probabilities could be calculated without difficulty and the model is "clean" without broken branches. Eventually, we add the property that the sum of the probabilities associated to the outgoing transitions of each states is equal to 1 (see line 16 of Algorithm 1).

We can conclude that the usage model is an extended Markov chain, where test cases can be generated by random walks.

4.6 Implementation

The theoretical foundations of the approach are implemented in MaTeLo Product Line Manager [4] (MPLM) tool [16]. MPLM is an Eclipse-based extension of the MaTeLo tool suite, which supports deriving usage models variants from a PL usage model. MPLM realizes the overall variability testing approach while all the described algorithms are part of the tool. Users can import an OVM model and a PL usage model, link features with requirements, configure variants for testing, and derive variant-specific usage model. In particular, the generated usage models variants can be exploited by the MaTeLo tool to produce automatically test cases for a given variant (product). We report in [10] an experimental case study conducted with the industrial partner Airbus Defence and Space in the frame of the ARTEMIS Joint Undertaking research project MBAT[5] in order to validate the approach from an industrial point of view.

5 Related Work

Our contribution relates to the automatic generation of test cases for a product line (PL). Pohl et al. [1] presented a PL framework, resulting outcome of European projects *Café, FAMILIES, ESAPS*. The framework is composed of two distinct phases. The *domain engineering* phase aims to define commonality and variability of a reusable set of artefacts. The OVM language has been proposed to document variability. The second phase, called *application engineering*, aims to derive new applications based on a desired combination of features and the actual reuse of artefacts.

Our PL approach promotes the use of functional requirements as an intermediate layer to link the variability model with the test model. The usage model and functional requirements act as reusable artefacts while the derivation phase

---

[4] http://people.irisa.fr/Hamza.Samih/mplm
[5] http://www.mbat-artemis.eu

produces specific test cases. It has the merit to enforce separation of concerns and to be non invasive with current practice – we simply reuse the specification of usage models and requirements. Metzger et al. distinguish software variability (hidden from customers and internal to implementation) from PL variability (visible to customers and external) [11]. They used an OVM model and a feature model for describing the two kinds of variability. We also separate the variability description in a distinct variability model. A notable difference is that we map the OVM model to a set of functional requirements itself connected to a usage model. A key contribution of the paper is to properly define the formal correspondences and to develop automated techniques to derive variants.

Validation and testing of PLs. Numerous research studies have focused on the validation of product lines, offering techniques to optimize and improve this costly phase. Thüm et al. [5] surveyed existing kinds of verification strategies for various kinds of artefacts, e.g., from the checking of feature-related code in isolation to the exploitation of variability information during analysis of the PL. Recent advances in behavioural modelling have also been provided by the model checking community (e.g., see [2]). As argued in [8], testing and model checking techniques can be combined to enforce quality assurance of PLs.

To the best of our knowledge, the only proposal to handle the specific formalism of usage models has been devised by Devroey et al. [17]. A key difference is that the authors assume the specification of a so-called feature transition system (FTS) to describe the variability of a usage model. The elaboration of a FTS requires a significant amount of work and is another formalism that practitioners need to handle. In our approach, we simply map variability to a set of functional requirements – it has the merit of reusing existing artefacts and current practice is slightly impacted. Another difference is that some variability expressed in the FTS may not be covered in the usage model. In our approach, practitioners start with the usage model and express the necessary and sufficient variability.

Combinatorial testing aims at reducing testing costs when dealing with large and complex systems with many input combinations to test. Different approaches have been proposed to help in this task. For instance, pair-wise techniques aim at minimizing the number of *feature configurations* (i.e., combinations of features) to test while covering each pair of features. Constraint Satisfaction Problem (CSP) [18] and algorithmic [19, 20] approaches have been proposed to obtain coverage configuration sets from a feature model – a widely used formalism for modelling variability.

In our context, the current practice is to manually choose configurations. A natural alternative is to apply combinatorial techniques for automatically generating a subset of configurations from the OVM model. Metzger et al. [11] showed that an OVM model can be translated into a feature model so that efficient automated techniques developed in the context of feature modelling can be reused. With our approach, we can thus envision a fully automated process for deriving usage model variants and test cases.

6 Conclusion

We presented a solution to use model-based testing in the context of product line engineering. The generation of test cases from a usage model (roughly a Markov chain test model) can be performed not only for one variant (product), but for many variants with specific features. The proposed approach augments the description of a usage model with variability information. Variability is described in a separate model in terms of features which are linked to functional requirements of a testable system. Practitioners can project the variability onto a usage model and automatically synthesize usage model variants.

The theoretical foundations of the approach are implemented in an industrial model-based testing tool (MaTeLo). An experimental case study was performed with the industrial partner Airbus Defence and Space in the frame of the ARTEMIS Joint Undertaking research project MBAT. Practitioners report a reduction of the cost for test case development and highlight the minimal invasiveness of the solution so that established requirements and usage models can be reused. A detailed description of the industrial report can be found in [10].

Future Work. We are now continuing the experiments of applying the tool-supported approach with other industrial uses cases in other domains, in order to complete our work with concrete quantitative and qualitative results of the industrial case studies. A study is underway to explore the possibility of achieving multiple profiles for each variant.

Acknowledgments. The research leading to these results has received funding from the ARTEMIS Joint Undertaking under grant agreement no. 269335 ARTEMIS project MBAT, French DGCIS and German BMBF.

References

1. Pohl, K., Böckle, G., van der Linden, F.J.: Software Product Line Engineering: Foundations, Principles and Techniques. Springer-Verlag New York, Inc. (2005)
2. Classen, A., Heymans, P., Schobbens, P.Y., Legay, A., Raskin, J.F.: Model checking lots of systems: efficient verification of temporal properties in software product lines. In: ICSE (2010)
3. Lochau, M., Schaefer, I., Kamischke, J., Lity, S.: Incremental model-based testing of delta-oriented software product lines. In: Brucker, A.D., Julliand, J. (eds.) TAP 2012. LNCS, vol. 7305, pp. 67–82. Springer, Heidelberg (2012)
4. Weißleder, S., Lackner, H.: Top-down and bottom-up approach for model-based testing of product lines. In: MBT (2013)
5. Thüm, T., Apel, S., Kästner, C., Schaefer, I., Saake, G.: A classification and survey of analysis strategies for software product lines. ACM Computing Surveys (2014)
6. Utting, M., Legeard, B.: Practical Model-based Testing. Morgan-Kaufmann (2007)
7. Le Guen, H., Thelin, T.: Practical experiences with statistical usage testing. In: Software Technology and Engineering Practice (2003)
8. Devroey, X., Cordy, M., Perrouin, G., Kang, E.-Y., Schobbens, P.-Y., Heymans, P., Legay, A., Baudry, B.: A vision for behavioural model-driven validation of software product lines. In: Margaria, T., Steffen, B. (eds.) ISoLA 2012, Part I. LNCS, vol. 7609, pp. 208–222. Springer, Heidelberg (2012)

9. Oster, S., Wubbeke, A., Engels, G., Schürr, A.: A survey of model-based software product lines testing. In: MBT for embedded systems (2011)
10. Samih, H., Acher, M., Bogusch, R., Le Guen, H., Baudry, B.: Deriving Usage Model Variants for Model-based Testing: An Industrial Case Study. In: ICECCS 2014, Tianjin, Chine. IEEE (2014)
11. Metzger, A., Pohl, K., Heymans, P., Schobbens, P.Y., Saval, G.: Disambiguating the documentation of variability in software product lines: A separation of concerns, formalization and automated analysis. In: RE 2007, pp. 243–253 (2007)
12. Zander-Nowicka, J.: Model-Based Testing of Real-Time Embedded Systems in the Automotive Domain. Fraunhofer-IRB-Verlag (2009)
13. Le Guen, H., Marie, R., Thelin, T.: Reliability estimation for statistical usage testing using markov chains. In: ISSRE (2004)
14. Utting, M., Pretschner, A., Legeard, B.: A taxonomy of model-based testing approaches. Softw. Test., Verif. Reliab. 22, 297–312 (2012)
15. Çinlar, E.: Introduction to stochastic processes. [nachdr.] edn. Prentice-Hall, Englewood Cliffs (1975)
16. Samih, H., Bogusch, R.: MPLM – MaTeLo Product Line Manager. In: SPLC 2014 Demonstrations and Tools track (to appear, 2014)
17. Devroey, X., Perrouin, G., Cordy, M., Schobbens, P.Y., Legay, A., Heymans, P.: Towards statistical prioritization for software product lines testing. In: VaMoS 2014 (2014)
18. Gotlieb, A., Hervieu, A., Baudry, B.: Minimum pairwise coverage using constraint programming techniques. In: ICST 2012, pp. 773–774 (2012)
19. Johansen, M.F., Haugen, O.Y., Fleurey, F.: An algorithm for generating t-wise covering arrays from large feature models. In: SPLC 2012, vol. 46 (2012)
20. Perrouin, G., Sen, S., Klein, J., Baudry, B., Traon, Y.: l.: Automated and scalable t-wise test case generation strategies for software product lines. In: ICST 2010. IEEE (2010)

AUTSEG: Automatic Test Set Generator for Embedded Reactive Systems

Mariem Abdelmoula, Daniel Gaffe, and Michel Auguin

LEAT, University of Nice-Sophia Antipolis, CNRS,
930 route des Colles, BP 145, 06903 Sophia Antipolis Cedex France
{Mariem.Abdelmoula,Daniel.Gaffe,Michel.Auguin}@unice.fr

Abstract. One of the biggest challenges in hardware and software design is to ensure that a system is error-free. Small errors in reactive embedded systems can have disastrous and costly consequences for a project. Preventing such errors by identifying the most probable cases of erratic system behavior is quite challenging. In this paper, we introduce an automatic test set generator called AUTSEG. Its input is a generic model of the target system, generated using the synchronous approach. Our tool finds the optimal preconditions for restricting the state space of the model. It only works locally on significant subspaces. Our approach exhibits a simpler and efficient quasi-flattening algorithm than existing techniques and a useful compiled form to check security properties and reduce the combinatorial explosion problem of state space. To illustrate our approach, AUTSEG was applied to the case of a transportation contactless card.

Keywords: AUTSEG, Test Sets, State Machines, States Space Covering, Sequences Generation, Contactless Smart Card, Specification, Synchronous Model.

1 Introduction

Verifying automatically and formally that a system is working correctly is not trivial nowadays due to the increasing complexity of computer programs and their strong interaction with the environment. An important class of systems facing such problems are reactive systems. They continuously react and respond to their environment. Reactive systems belong to the large family of FSMs (Finite State Machines). They are ubiquitous in everyday life, varying from simple thermostats to the control of nuclear power plants, avionics, telesurgery, and online payment. Security for these systems is critical; even minor errors are unacceptable. In this paper, we focus on verification of embedded software controlling the reactive system behavior. To illustrate our approach, we aim to verify the implementation of the OS integrated in a contactless smart card for transportation. We specifically target the verification of the card's functionality and security features. Smart Cards are ubiquitous, with more than 200 million used across the globe for transportation, telephony, health insurance, banking, ID,

M.G. Merayo and E. Montes de Oca (Eds.): ICTSS 2014, LNCS 8763, pp. 97–112, 2014.

etc. Frauds are especially critical for banking cards, as counterfeiters are able to exploit the vulnerabilities of coding systems.

Furthermore, the card's complexity makes it difficult for a human to identify all possible sensitive situations or to validate it by classical methods. We need approximately 500 000 years to test the first 8 bytes if we consider a classical Intel processor that generates 1000 test sets per second. As well, combinatorial explosion of possible modes of operation makes it nearly impossible to attempt a comprehensive simulation. The problem is exacerbated when the system integrates data processing, so results have significant effects on system behavior. Thus, we strive for highly-automated testing techniques. We aim as well to describe with symbolic means the reachable state space model of the card specification for a particular security property. Expertise in symbolic verification and synchronous languages are required to automatically generate exhaustive test sets that represent critical situations.

We hence focus on a set of techniques known as formal methods, based on the Binary Decision Diagram BDD [1] that are used in computer science to ensure correct system behavior. We propose in this paper, an automatic test set generator called AUTSEG. Generating automatic test sets and covering all transitions is not a new research area. However, we notably address in this paper the state space explosion problem. We first generate a powerful quasi-flattening algorithm which performs a simple and deterministic model, thus facilitating code generation. We qualify by a second algorithm the correct behavior of the global system, without requiring coverage of all system states and transitions.

In the remainder of this paper, we give an overview of related work in Section 2. We present in Section 3 our global approach for test generation. AUTSEG and details on its capabilities are presented in Section 4. Section 5 presents the application of our generator to a specific contactless card for transportation. Experimental results are shown in Section 6. Finally, Section 7 concludes the paper with some directions for future work.

2   Related Work

Lutess V2 [2] is a test environment, written in Lustre, for synchronous reactive systems. It automatically generates tests that dynamically feed the program under test from the formal description of the program environment and properties. This version of Lutess deals with numeric inputs and outputs unlike the first version [3]. Lutess V2 is based on Constraint Logic Programming (CLP) and allows the introduction of hypotheses to the program under test. Due to CLP solvers' capabilities, it is possible to associate occurrence probabilities to any Boolean expression. However, this tool requires the conversion of tested models to the Lustre format, which may cause a few issues in our tests.

B.Blanc presents in [4] a structural testing tool called GATeL, also based on CLP. GATeL aims to find a sequence that satisfies both the invariant and the test purpose by solving the constraints problem on program variables. Contrary to Lutess, GATeL interprets the Lustre code and starts from the final state and ends with the first one. This technique relies on human intervention, which is stringently averted in our paper.

C.Jard and T.Jeron, present TGV (Test Generation with Verification technology) in [5], a powerful tool for test generation from various specifications of reactive systems. It takes as inputs a specification and a test purpose in IOLTS (Input Output Labeled Transition System) format and generates test cases in IOLTS format as well. TGV allows three basic types of operations: 1. It identifies sequences of the specification accepted by a test purpose, based on the synchronous product; 2. It then computes visible actions from abstraction and determinization; 3. Finally, it selects test cases by computation of reachable states from initial states and co-reachable states from accepting states. A limitation lies in the non-symbolic (enumerative) dealing with data. The resulting test cases can be big and therefore relatively difficult to understand.

D.Clarke extends this work in [6], presenting a symbolic test generation tool called STG. It adds the symbolic treatment of data by using OMEGA tool capabilities. Test cases are therefore smaller and more readable than those done with enumerative approaches in TGV. STG produces the test cases from an IOSTS specification (Input Output Symbolic Transition System) and a test purpose. Despite its effectiveness, this tool is no longer maintained.

[7] describes STS (Symbolic Transition Systems), quite often used in systems testing. STS enhances readability and abstraction of behavioral descriptions compared to formalisms with limited data types. STS also addresses the state explosion problem through the use of guards and typed parameters related to the transitions. At the moment, STS hierarchy does not appear very enlightening outside the world of timed/hybrid systems or well-structured systems. Such systems are outside of the scope of this paper.

ISTA (Integration and System Test Automation) [8] is an interesting tool for automated test code generation from High-Level Petri Nets. ISTA generates executable test code from MID (Model Implementation Description) specifications. Petri net elements are then mapped to implementation constructs. ISTA can be efficient for security testing when Petri nets generate threat sequences. However, it focuses solely on liveness properties checking, while we focus on security properties checking.

J.Burnim presents in [9], a testing tool for C called CREST. It inserts instrumentation code using CIL (C Intermediate Language) into a target program. Symbolic execution is therefore performed concurrently with the concrete execution. Path constraints are then solved using the YICES solver. CREST currently reasons symbolically only about linear, integer arithmetic. Closely related to CREST, KLOVER [10] is a symbolic execution and automatic test generation tool for C++ programs. It basically presents an efficient and usable tool to handle industrial applications. Both KLOVER and CREST cannot be adopted in our approach, as they accommodate tests on real systems, whereas we target tests on systems still being designed.

3 Global Process

Let us start with a description of the global architecture we have designed for our test. Fig.1 shows 4 main operations explained in detail in the following sections.

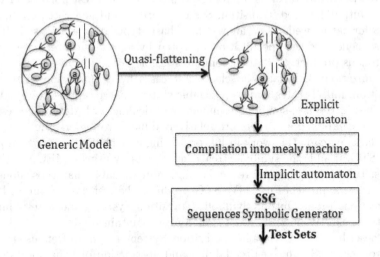

Fig. 1. Global process structure

1. Generic model: it presents the principal input of our test. The global architecture is composed of hierarchical and parallel concurrent FSM based on the synchronous approach. It should conform to the specification of the system under test.

2. Quasi-flattening process: we flatten only hierarchical automata, the rest of automata remaining parallel. This offers a simple model and brings more flexibility to identify all possible evolutions of the system.

3. Compilation process: it generates an implicit automaton represented by a Mealy machine from an explicit automaton. This process compiles the model, checks the determinism of all automata and ensures the persistence of the system behavior.

4. SSG (Sequences Symbolic Generator): it extracts necessary preconditions which lead to specific, significant states of the system from generated sequences.

3.1 Quasi-flattening Process

The straightforward way to analyze a hierarchical machine is to flatten it (recursively substitute in a hierarchical FSM each super state with its associated FSM), then apply as an example a model-checking tool on the resulting FSM. Let's consider the model shown in Fig.2, which shows automata interacting and communicating between each other. Most of them are sequential, hierarchical

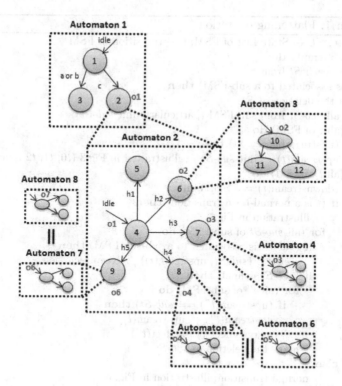

Fig. 2. Model Design

automata (e.g. automata 1 and 2), while others are parallel automata (e.g. automata 6 and 8). We note in this architecture 13122 ($3 \times 6 \times 3 \times 3 \times 3 \times 3 \times 3 \times 3$) possible states derived from parallel executions (graphs product) while there are many fewer active states at once. Indeed, this model is designed by the graphical formalism SyncChart [11]. A classical analysis is to transform this hierarchical structure to the synchronous language Esterel [12]. Such transformation is not quite optimized. Furthermore, Esterel is not able to realize that there is only one active state at once. In practice, compiling such structure by Esterel generates 83 registers making roughly 9.6×10^{24} states. Hence, the behoof of our process. Opting for a quasi-flattening, we have flattened only hierarchical automata. Thus, state 2 of automaton 1 is substituted by the set of states 4,5,6,7,8,9 of automaton 2 and so on. Required transitions are rewritten thereafter. Parallel automata are acting as observers that manage the model's control flags. Flattening parallel FSMs explodes usually in number of states. Thus there is no need to flatten them, as we can compile them separately, then concatenate them with the flat model retrieved at the end of the compilation process.

Algorithm 1 details our quasi-flattening operation. We denote downstream the initial state of a transition and upstream the final one. This algorithm implements three main operations. Overall, It replaces each macro state with a corresponding FSM. It first interconnects the internal initial states. It then

Algorithm 1. Flattening operation

$St \leftarrow$ State; $SL \leftarrow$ State List of FSM; $t \leftarrow$ transition in FSM
while $SL \neq$ empty **do**
  Consider each St from SL
  if (St is associated to a sub-FSM) **then**
    mark the deletion of St
    load all sub-St from sub-FSM (particularly init-sub-St)
    for (all t of FSM) **do**
      if (upstream(t) == St) **then**
        upstream(t) $\leftarrow$ init-sub-St // illustration in Fig.3 ($t0$, $t1$, $t2$ relinking)
    for (all t of FSM) **do**
      if (downstream(t) == St) **then**
        if (t is a normal-term transition) **then**
          // illustration in Fig.5
          for (all sub-St of sub-FSM) **do**
            if (sub-St is associated to a sub-sub-FSM) **then**
              create t' (sub-St, upstream(t)) // Keep recursion
            if (sub-St is final) **then**
              for (all t'' of sub-FSM) **do**
                if (upstream(t'') == sub-St) **then**
                  upstream(t'') $\leftarrow$ upstream(t)
                  merge effect(t) to effect(t'')
            mark the deletion of sub-St
      else
        // normal transition: illustration in Fig.3
        // For example $t3$ is less prior than $t6$ and replaced by $\overline{t6}.t3$ and $t6$
        for (all sub-St of sub-FSM) **do**
          create t'(sub-St,upstream(t),trigger(t),effect(t))
          for (all sub-t of sub-FSM) **do**
            turn-down the sub-t priority (or turn up t' priority)
      delete t
    add and rename all sub-t transitions from subFSM to SL
    add and rename all sub-St state from subFSM to SL
    cancel marked states

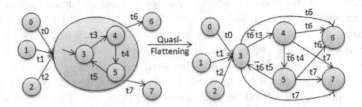

Fig. 3. Initial and Normal Transition Linking

replaces normal [1] terminations with internal transitions in a recursive manner. Finally, it interconnects all states of the internal FSM.

---

[1] Refers to SyncCharts "normal termination" transition [11].

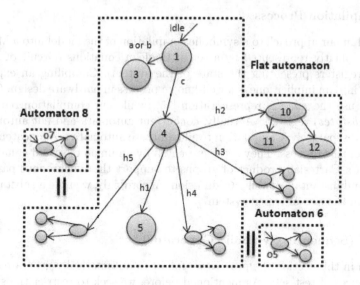

Fig. 4. Flat Model

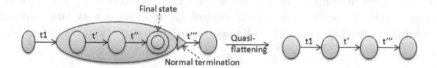

Fig. 5. Terminal Transition Linking

Flattening the hierarchical model of Fig.2 results in a flat structure shown in Fig.3.1. As the activation of state 2 is a trigger for state 4, these two states will be merged, just as state 6 will be merged to state 10, etc. Automata 6 and 8 (observers) remain parallel in the expanded automaton; they are small and do not increase the computational complexity. The model in Fig.3.1 contains now only 144 (16 × 3 × 3) state combinations. In practice, compiling this model according to our process generates merely 8 registers, equivalent to 256 states.

Our flattening differs substantially from those of [13] and [14]. We assume that a transition, unlike the case of statecharts, cannot exit different hierarchical levels. Several operations are thus executed locally, not on the global system. This yields a simpler algorithm and faster compilation. To this end, we have integrated the following assumptions in our algorithm:

-Normal termination. Fig.5 shows an example of normal termination carried when a final internal state is reached. It allows a unique possible interpretation and facilitates code generation.

-Strong preemption. Unlike classical preemption, internal outputs of the preempted state are lost during the transition.

3.2   Compilation Process

We proceed in our approach to a symbolic compilation of the model into a Mealy machine, implicitly represented by a set of Boolean equations (circuit of logic gates and registers presenting the state of the system). Compiling an explicit automaton into an implicit one is a well-known process in hardware design. Classical works use the *one-hot* representation [15], while our compilation requires only $log_2(nbstates)$ registers. Actually, concurrent automata and flat automata are compiled separately. Compilation results of these automata are concatenated at the end of this process. They are represented by an union of sorted equations rather than a Cartesian product of graphs to support the synchronous parallel operation and instantaneous signals diffusion. Accordingly, we note a substantial reduction on the size of tested system.

3.3   SSG (Sequences Symbolic Generator)

We explain in this section the process we follow to automatically generate symbolic sequences of test sets. As mentioned before, we seek to restrict the states space and confine only to significant states. The model of Fig.6 presents all possible sequences of commands describing the system behavior. It is a classical representation of the dynamic system evolutions. It shows a very large tree or even infinite tree. Thus, exploring all possible program executions is not feasible.

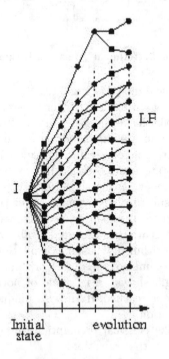

Fig. 6. Classical Sequences Generation

We will show in section 6 the weakness of this classical approach. If we consider the representation of the system by a sequence of commands executed iteratively, the previous sequences tree becomes a *repetition of the same subspace pattern* as shown in Fig.7. We will focus in our approach only on this subspace. This represents a specific system command which can be repeated through possible generated sequences.

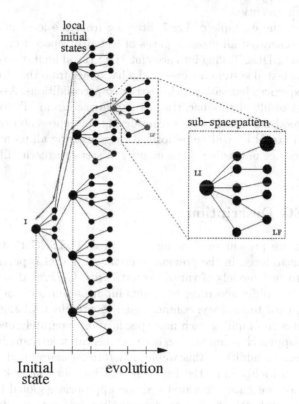

local
initial
states

sub–spacepattern

LI

LF

I

Initial   evolution
state

Fig. 7. Model Representation

Each state in the subspace is specified by the symbolic values of the program variables, the path condition and the command parameters (next byte-code to be executed). The path condition represents constraints that should be satisfied by the symbolic values to progress the execution of the current path. It defines the preconditions to successfully follow that path. Our work targets extracting these preconditions from the subspace check. Indeed, we have applied BDD-analysis from the local initial state to local final states of the specified subspace. For each combination of registers, BDD manipulations allow the extraction of the next awaited variables, that lead to the next state and required preconditions. Outputs are then pushed into a stack, in conjunction with resulting preconditions. Finally, sequence generation pops the constructed stack. Once the necessary preconditions are extracted, a next step is to backtrack the tree until finding the initial sequence fulfilling these preconditions. The backtrack operation is ensured by the compilation process which kept enough knowledge to find later the previous states.

Contrary to the classical sequence generator, our tool constantly generates a tree of pure future states, thus preventing loops from occurring. In other words, previous states always converge to the global initial state. This approach easily favors backtrack execution.

Let's consider the example of Fig.7. Starting from the local initial donated state "LI", we generated all possible paths of tested subspace to reach the final local states using BDDs. Taking into account "LF" (local final state) as a critical final state of the tested system, we executed a backtrack from the "LI" state until covering the sequence that satisfies the extracted preconditions. Assuming state "I" as the final result of this backtrack, the sequence from "I" to "LF" is an example of a good test set. However, considering the representation of Fig.6, a test set from "I" to "LF" will be performed by generating all paths of the tree. Such a test becomes unfeasible if the number of steps to reach "LF" is greatly increased.

4   AUTSEG Description

In this section, we present our testing tool called AUTSEG that implements the approach introduced in the previous section. AUTSEG is particularly used in this paper to test models of various smart cards. Generated automatic test sets typically must differ according to system input parameters, for example the adopted smart card technology: contact versus contactless. Changing card parameters requires recompiling each new specification separately and re-running the tests. This approach is unrealistic, because this can take many hours or even days to compile. In addition, this would generate as many models as system types, which can highly limit the legibility and increase the risk of specification bugs. Hence, we have generated a single appropriate global model for all card types and applications, The model's explicit test sets are to be filtered

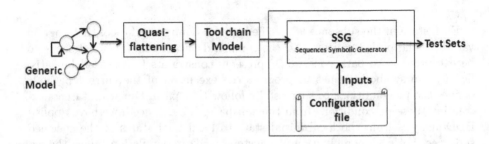

Fig. 8. AUTSEG structure

thereafter by AUTSEG. To this end, AUTSEG will query via predefined signals a configuration file specific to each system application. As shown in Fig.8, AUTSEG operation is carried by 5 main entities: (1) The generic model, (2) Quasi-flattening, (3) Compilation, (4) SSG and (5) The configuration file.

After quasi-flattening the hierarchical structure by the "autom-expand" [16] tool implemented according to Algorithm 1, the expanded automaton is compiled separately and linked later with other compiled parallel automata, as shown in Fig.9.

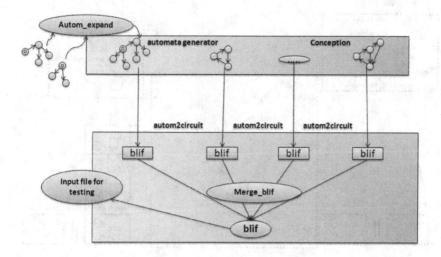

Fig. 9. Model Tool chain

Compilation process is carried out by the "autom2circuit" tool [16], explained in section 3.2. The execution of "autom2circuit" generates a blif file [17] as shown in Fig.9. A blif file is a compact format to express a netlist and is well-suited to represent Boolean equation systems. Using the "merge-blif" tool [16], the generated blif files are concatenated at the end of the compilation process to produce the final global blif file (SSG input file).

In fact, AUTSEG defines two types of preconditions: (1) preconditions related to command parameters as described in section 3.3 and (2) preconditions defined by the configuration file. For a particular test generation, AUTSEG will extract the basic characteristics of the system from the configuration file unit. They are presented as Boolean variables, characterizing the preconditions of the system execution. If preconditions are not satisfied , the tested model will be refined, thus reducing the combinatorial explosion problem during sequence generation.

5   Use Case

To illustrate our approach, we studied the case of a contactless smart card designed for the transportation sector. We aim to verify the correct and secure behavior of this card using AUTSEG.

5.1   Smart Card Model

The generic model of the studied smart card is designed from a given transport standard called Calypso. This standard defines 33 commands. The succession of these commands (e.g. Open Session, SV Debit, Get Data, Change Pin) presents possible scenarios of the card operation. All commands have been modeled with the Galaxy tool[16].

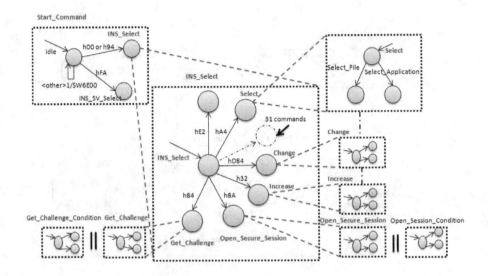

Fig. 10. Calypso smart card model

Galaxy is an automata editor of finite state machines, able to generate four types of automata: simple (basic automata), parallel automata, hierarchical (light Esterel [18]) and syncChart. We chose to use light Esterel (a light version of SyncChart), a synchronous graphical model that integrates high-level concepts of synchronous languages in an expressive graphical formalism. The resulting model presents 52 interconnected automata including 765 states. Forty-three of them form a hierarchical structure. The remaining automata operate in parallel and act as observers for control data of the hierarchical automaton. Fig.10 shows a small part of our model introducing the beginning of card scenarios. Applying "autom-expand" to the hierarchical automata shows in Fig.11 a flattened structure running in parallel with the observers. Due to "autom-expand", we moved from 477 registers to only 22.

5.2   Configuration and Tests

According to the Calypso standard, several types and configurations of the card are defined (contact/contactless, maximum buffer size, etc.). We present these

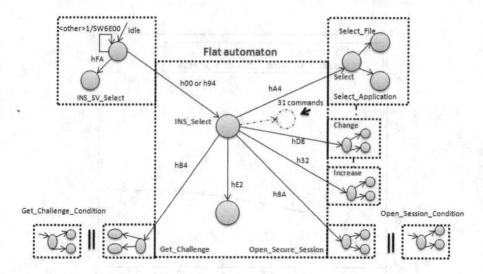

Fig. 11. Calypso Flat Model

characteristics as preconditions of the system execution (*AUTSEG_Contact_
Mode*, *AUTSEG_ch1_Selected*, etc). The remaining preconditions are established during the execution of Calypso commands. They inform about system
status, for instance, *AUTSEG_V_Select_File* is true if the command "Select
File" is executed normally, generating the output code SW9000.

6   Experimental Results

In this section, we show experimental results of applying AUTSEG to the contactless transportation card. We intend to test the security of all possible combinations of 33 commands of the Calypso standard. Each command in the Calypso
standard is encoded on a minimum of 8 bytes. We conducted our experiments
on a PC with Intel Dual Core Processor, 2 GHz and 8 GB RAM. A classical
test of this card can be achieved by browsing all possible paths of the model as
represented in Fig.6.

Such a test shows in Fig.12 an exponential evolution of the number of sequences versus the number of tested bytes. We are not even able to test more
than 2 commands of the model. Our model explodes by 13 bytes generating
3,993,854,132 possible sequences.

A second test applies AUTSEG on the card model represented in the same
manner as Fig.7. Results show that our approach enables coverage of the global
model in a substantially short time. It allows separately testing 33 commands
(all the system commands) in only 10 steps, generating a total of 1784 paths.
These results are highlighted in Fig.12 by a comparison of our approach to the
classical generation method. We note from the AUTSEG curve a lower evolution
that stabilizes at 10 steps and 1784 paths, allowing for coverage of all states of

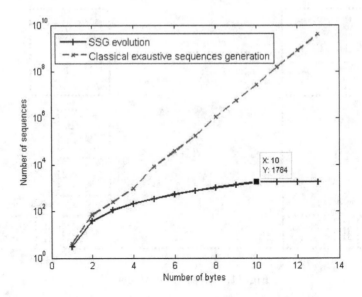

Fig. 12. Combinatorial explosion of classical tests

the tested model. Covering all states in only 10 steps, our results demonstrate that we test seperately one command (8 bytes) at once in our approach. Few additional bytes (2 bytes in our case) are required to test system preconditions.

We show below an excerpt of generated sequences presenting the two last paths. We observe the extraction of necessary preconditions that should be satisfied for each sequence. *AUTSEG_Contact_Mode* and *AUTSEG_ch1_Selected* are preconditions from the configuration file. They serve to specify the execution context and thus possible resulting sequences. The remaining preconditions (*AUTSEG_V_Select_File*, *AUTSEG_Verif_Always_DF*, etc) will be used to play iteratively the backtrack (e.g, check Setlect File command) until the source sequence is found. We notice the END of sequence generations by 1784 paths, thus covering the entire system execution.

```
AUTSEG TEST SET
-------------------------------------------------
PATH: 1

   .
   .
   .

-------------------------------------------------
PATH: 1783
PRECONDITIONS:
AUTSEG_Contact_Mode
AUTSEG_CH1_Selected
AUTSEG_Verif_Always_DF and AUTSEG_V_Select_File
not AUTSEG_Too_many_modifications_In_session
```

```
SEQUENCE:
- h00
- h04
- h00 ---> SW9000 Next_command
------------------------------------------------
PATH: 1784
PRECONDITIONS:
AUTSEG_CH1_Selected
AUTSEG_Verif_Always_DF and AUTSEG_V_Select_File
AUTSEG_Too_many_modifications_In_session
SEQUENCE:
- h00
- h04
- h00 ---> SW6400 Next_command
------------------------------------------------

EXPLORATION END FINDING 1784 PATHS...
```

7 Conclusion

We have proposed AUTSEG, an Automatic Test Set Generator for embedded reactive systems. We particularly focused in this paper on systems executing iterative commands. Our tool is able to handle large models, where the risk of combinatorial explosion of states space is important. This has been achieved by essentially (1) providing an algorithm to quasi-flatten hierarchical FSM and reduce the states space, and (2) focusing on pertinent subspaces and restricting the tests. This enables coverage of the global system behavior and generates the list of all possible system evolutions according to the configuration file. Since our tool ensures communication with an interactive specification block, this approach can be adapted to process in parallel several types of system specifications.

In the near future, we will integrate data evaluation during the test process. We aim to use the Linear Decision Diagram LDD [19] to accomplish this. LDD allows the characterization and expression of the given preconditions by numerical constraints. It checks several constraints and concludes about the feasibility of the corresponding sequence. For example, if the union of constraints is unsuccessful by LDD, then we can confirm that tested sequence is impossible and remove it. With this approach, we can reduce the states space and avoid large calculations.

References

1. Bryant, R.E.: Graph-based algorithms for boolean function manipulation. IEEE Transaction on Computers C-35(8), 677–691 (1986)
2. Seljimi, B., Parissis, I.: Automatic generation of test data generators for synchronous programs: Lutess v2. In: Workshop on Domain Specific Approaches to Software Test Automation: in conjunction with the 6th ESEC/FSE Joint Meeting, DOSTA 2007, pp. 8–12. ACM Press, New York (2007)
3. DuBousquet, L., Zuanon, N.: An overview of lutess: A specification-based tool for testing synchronous software. In: ASE, pp. 208–215 (1999)

4. Blanc, B., Junke, C., Marre, B., Le Gall, P., Andrieu, O.: Handling state-machines specifications with gatel. Electron. Notes Theor. Comput. Sci. 264(3), 3–17 (2010)
5. Calam, J.R.: Specification-Based Test Generation With TGV. CWI Technical Report SEN-R 0508, CWI (2005)
6. Clarke, D., Jéron, T., Rusu, V., Zinovieva, E.: STG: A symbolic test generation tool. In: Katoen, J.-P., Stevens, P. (eds.) TACAS 2002. LNCS, vol. 2280, pp. 470–475. Springer, Heidelberg (2002)
7. Bentakouk, L., Poizat, P., Zaïdi, F.: A formal framework for service orchestration testing based on symbolic transition systems. In: Núñez, M., Baker, P., Merayo, M.G. (eds.) TESTCOM 2009. LNCS, vol. 5826, pp. 16–32. Springer, Heidelberg (2009)
8. Xu, D.: A tool for automated test code generation from high-level petri nets. In: Kristensen, L.M., Petrucci, L. (eds.) PETRI NETS 2011. LNCS, vol. 6709, pp. 308–317. Springer, Heidelberg (2011)
9. Burnim, J., Sen, K.: Heuristics for scalable dynamic test generation. In: Proceedings of the 2008 23rd IEEE/ACM International Conference on Automated Software Engineering, ASE 2008, pp. 443–446. IEEE Computer Society, Washington, DC (2008)
10. Li, G., Ghosh, I., Rajan, S.P.: KLOVER: A symbolic execution and automatic test generation tool for C++ programs. In: Gopalakrishnan, G., Qadeer, S. (eds.) CAV 2011. LNCS, vol. 6806, pp. 609–615. Springer, Heidelberg (2011)
11. André, C.: Representation and analysis of reactive behaviors: A synchronous approach. In: Computational Engineering in Systems Applications (CESA), Lille (F), pp. 19–29. IEEE-SMC (1996)
12. Berry, G., Gonthier, G.: The esterel synchronous programming language: Design, semantics, implementation. Sci. Comput. Program. 19(2), 87–152 (1992)
13. Paiva, A.C.R., Tillmann, N., Faria, J.C.P., Vidal, R.F.A.M.: Modeling and testing hierarchical guis. In: Proc. ASM 2005, Universite de Paris, vol. 12, pp. 8–11 (2005)
14. Wasowski, A.: Flattening statecharts without explosions. SIGPLAN Not. 39(7), 257–266 (2004)
15. Chiuchisan, I., Potorac, A.D.: G.A.: Finite state machine design and vhdl coding techniques. In: 10th International Conference on Development and Application Systems, Suceava, Romania, pp. 273–278. Faculty of Electrical Engineering and Computer Science (2010)
16. Gaffé, D.: Research web site, http://sites.unice.fr/dgaffe/recherche/research.html
17. Berkeley University: Berkeley logic interchange format, blif (1998)
18. Ressouche, A., Gaffé, D., Roy, V.: Modular compilation of a synchronous language. In: Lee, R. (ed.) Soft. Eng. Research, Management and Applications, best 17 Paper Selection of the SERA 2008 Conference, Prague, vol. 150, pp. 157–171. Springer, Heidelberg (2008)
19. Chaki, S., Gurfinkel, A., Strichman, O.: Decision diagrams for linear arithmetic. In: FMCAD, pp. 53–60. IEEE (2009)

Well-Defined Coverage Metrics for the Glass Box Test

Rainer Schmidberger

ISTE (Institute for Software Technology), Stuttgart University, Germany
rainer.schmidberger@informatik.uni-stuttgart.de

Abstract. The Glass Box Test (GBT), also known as White Box Test or Structural Test, shows which parts of the program under test have, or have not, been executed. Many GBT tools are available for almost any programming language. Industry standards for safety-critical software require a very high or even complete coverage. At first glance, the GBT seems to be a well-established and mature testing technique that is based on standardized metrics. But on closer inspection, there are several serious shortcomings of the underlying models and metrics which lead to very imprecise, inconsistent coverage results of the various GBT tools. In this paper, a new and precise model for the GBT is presented. This model is used as a reference for the precise definition of all the popular coverage metrics that are around. The tool CodeCover which was developed in the University of Stuttgart is an implementation that strictly follows those definitions.

Keywords: Glass Box Test, White Box Test, Structural Test, coverage testing, coverage tools.

1   Introduction

In industrial practice testing is the technique most widely used to find errors in programs or to demonstrate a certain quality of a program. Accordingly, companies spend a significant part of their project budgets on testing, which in many cases does not achieve the desired quality – (too) many serious defects remain undetected. As a starting point for the improvement of the test, the Glass Box Test (GBT) can be used, also known as White Box Test or Structural Test, that shows which parts of the program under test have, or have not, been executed. This degree of execution is called coverage. It can be used as a test completion criterion or as input for developing test cases [1, 3, 8, 14, 18]. Many GBT tools are available for almost any programming language. Industry standards for safety-critical software require a very high or even complete coverage (e.g. [8, 12]). Empirical studies clearly indicate that higher GBT coverage correlates with lower post-release defect density [2, 4, 13].

At first glance, the GBT seems to be a well-established and mature testing technique, but it is worth having a closer look at the underlying models and metrics.

For the GBT, typically the control flow graph (CFG) is used to build an abstraction model of the original program code. Most popular GBT metrics are defined with respect to the CFG [1, 3, 10, 11]. The statement coverage of a program execution, for

M.G. Merayo and E. Montes de Oca (Eds.): ICTSS 2014, LNCS 8763, pp. 113–128, 2014.

example, is defined as the node coverage of the program's corresponding CFG. The branch coverage is defined as the edge coverage.

Thus, while the GBT metrics based on the CFG are precisely defined, the transformation of the real programs into the model is imprecise and ambiguous. For example, it is undefined whether the CFG representation of an if- or while-statement has a distinct end node which corresponds to "EndIf" or "EndWhile". Fig. 1 shows an example. The classification of nodes as entry or exit nodes is ambiguous as well: Some authors add a distinct entry and exit node to the CFG, others do not.

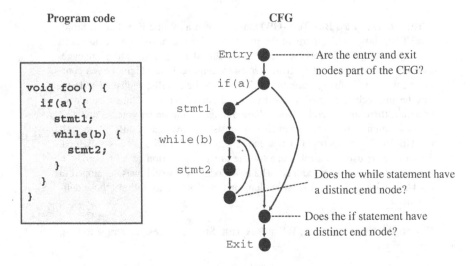

Fig. 1. Ambiguities in CFG modelling

What is more severe than these details is the fact that there is no representation of exception handling in the CFG. But exception handling is an important part of modern programming languages. In addition, the CFG does not provide any means for handling the GBT-relevant expressions such as the conditional expression or the short-circuit operations of Boolean expressions [9]. As a result, it is not possible to model compound Boolean operations for handling logic-based coverage criteria like term coverage [19] or MC/DC [1, 19]. As a consequence of this unsatisfactory model and metric definition, the most important GBT tools for Java [17] show completely different coverage results (Table 1) for the same execution of a given 45-statement reference program [16]. Furthermore, those tools are not based on well-defined metrics. (What does line coverage or instruction coverage mean?)

While these differences can be explained partly by the different instrumentation techniques of the GBT tools, there is no "reference" which the tool developer could use as a specification and for comparing results.

Table 1. Coverage results for the same reference execution

	Statement coverage	Branch coverage
CodeCover Version: 1.0.2.2	62,8 %	Branch: 50,0 % Block: 52,2 %
Clover Version: 3.1.0	58,5 %	
Emma Version: v2.1.5320	Line: 62,0 %	Block: 54,0 %
EclEmma Version: 2.2.1	Instruction: 56,7 % Line: 63,6 %	Block: 50,0 %
eCobertura Version: 0.9.8	64,3 %	Branch: 50,0 %
CodePro Version: 7.1.0	Instruction: 57,7 % Line: 58,5 %	Block: 60,6 %
Rational Application Developer Version 9.0.0	Line: 67,0 %	

2   A New and Precise Model for the GBT

The GBT model described below is intended to provide such a reference. It should meet the following requirements:

- The model forms the basis on which both the popular control-flow based metrics as and the logic and conditional expression based metrics can be defined.
- The model supports exception handling and provides an easy and clear definition of how coverage metrics are applied to exception handling.
- There is an easy and precise transformation rule to transform real programs into the model.
- The model does not depend on any particular programming language. An algorithm implemented in different programming languages should have the same model representation.
- The model specifies how to place the probes that count the execution of the relevant code items in the instrumented program.

Such a GBT model is now presented in three steps:

1. Definition of a primitive language (RPR = Reduced Program Representation) which is reduced to the GBT-relevant aspects of the real programming languages. It provides control flow, exception handling, and expressions. These GBT-relevant

aspects are mapped in so-called GBT items such as statements, statement blocks, and Boolean or conditional expressions. This abstraction has two goals: First, to make metric definition easier because the metrics are based on only a few distinct elements. And, second, to keep the model independent of a particular programming language.

2. Definition of the execution semantics using Petri nets. This part of the model precisely defines the control flow inside and between the GBT items for both normal and abrupt completion. The Petri net model specifies precisely how the original program has to be instrumented.

3. Definition of the coverage metrics based on the Petri nets.

2.1   The Reduced Program Representation (RPR)

RPR defines all GBT-relevant aspects of the original program code and suppresses all irrelevant attributes like numerical expressions or design elements such as inheritance, interface or visibility. RPR is subdivided into two parts: First, the control flow part which covers the typical control flow statements like decision, loop, and switch statement. In the second part the GBT-relevant expressions such as the conditional expression or Boolean terms are described. The control structures of RPR correspond to the principles of structured programming as described by Dahl, Dijkstra, and Hoare [18]. In addition, a try-statement covers the typical exception handling of modern languages. *Program* represents a method or procedure. The *StatementBlock* subsumes all blocks and branches like then or else blocks, method blocks, and catch blocks. *Statement* and *StatementBlock* are given a unique identifier that does not exist in the original program. This identifier builds the reference between the static model and the dynamically recorded protocol of the executed items. These identifiers are automatically generated.

The meta syntax of the following grammar is easy to understand: terminals are quoted, "empty" is the empty sequence of terminals, and each production ends with a dot.

```
Program             = Identifier StatementBlock.
StatementBlock      = Identifier "{" StatementList "}".
StatementList       = Statement StatementList | empty.
Statement           = Identifier
                        ( PrimitiveStatement
                        | TerminateStatement
                        | WhileStatement
                        | IfStatement
                        | SwitchStatement
```

```
                          |  TryStatement )
                         SubExpressions.
IfStatement             = "if" "(" BoolExpression ")"
                          "then" StatementBlock
                          "else" StatementBlock.
WhileStatement          = "while" "(" BoolExpression ")"
                          StatementBlock.
SwitchStatement         = "switch" CaseHandler.
CaseHandler             = "case" StatementBlock CaseHandler
                          | "default" StatementBlock.
TryStatement            = "try" StatementBlock CatchHandler.
CatchHandler            = "catch" StatementBlock CatchHandler
                          | empty.
PrimitiveStatement      = "stmt".
TerminateStatement      = "throw" | "return" |
                          "break" | "continue".
```

The decision of an if statement and the loop condition of a while statement are Boolean values, and therefore, they are represented in the model to be used in logic-based coverage metrics such as MC/DC or term coverage. In contrast, the numerical expression of the switch statement and the exception types in the catch part of the try statements are not represented because no coverage metric is based on these types. The following second part of the language covers the Boolean and conditional expressions:

```
Expression          = BoolExpression
                      | ConditionalExpression.
BoolExpression      = Identifier
                      ( Condition | CompoundExpression ).
Condition           = "expr" SubExpressions.
CompoundExpression  = ("andThen"|"orElse"|"and"|"or")
                          "(" BoolExpression ","
                                    BoolExpression ")".
ConditionalExpression = Identifier BoolExpression "?"
            SubExpressions ":" SubExpressions ).
```

```
SubExpressions = "[" ExpressionList "]".
ExpressionList = Expression ";" ExpressionList | empty.
```

Because *BoolExpression* and *ConditionalExpression* are referenced in metric definitions, they have an identifier like the *Statement* and *StatementBlock*. The definition of *Condition* complies with [9]: "A Boolean expression containing no Boolean operators". The compound Boolean expressions like "A orElse B" are handled by *CompoundExpression*. For this, the model includes the (binary) tree structure of the Boolean expression's derivation tree. Thanks to the distinction between the operands *and* and *andThen*, the so-called short-circuit behavior can be applied to the GBT metrics. The *SubExpressions* are used to handle GBT-relevant expressions that are embedded in a primitive expression or statement. For example, let us consider the following Java expression:

```
A && f(B && C)
```

According to the definition of Condition, the complete term f(...) is a (primitive) condition. In order not to "lose" the embedded expression B && C, it is handled as an element of the embedded SubExpressions of the condition f(...). For determining expression-based metrics like MC/DC, these embedded expressions are also taken into consideration.

In the following example, a factorial function is transferred from Java into RPR. The unique identifiers are built with "S" for statements, "B" for statement blocks and "E" for expressions, followed by an ascending number.

Java	RPR
`int factorial(int n) {`	`P1 B1 {`

`if(n < 0 || n > MAX) {`	`S1 if(`
	 `E1 orElse(E2 expr [],`
	 `E3 expr [])`
	 `) then B2 {`

`  return -1;` `}`	`S2 return []` `} else B3 { } []`
`int result = 1;`	`S3 stmt []`
`while (n > 1) {`	`S4 while(E4 expr []) B4 {`

`  result *= n;`
 `  n--;`
 `}`
	`S5 stmt []`
	 `S6 stmt []`
	 `} []`

`return result;` `}`	`S7 return []` `}`

One major advantage of RPR is that the transformation of a given real language into the model can be clearly defined by mapping the right sides of the grammar productions. The mapping of a Java if statement, for example, into the model language can be described is as follows:

Java	RPR
"if" "(" Expression ")" Statement ["else" Statement]	"if" "(" BoolExpression ")" "then" StatementBlock "else" StatementBlock

It is easy to see that the Java "statements" in the *then* and *else* parts are mapped into statement blocks in the GBT model. In addition, the else part in Java is optional while the else part in the GBT model is not. If an if statement in the original program has no else block, it is added as an empty block in the GBT model.

2.2   Execution Semantics

Every (primitive) GBT item such as a primitive statement or a primitive Boolean expression is described as a place-bordered and token-preserving Petri (sub)net called GBT model net (or short: model net). The model net of a primitive statement is shown in Fig. 2, the model net of the primitive Boolean expression in Fig. 3 on the left side.

Loosely speaking, a model net is a Petri net with distinguished input and output places. Each model net has exactly one input place and one or more output places for normal and abrupt completion. The input place has no input transition relative to the model (sub)net. The output places have no output transition, respectively. In Fig. 2, Fig. 3, and Fig. 4 these input and output places are located on the dashed border line of the GBT item. The initial marking of a model net has exactly one token in the input place while all other places are empty. Due to the token-preserving property the model net's end marking has exactly one token in one of the net's output places.

Because all model nets are place-bordered and token-preserving, they can be abstracted into both sub nets, which are reduced to the border places and super places [22]. Fig. 2 shows this abstraction of a statement's model net. The abstractions are used for theoretical net analysis like the reachability analysis as well as for describing the compound model nets of the complex GBT items.

In Fig. 2 the conflict in the model net between the transitions $t_{ENormal}$ and $t_{EAbrupt}$ and their common input place s_E models the non-determinism of the statement's execution behavior, in Fig. 3, between the three transitions t_{EFalse}, t_{ETrue}, and $t_{EAbrupt}$ of a Boolean Expression): On the basis of the model net, it is not decidable whether a statement or expression completes abruptly or which Boolean result the real expression returns. But this execution behavior can be observed in the program under test by adding so-called probes to the program code. Fig. 3 shows this connection between the instrumented program code of a GBT item and its corresponding model net: The execution area of the model net abstracts the statically undecidable behavior of the real program's expression or statement. The places s_{CIn}, s_{CT}, s_{CF} and s_{CA} abstract the execution counters of the program under test and build a specification for the source code's instrumentation.

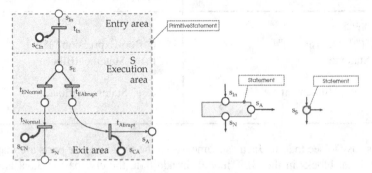

Fig. 2. (Petri)-model net for a primitive statement

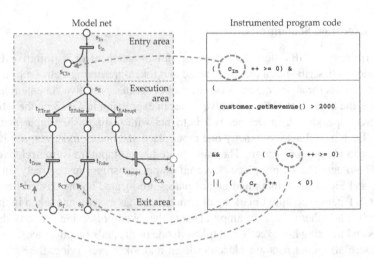

Fig. 3. (Petri)-model net for a primitive Boolean expression

The example of Fig. 3 shows the instrumentation technique used by the GBT tool CodeCover [5, 6, 7]. In order to avoid additional method invocations, increment expressions using the so-called shortcut semantics "surround" the original expression. Details about this instrumentation can be found in [6].

While the values of the "not-abrupt" execution counters c_{In}, c_T and c_F directly determine the markings of the model nets corresponding counter places, the value of the counter place for abrupt completion is not given by an instrumented counter. But due to the mathematically sound model net, after reaching a final marking, theese counter place markings can be derived:

$$| M(s_{CA}) | = | M(s_{CIn}) | - | M(s_{CT}) | - | M(s_{CF}) |$$

In the model net of the primitive expression in Fig. 3 the proof is easy to see, for the more complex items the proof can be provided by using the Petri net's reachability analysis. Also by using the reachability analysis for all model nets of the various GBT items it can be proven that each (sub-)net is token-preserving and, as a consequence for each firing sequence starting from the initial marking a final marking is reached with exactly one token in one of the output places.

In contrast to the primitive GBT items the complex GBT items contain other GBT items as part of their own structure. E. g. an *if* statement contains a Boolean decision and a *then* and *else* statement block. Fig. 4 shows the model net of such an *if* statement. Parts of this model net are embedded model (sub)nets of the embedded GBT-items which are abstracted into place-bordered boxes.

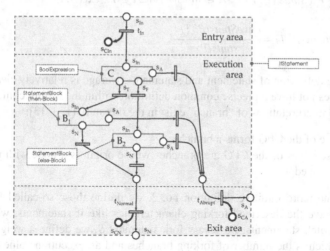

Fig. 4. (Petri)-model net for an if statement

This embedding technique automatically provides a dominance relationship between the GBT items. The embedded items are direct dominated:

A ddom B ⇔   the model net of B is directly embedded in the model
               net of A

As already described, an important aspect of the model net is that there is a formal basis for the execution counters which have been generally used since the early beginnings of coverage testing [13]. The net model provides both a precise placement for the counters for normal completion and a (sound) basis for calculating counters for abrupt completion. As a result, the execution state of a GBT item A for a given test case t – "A is executed by test case t at least once" – can now be defined:

$$exe(A, t) \Leftrightarrow | M(s_{CIn}(A)) | > 0$$

This ability to report the execution of a GBT item for a particular test case (and not only for the entire test suite) is called "test-case selective GBT". While most GBT metrics are defined for the entire test suite, many useful GBT evaluations like test suite reduction, selective regression test and development of new test cases require the test-case selective GBT.

2.3   Metric Definition

On the basis of the GBT items and their execution property we can now clearly and precisely define the GBT metrics. E. g. the statement coverage for an execution of a given program P can be defined as the proportion of executed statements; stmts(P) is defined as the set of all statements of P. The precise definition of "statement" is given by the grammar of the model language.

$$A \in exeStmts\ (P, T) \Leftrightarrow A \in stmts(P) \wedge \exists t \in T : exe(A, t)$$

$$stmtCov(P,\ T) = \frac{|\ exeStmts(P,\ T)\ |}{|\ stmts(P)\ |}$$

While the definition of statement and statement coverage is relatively clear, branch coverage does not have a precise common definition within the testing community. In general, two interpretations of "branch" exist in the literature [1, 3, 13]:

1. Every edge of the CFG forms a branch
2. Only those edges of the CFG are branches whose origin is a node with more than one outgoing edge.

Following the more intuitive definition no. 2, we define those so-called fork statements that have the described forking characteristics like if statements, while statements, or switch statements. For every fork statement S, we define a weight $w(S) \rightarrow \mathbb{N} \setminus \{ 1 \}$, which is the number of forking branches and an execution value $e(S, T) \rightarrow \mathbb{N}$ with $0 \leq e(S, T) \leq w(S)$, which is the number of executed branches for S with a test suite T. Thus, the branch coverage is defined as follows:

$$S \in forkStmts\ (P) \Leftrightarrow S \text{ is a statement with forking branches}$$

$$branchCov(P, T) = \frac{\sum_{i \in forkStmts(P)} e(i, T)}{\sum_{i \in forkStmts(P)} w(i)}$$

For some good reasons we also include the try statement in the forking statements, even though there is no distinct forking point. Otherwise, it would be possible to achieve full branch coverage without executing the catch blocks. In addition to the branch coverage we propose block coverage which defines the degree to which statement blocks are executed, similar to the statement coverage. A statement block is defined within RPR and e. g. is a *then* or *else* block of an *if* statement, a procedure body, or a catch block. Again, P is a program and T is a test suite.

$$B \in exeBlocks\ (P, T) \Leftrightarrow B \in blocks(P) \wedge \exists t \in T : exe(B, t)$$

$$blockCov(P, T) = \frac{|\ exeBlocks(P, T)\ |}{|\ blocks(P)\ |}$$

Generally, block and branch coverage are very similar because nearly all branches flow into a statement block and vice versa. A difference exists in the while statement where the branch that leaves the loop does not lead to a statement block. The procedure body constitutes a statement block but is no branch. Compared to the branch coverage, the block coverage has some practical advantages:

- The definition is easier and hence the understanding for the tester and the implementation in a GBT tool are easier.
- Unlike branches, statement blocks have a concrete representation in the program code. This makes the visualization of the coverage in the code easier and clearer.
- For block coverage, it is clear that catch blocks are taken into account, while most definitions of branch coverage do not address exception handling.

Some other coverage metrics which address control flow in expressions are described in [15].

3   Related Work

Most of the coverage metrics have their beginning in Myers' book [14] and in Huang's article [11]. While there is a lot of work using the CFG for coverage testing topics, there is only little attention from the testing community to the CFG's disadvantages described in Section 1. In [21] Binder describes a GBT model based on "code segments" which covers both (traditional) control flow and control flow in expressions. But he does not present this model in detail and does not develop a theory based on it. Ammann, Offutt, and Hong develop a theory for logic expressions in [1], but do not cover control flow or GBT-relevant expressions like the conditional expression. Zhu, Hall, and May shortly cover the topic of transformation (structured) program code into a CFG, but do not develop a GBT-language like the RPR. A detailed coverage tool investigation is conducted in [9]. The authors develop a test suite to test whether the performance of a structural coverage analysis tool is consistent with the structural coverage objectives in DO-178B [22]. While the authors describe a complete set of test cases concerning control flow, control flow in expression, and logic expressions, they do not develop a model that "abstracts" the given test cases.

Lui et al. define in [23] coverage metrics based on Petri nets in the context of workflow applications. Comparable to this work the authors combine predefined subnets, but their scope is limited on the workflow aspects.

4   CodeCover

CodeCover is an open-source GBT tool that was initially developed 2008 in a student project at the University of Stuttgart. More information about that project is available in [5, 6]. Although stable releases have been available since 2008, CodeCover is still being extended and improved. Many enhancements have been implemented over the last years. CodeCover was developed to support both relatively small student projects and large industrial projects. For small projects, CodeCover provides an easy-to-use Eclipse integration. For larger projects, CodeCover can be used with the popular "Apache Ant" build tool or in batch mode. All information about installation and usage can be obtained from the CodeCover web page [7]. Currently, CodeCover supports the languages Java, C and COBOL. The GBT metrics provided are the control-flow based metrics introduced in Section 2, the loop coverage, conditional expression coverage, and term coverage [19], which is very similar to MC/DC.

4.1   User Interface

The easiest way to use CodeCover for Java programs is using the Eclipse integration. A typical picture of the CodeCover-Eclipse user interface is shown in Fig. 5.

To use CodeCover in an existing Java project only the following three steps must be performed:

1. Open "Properties" and select the CodeCover page. The desired GBT metrics can be selected here.
2. In "Project Explorer" select the packages or classes to be included in the GBT evaluation. Open popup menu and select "Use For Coverage Measurement".
3. If JUnit tests are used, run the test cases with "CodeCover Measurement for JUnit", otherwise open the "Run Configurations" and select the CodeCover dialog. Select "Run with CodeCover".

4.2   Instrumentation and data flow

CodeCover works with so-called source-code instrumentation, where the execution counters for the GBT items are added into the program's source code. Fig. 6 shows the activities and artifacts which are visible for a tester using the CodeCover batch interface. The model representation of the program code is stored in a so-called TestSessionContainer (TSC).

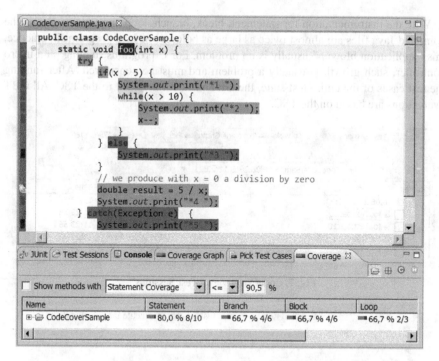

Fig. 5. CodeCover Eclipse integration

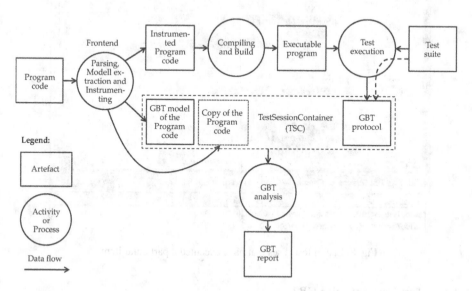

Fig. 6. Data flow

With the instrumentation for statement, block, branch, loop and term coverage, the compiled Java files are almost twice as large as before. For Java programs in practice, this "application blowup" usually is no problem. For C programs running on a micro controller, such growth is usually a problem and must be considered. After running the test cases of the entire test suite, the GBT protocol is added to the TSC. All GBT evaluations are based on the TSC.

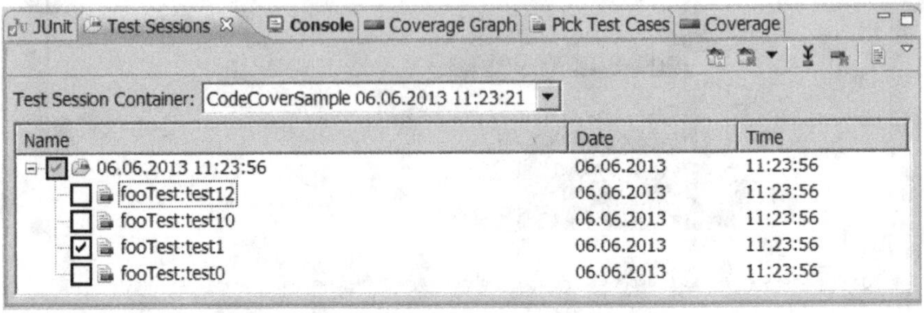

Fig. 7. CodeCover view "Test Sessions"

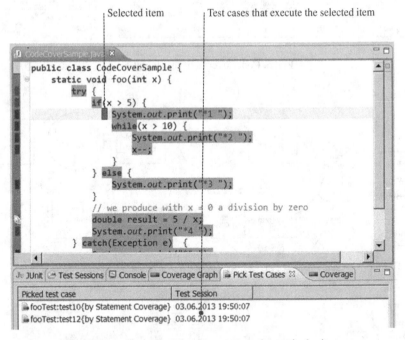

Fig. 8. List of test cases that have executed a particular item

4.3 Test Case Selective GBT

Beyond the functionality that most GBT tools offer, CodeCover can analyze the execution of individual test cases. In Fig. 7 ("Test Sessions") all the test cases of the entire test suite are listed. For a JUnit test, the identifiers of the test cases are derived from the JUnit test case names. Four test cases are executed but the user has selected only one test case ("fooTest:test1"). In this case the coverage visualization and summary report are generated only for this selected test case. Using this, the execution of a particular test case can be visualized. CodeCover can also list those test cases that executed an item the user selected by putting the cursor in the code area of the item. These test cases are listed in the view "Pick Test Cases" (Fig. 8). This function that is not found in other test tools provides useful information about the execution behaviour of the program under test.

5   Conclusion

To date, most GBT metrics are defined either intuitively or based on the CFG. In the approach described above, the GBT metrics are precisely defined using a notation (RPR) which is applicable to a large class of programming languages. Expressions and exception handling are well integrated. Based on this model, the popular metrics are precisely defined. The tool CodeCover is an implementation that strictly follows these definitions.

When new GBT metrics are introduced, RPR can easily be extended to support the collection of these metrics. An example – and a topic for future work – are polymorphic expressions of object-oriented languages whose behavior is similar to that of switch statements.

Acknowledgements. I would like to thank Prof. Jochen Ludewig for his valuable support and advice, as well as Kornelia Kuhle and the anonymous reviewers for their comments.

References

1. Ammann, P., Offutt, A.J., Hong, H.S.: Coverage Criteria for Logical Expressions. In: Proc. International Symposium on Software Reliability Engineering, pp. 99–107 (2003)
2. Andrews, J.H., et al.: Using Mutation Analysis for Assessing and Comparing Testing Coverage Criteria. IEEE Trans. Softw. Eng. 32(8), 608–624 (2006)
3. Beizer, B.: Software Testing Techniques. Van Nostrand Reinhold, New York (1990)
4. Berner, S., Weber, R., Keller, R.K.: Enhancing Software Testing by Judicious Use of Code Coverage Information. In: Proceedings of the 29th International Conference on Software Engineering, ICSE 2007 (2007)
5. Hanussek, R., et al.: CodeCover - Glass Box Testing Tool, Design, Student Project "OST-WeST", University of Stuttgart (2008), http://codecover.org/development/Design.pdf
6. Starzmann, M., et al.: CodeCover - Glass Box Testing Tool, Specification, Student Project "OST-WeST" (2008), http://codecover.org/development/Specification.pdf
7. CodeCover Homepage, http://codecover.org

8. Dupuy, A., Leveson, N.: An empirical evaluation of the MC/DC coverage criterion on the HETE-2 satellite software. In: Proc. Digital Aviation Systems Conference (DASC 2000), Philadelphia (2000)
9. Federal Aviation Administration, Software Verification Tools Assessment Study, DOT/FAA/AR-06/54 (2007), http://www.tc.faa.gov/its/worldpac/techrpt/ar0654.pdf
10. Fenton, N., Pfleeger, S.L.: Software Metrics: A Rigorous and Practical Approach, 2nd edn. PWS Pub. Co., Boston (1997)
11. Huang, J.C.: An Approach to Program Testing. ACM Comput. Surv. 7(3), 113–128 (1975)
12. IEC 61508. Functional safety of electrical/electronic/programable electronic (E/E/PE) safety related systems. Part 1–7, Edition 1.0
13. Mockus, M., Nagappan, N., Dinh-Trong, T.T.: Test coverage and post-verification defects: A multiple case study. In: Proceedings of the 2009 3rd International Symposium on Empirical Software Engineering and Measurement (ESEM 2009), pp. 291–301. IEEE Computer Society, Washington, DC (2009)
14. Myers, G.J.: Art of Software Testing, John Wiley & Sons, Inc., New York (1979)
15. Schmidberger, R.: Wohldefinierte Überdeckungsmetriken für den Glass-Box-Test (Well-defined Coverage Metrics for the Glass Box Test; in German). Doctoral Dissertation; to be submitted to the Department of Informatics and Electrical Engineering, University of Stuttgart (2013)
16. Yang, Q., Li, J.J., Weiss, D.: A Survey of Coverage-Based Testing Tools. Comput. J. 52(5), 589–597 (2009)
17. Zhu, H., Hall, P.A.V., May, J.H.R.: Software unit test coverage and adequacy. ACM Computing Surveys 29(4), 366–427 (1997)
18. Dahl, O.-J., Dijkstra, E.W., Hoare, C.A.R.: Structured Programming. Academic Press (1972)
19. Chilenski, J.J., Miller, S.P.: Applicability of modified condition/decision coverage to software testing. Software Engineering Journal 9(5), 193–200 (1994)
20. Binder, R.V.: Testing Object-Oriented Systems: Models, Patterns, and Tools. Addison-Wesley Longman Publishing Co., Inc., Boston (1999)
21. RTCA-DO-178B, 1992, Software considerations in airborne systems and equipment certification (December 1992)
22. Reisig, W.: A Primer in Petri Net Design. Springer, Berlin (1992)
23. Liu, Z., et al.: Test Coverage for Collaborative Workflow Application based on Petri Net. In: Proceedings of the 2010 14th International Conference on Computer Supported Cooperative Work in Design (2010)

Cutting Time-to-Market by Adopting Automated Regression Testing in a Simulated Environment

Manuel Palmieri[1], Antonio Cicchetti[2], and Anders Öberg[3]

[1] Bombardier Transportation, Västerås, Sweden
manuel.palmieri@se.transport.bombardier.com
[2] Mälardalen University, Västerås, Sweden
antonio.cicchetti@mdh.se
[3] MAXIMATECC, Västerås, Sweden
anders.oberg@maximatecc.com

Abstract. Industrial system development is facing an ever growing complexity of the target applications together with market demands of reducing time and costs of products. This issue is even more relevant in safety critical domains, where the quality of the system has to be necessarily validated before any release can be placed on the market. Bombardier Transportation works in one of such domains, namely rail-equipment development, and has to deal with problems related to testing the developed applications in an efficient and effective way while trying to reduce costs and time-to-market.

This work illustrates the concrete solutions adopted by the company in order to effectively test their systems; in particular, they adopt automated regression testing and simulated environments to speed-up the process and alleviate the problems due to hardware costs and size as well as the non-reversibility of reality.

Keywords: Industrial System Testing, Automated Regression Testing, Simulation Environments, Rail Equipment Development.

1 Introduction

Nowadays' needs to increase software quality assurance and reduce development time is making manual testing not appropriate to meet market demands [10]. Moreover, companies that produce artefacts for safety-critical applications, notably automotive, aviation, medicine, nuclear engineering, transport, etc., have to face some additional issues. In particular, they have to deal with high costs for buying hardware units devoted to developers and testers; they have to face the impossibility to perform certain types of tests because of their dangerousness and destructiveness, and management of timing issues related to the execution of tests.

Bombardier Transportation is one of the world's largest companies in rail-equipment manufacturing and servicing industries with a wide product range

M.G. Merayo and E. Montes de Oca (Eds.): ICTSS 2014, LNCS 8763, pp. 129–144, 2014.

of passenger trains, locomotives, and boogies [11]. MAXIMATECC is a Swedish company whose purpose is to support manufacturers of industrial vehicles with solutions that deal with humans in control of vehicles working in critical environments [13]. Besides providing mechanical and electrical parts, Bombardier Transportation also produces software for its vehicle control systems. One of the most important parts of such software is the Train Control and Management System (TCMS), which is a high capacity, infrastructure backbone that allows easy integration of all controls and communications requiring functions on-board the train [11][12].

This article discusses about the exploitation of automated regression testing in a simulated environment by illustrating its concrete implementation in an industrial setting. The aim is to clarify the general needs, implementation solutions, advantages, and drawbacks of adopting such a testing methodology in industrial practice. To the best of our knowledge, despite the relevance of the problem, this is the first work that illustrates the issues and possible solutions due to the introduction of regression testing techniques and simulated environments in the railway industrial domain.

The paper is structured as follows: Sect. 2 describes the basic concepts that underpin the contribution of this work, while Sect. 3 illustrates the main characteristics of the TCMS and its complexity. Sect. 4 presents the Bombardier Transportation and MAXIMATECC framework that supports automated regression testing and its interconnection with the simulated environment, while Sect. 5 clarifies the fundamental steps the brought Bombardier Transportation and MAXIMATECC to obtain the desired support for simulation. The paper then shows concrete results of the comparison between manual versus automated testing procedures both in a real and in a simulated environment in Sect. 6. The work is concluded in Sect. 7 by drawing considerations on the lesson learned in the realization of the automated regression testing support including its interconnection with simulated environments, and outlines some future investigation directions.

2   Background

Software testing has been traditionally meant to be a manual activity, where people sitting in front of the computers test the software by trying various usage and input combinations. In the last decade, due to the need of increasing the effectiveness, efficiency and coverage of the testing, companies are investing more and more on the automation testing. [16]. In this work we refer to automated testing as the process to analyse software by using special tools to automatically control the execution of tests and detect differences between existing software conditions and expected results [1] [17]. Its introduction has given a significant boost to the testing area, by allowing to speed-up testing activities and hence the whole Software Development Life-Cycle (SDLC). Moreover, it has contributed to alleviate relevant disadvantages of manual testing by reducing test execution time, human mistakes in performing and evaluating tests, and limitations related to the dangerousness and time extension of tests [2] [16]. Besides, automated testing has also favoured the use of regression testing, which was considered an expensive and time consuming testing technique. The combination of automated and regression testing has given life to a practice that is usually called automated regression testing [15].

Regression Testing is a particular type of software testing that prescribes retesting the software during its SDLC, with the aim to detect defects deriving from software changes. When a new version of the software is released, existing test suites have to be partly or completely rerun to verify and validate that software changes did not introduce new faults, and that the software behaviour is still matching the requirements. During the re-testing phase, developers and testers have to continuously revise and refine test cases with the aim to make them as much as possible accurate for the new software release [2].

The combination of automated and regression testing has the benefit that they compensate the disadvantages of one another. On the one hand, automated testing has the advantage to automatically perform tests avoiding human resources to step by step verify and validate the correctness of the software, but has the disadvantages of high initial costs, time-consuming setup and configuration operations needed to prepare the environment to run tests. On the other hand, regression testing has the advantage to have a short setup phase to run tests, but has the disadvantage that for each software change tests should be rerun and consequently very time-consuming if manually done. Therefore, benefits of automated regression testing become evident in long-term SDLCs, where the testing phase is quite long and there is the necessity to frequently run tests [2] [3].

Among possible implementations, automated regression testing in a simulated environment represents an important possibility for companies since it magnifies the advantages gained through automation [4]. In particular, it allows to improve accuracy, coverage, and reusability by setting and possibly enforcing certain system states that constitute the pre-conditions for a given test to be run. It is worth noting that in real environments it can be very difficult (and even impossible in some cases) to reproduce particular conditions due to timing issues as well as because of the potential destructiveness of the test. For the same reasons, simulated environments permit to save time and money (e.g by avoiding to buy multiple hardware components) in selecting the best alternative among several acceptable design solutions.

In the following, we first illustrate the TCMS system in order to let the reader grasp the complexity of a modern train application; then, we describe how Bombardier Transportation and MAXIMATECC provided an integrated solution for automated regression testing in a simulated environment.

3   The TCMS System

Bombardier Transportation produces software for its Vehicle Control Units (VCU) and Intelligent Display Units (IDU). One of the most important parts of the developed software is the TCMS, which is a high capacity, infrastructure backbone that allows easy integration of all controls and communications requiring functions

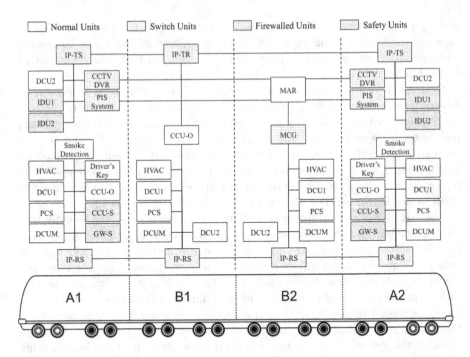

Fig. 1. General architecture of the TCMS system

on-board the train. It provides a high processing capability and bandwidth for real time exchange of data, both throughout the train and with the outside world, via up to date mobile communications [5].

TCMS interacts with all train subsystems, notably brakes, pantographs, doors, lights, toilets, and so forth. The architecture of TCMS consists of mainly three networks, namely Internet Protocol Train Communication (IPTCom), Multifunction Vehicle Bus (MVB), and Serial. In Fig. 1 is shown an example of an IPTCom network [1], where it is illustrated how involved sub-units communicate with each other. Even though the architecture in the picture is train specific, it is noteworthy that train architectures adhere to a generic design pattern that is detailed in the following.

Usually, each train consists of multiple cars, where the first and the last are a combination of control and passenger cars, whereas the ones in between are usually only passenger cars. As expected, control cars (which in this figure are named with A1 and A2) are the places where the driver can sit and where most of the train controls are contained. Moreover, they contain most of the TCMS units and those units that are classified as safety critical. Instead, B1 and B2 contain only units to control normal actions and reactions that are executed in all cars (e.g, activate driver's desk, raise pantograph, open battery contact, activate emergency brakes). A relevant characteristic of the TCMS architecture is its

---

[1] For the sake of space and readability, in this paper we only show part of the IPTCom network to let the reader grasp the complexity of the TCMS system.

redundancy: almost all units included in both control/passenger and passenger cars are replicated. This serves to increase the reliability of the system in case of malfunctions, damages, etc. of architecture units. Moreover, safety critical devices have the capacity to take decisions and act on the train in case of system malfunctions, driver absence, etc. These actions depend on the status of TCMS units, the status of the train and its location, the communication with the outside world, etc.

By looking deeper at the TCMS architecture example, it is possible to notice that most of the units contained in A1 are duplicated in A2 and the same happens for B1 and B2. In particular, B1 and B2 contain Heating, Ventilation and Air-Conditioning (HVAC), Driver Control Unit 1 (DCU1), Driver Control Unit 2 (DCU2), Passenger Counting System (PCS), and Drive Control Unit Motor (DCUM) converter units. A1 and A2 include a majority of the passenger car units, and additionally locate units such as Driver's Key, those classified safety critical such as IDUs, Central Computing Unit Safety (CCU-S), and GateWay Safe (GW-S), those protected by firewall (exclusion MCG) such as Closed Circuit TeleVision Digital Video Recorder (CCTV DVR) and Passenger Information System (PIS) System, and the Central Computing Unit Operation (CCU-O).

Since TCMS communicates with other systems (both inside and outsite the train), it needs to be protected with firewall units. In the IPTCom network of the TCMS architecture there are five devices that are protected by the firewall and they are CCTV DVR, PIS System and MCG as shown in Fig. 1. Moreover, TCMS is responsible to read Input and Output (IO) signals connected to the driver control and communicate their states to the dedicated hardware to process their values and perform corresponding actions. Additionally, it is also responsible to evaluate reactions, which can be generally described as consequences to actions, e.g., open doors, release brakes, activate heating, turn on lights [14].

Over the years, this system has become more and more complex and customer's requirements of shorter time-to-market became more stringent. Bombardier Transportation, with the aim to meet these requirements, keep its global leader position, improve its competitiveness and quality, and reduce the development time and costs, has revolutionized its development process by creating, i) an automated testing environment and, ii) a simulated environment able to replicate the behaviour of the real system, both in its software and hardware parts. The need to perform critical tests and regression testing has encouraged the use of automated testing versus manual testing. Furthermore, the decision to create a simulated environment has been mainly due to the impossibility to have the real train in the office because of space, costs, and because typically software development is distributed across different company sites.

4   Automated Regression Testing Support at Bombardier Transportation

This section describes how automated regression testing and simulated environment techniques are combined in the state of practice at Bombardier. In particular, we first introduce the overall environment that supports testing for both

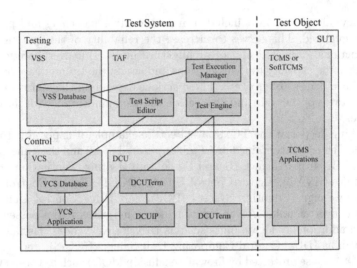

Fig. 2. General architecture of the test environment

real and simulated artefacts. Then, we illustrate how simulation mechanisms are integrated to test the System Under Testing (SUT).

4.1   Test Environment

Bombardier Transportation has created a testing environment with the aim to speed-up and automate as much as possible the testing process, and ease the adoption of regression testing. The result is a simple architecture, but at the same time complex in software components, consisting of two blocks, namely Test System and Test Object, as depicted in Fig. 2.

Test System consists of two sub-systems, i.e. Testing and Control, that provide automation support for the testing process and a controller tailored to the Test Object, respectively. The former includes the Test Automation Framework (TAF) and Visual Source Safe (VSS), whereas the latter encompasses a Vehicle Control Simulator (VCS) and Driver Control Unit (DCU).

TAF is a set of applications devoted to the specification of tests and their automated execution. In particular, the Test Script Editor (TSE) serves to create and edit test scripts and snippets [2] based on the definition of test specifications. TSE requires the communication with the VCS and VSS databases (as shown by means of interconnection lines in Fig. 2), in order to gather on one hand train signals and controls, and on the other hand test scripts, snippets, and sessions, respectively. Train signals and controls are categorized as *action*, *reaction*, and *neutral* instructions. Actions are the operations the SUT is subject to, reactions are the corresponding effects triggered in the SUT and observable in terms of changes to the system, and neutrals have no effects on the SUT, but serve to support the execution of test scripts, such as the execution of parallel reactions,

---

[2] Snippets allow the modularization of test scripts by grouping testing operations.

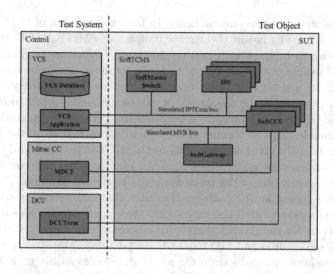

Fig. 3. General architecture of the simulated environment

the displaying of comments, etc. The Test Engine (TE) is in charge of running test scripts against the SUT. It consists of a GUI application that initializes the SUT and test scripts, and a library containing validation rules to compare testing against expected results. Therefore, TE takes care to perform actions against the SUT and verify the correctness of SUT reactions. In this respect, DCUTerm and DCUIP are exploited to access TCMS's built-in logging functionality for monitoring the status of signal values at millisecond resolution, and to generate test reports for each test script execution in various formats (i.e., PDF and XML documents), respectively. Finally, the Test Execution Manager (TEM) is used to create advanced testing workflows, notably collections of one or more test scripts scheduled by following a user's defined logic known as sessions. In the session the user can set a number of repetitions and conditional jumps for each test script, as well as define termination policies.

Test Object is the block that represents the SUT and can be either TCMS or SoftTCMS. TCMS differs from SoftTCMS since the latter is a simulated environment of the former. Test System, excluded the VCS, is the part of the Test Environment that is considered static, since all the included components are invariants of the testing support. Instead, the VCS and Test Object change depending on the project definition and can vary between the real and simulated environments, simply by selecting TCMS or SoftTCMS. In this manner the test object can be totally real, hybrid, or totally simulated.

4.2   Simulated SUT

The simulation of VCUs and the TCMS software loaded into them consists in creating several applications that replicate the behaviour of VCUs allowing the execution of the same TCMS software that is executed in real VCUs (called SoftTCMS in fig. 3). This provides the advantage to have the same application in both simulated and real environments. In fact, the creation of train software applications is done by means of the same tool, namely MITRAC CC, regardless they are going to interact with real or simulated environments. This has the remarkable advantage that once specified, the application can be compiled to be executed on a general purpose operating system (OS), notably Microsoft Windows in this case, to be simulated, or can be compiled to be executed on a train-specific OS, to be run on real VCUs. Software systems are designed in terms of Programmable Logic Controller (PLC) applications written in the Function Block Diagram (FBD) language specified by the IEC 61131-3 standard [9]. Then, the phases to generate applications for both environments are two and they consist in the generation of the framework and in the compilation. The former addresses the generation of configuration files that are necessary to compile the final application toward the target OS. Once configuration files are ready, the applications for the simulated and real environments are compiled by using Microsoft Visual Studio and MITRAC CC, respectively. Moreover, a glue layer has been developed to make train OS applications compatible with Microsoft Windows OSs and hence properly interface them with the simulation layer.

The information about the status of the train is mainly provided to drivers by using IDUs, while the communication among VCUs, IDUs, etc. and their startup-setup is done by using IP Switches and Gateways. As a consequence, during the realization of the train also IDUs, IP-Switches and Gateways are subject to testing and need to be simulated. IDUs are simulated following a similar procedure of VCUs, whereas IP-Switches and Gateways are simulated by means of a single application that provides network services, such as DHCP, DNS, etc., as depicted in Fig. 3. The use of this application makes easier and faster the preparation of the simulated environment since there is no need to use real IP-Switches and Gateways.

Ultimately, with the aim to improve the debugging and testing experience, some additional tools have been developed, namely DCUTerm and the Mitrac Desktop Component Tester (MDCT). These tools allow debugging and testing whole as well as partial device applications, disclosing the opportunity to perform unit, integration, and system testing at software level.

To summarize, the development of the simulation environment and its supporting applications allowed the remote control and management of the real hardware, avoiding the uncomfortable need to have it on developer and tester's desks. In this respect, we discuss a sample testing scenario in the following, in order to illustrate a typical testing scenario in BT and clarify the potentials of exploiting simulated environments.

4.3   A Sample Testing Scenario

The example shown in Fig. 4 illustrates an excerpt of a test case that serves to verify the correctness of the closing of load shed contactors. It consists in verifying a series of requirements that are part of the Technical Requirements Specification, localised at system level. The approach that is used at this test

Action	Reaction
- Activate a cab. - Deactivate HV and remove external 3-phase. - Log battery voltage and current.	- Check that the battery chargers are indicated as not started on the IDU. - Check that battery voltage, current and temperature for each battery are shown on IDU. - Check that battery currents are negative as no charging is active. - Check that battery voltage for both battery buses are shown on IDU. - Check that event "Battery charger does not start" is not set, wait for 60 seconds.
Wait 5 minutes with battery discharging	- Check that the BC4 contactors are opened after 5 minutes with discharging current more than 10A. - Check that the battery discharging current is not less than 10A as then the limit for detecting discharging is not correct. - Check that no incorrect events are set when BC4 contactors are opened.
Wait total 30 minutes with battery discharging	- Check that the BC3 contactors are opened after 30 minutes with discharging current more than 10A. - Check that the battery discharging current is not less than 10A as then the limit for detecting discharging is not correct. - Check that no incorrect events are set when BC3 contactors are opened.

Fig. 4. A test case excerpt (from ComTS-IVVP-0181)

level is requirements based, which means that all test cases are created against specific requirements.

A typical test case is made up of a sequence of steps composed of actions and reactions (see Fig. 4). Moreover, all actions and reaction listed in the test cases are available in the TAF to design corresponding test scripts [3]. This means that each test script reflects exactly a test case and vice-versa. A further benefit that this approach gives to testers is the possibility to first create test scripts that can be immediately tested against the system and then create "official" test cases for documentation purposes.

The explanation of the whole test case goes beyond the purpose of this work; what is worth noting in Fig. 4 is the frequent exploitation of timed events, notably deadlines, delays, and so forth. The combined use of automation testing and simulation gives to testers the possibility to perform "short-cut" actions during tests in order to reduce the execution time. For example, when a test case introduces delays due to hardware parts, they can be easily reduced by performing additional actions against the system. The benefit of this approach is the possibility to cut the testing execution duration while preserving its reliability. In fact, if a tester has to check that the BC3 contactors are opened after 30 minutes with the discharging of the current of more than 10A, she/he can avoid waiting 30 minutes in the simulated environment by introducing an action that speeds up the discharging of the battery in the test script.

In the following, a deeper discussion of the simulation techniques is provided, in order to better illustrate available features and challenges faced in their realization.

---

[3] We refer to test cases for the manual testing and test scripts for automated testing.

5   Towards a Completely Simulated Train

The simulation of the TCMS has been a long-lasting and intense activity demanded an in-depth analysis and understanding of how to create an appropriate simulation and how to make the simulation as much as possible close to the real environment. The first simulation step has been addressed with the VCS, which is the control simulator of all TCMS subsystems, including physical and electrical models, driver desks (e.g. LEDs, buttons, hand levers, displays, etc.), and IO modules (i.e. sensors, actuators, etc.). The simulation of the VCS reproduces all possible train controls and signals by using graphical panels, with the purpose to enable users to control and manage the TCMS system by using GUI simulators instead of real hardware. Furthermore, the VCS simulator has been designed and developed to be reusable across different projects making minor adjustments. In this respect, a database has been created where information about train controls and signals are contained. The database is not common across train projects, rather it is project specific; however, it allows to decouple the VCS GUI from the corresponding signals exchanged when acting on the VCS, making the simulation support more scalable and re-usable.

After the realization of the VCS, Bombardier Transportation was able to run a hybrid system made up on the interaction between the VCS and VCUs. The non-simulated part of the hardware was still built up in rack cabinets and connected with the VCS through IO boards. Although this was a relevant step forward to speed up the testing, availabilities and costs to build up rack cabinets still represented a relevant limitation to perform parallel tests. Furthermore, the application update on TCMS devices still constituted a bottle-neck in the testing procedures. In fact, that is a complex and time-consuming process due to a careful (and often tricky) management of safety devices and because of the update speed. The application update requires a specific process that takes about 30 minutes for each safety device and only a bit less for non-safety devices. Furthermore, for safety devices if the update is not performed by strictly following a step-by-step well-defined procedure and respecting all its pre-conditions, it is very likely to get a failure during the update. This is mainly due to the fact that the update has to take into consideration a lot of information of the device, such as version match among software components, Cyclic Redundancy Check (CRC) of files, and so forth. As a consequence, by considering the complexity of the train architecture, the update of all installed devices is a procedure that takes several hours with a high probability of making mistakes during the update. Even worse, taking into account the typical change rate of VCU applications during the train development process, TCMS updates constituted one of the main time costs in debugging and testing activities.

As an additional remark, the difficulty or impossibility to debug VCU applications during their execution in the real environment contributed to make the work for developers and testers harder. In particular, because of timing problems when applications run asynchronously it is very difficult (and even not possible at all) to perform tests on time-dependent actions and reactions, especially when several events are expected to happen in parallel. As a consequence,

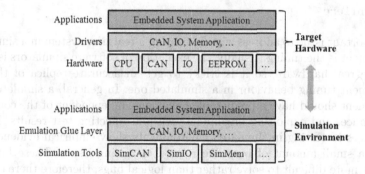

Fig. 5. Architecture of the Hardware Abstraction Layer [6]

Bombardier Transportation decided to simulate the remaining TCMS hardware units and communication buses with simulators compiled for Microsoft Windows OSs. Nowadays Bombardier Transportation is able to run the whole train system on a computer, which marked a major turning point in the context of application development and testing for TCMS. In today's practice, the main goal for this company is to set up a test system able to perform the automated regression testing on the realized simulated environment.

5.1   Architecture

In general, when a real environment is replicated with a simulated one, the main goal is to make the simulation as accurate as possible, in order to get reliable results and reduce efforts due to tuning the environment itself. In this respect Bombardier Transportation and MAXIMATECC adopted a well-defined layered architecture rather than simply developing simulators specific to each project, since empirical experience has shown its efficacy. In particular, MAXIMATECC proposed a Hardware Abstraction Layer (HAL), that is a simulation architecture where each layer and its components are simulated by preserving the same characteristics and intercommunications of the real environment. Fig. 5 depicts the core concept of the HAL: it mainly consists of three layers that represent different levels of abstraction, namely software, driver, and hardware.

The Applications layer comprises a single component that is the Embedded System Application. It represents the applications that are executed on the real environment as well as on the simulated environment. It is worth to recall here that this layer remains unchanged in both environments, making an application developed and tested with a simulated environment ready to be executed on the real environment. The layer of Drivers includes the Controller Area Network bus, IO interfaces, memory, and so forth. It is replaced in the simulated environment with the Emulation Glue Layer, which is a connection wrapper between Applications and Simulation Tools. Finally, the Hardware layer comprises the CPU, Control Area Network (CAN) connection, IO interfaces, Electrically Erasable Programmable Read-Only Memory (EEPROM), etc., and it is replicated component by component in the simulated environment with simulation tools.

5.2   SimTecc

One important issue to address when executing a real time system in a simulated environment is the timing. Usually, the execution of software simulators is faster than the real hardware, so it is tricky to get an accurate replica of the real environment timing behaviour in a simulated one. In general, a simulated test environment should have a predictable behaviour, independent of the computer performance, and exploiting breakpoints without affecting test results. Recent experiences in testing in simulated environments show empirical evidence that usually a small amount of bugs are related to timing issues. These bugs are typically more difficult to solve rather than logical bugs, therefore there exists a general pressure on tool providers to invest time and money for improving the time management accuracy.

In order to face the timing issues mentioned so far, MAXIMATECC has developed a platform that enables the simulation of hardware and buses on ordinary computers running Microsoft Windows OSs. This platform, called SimTecc, is mainly designed for testing distributed embedded systems [6]. MAXIMATECC addressed timing issues by developing a software component called TimeSync that operates as a clock and scheduler for simulated environments. The idea behind the development of this clock is to keep aligned the tick pace of all simulators and offer the possibility to *speed-up* the simulation according to the availability of operating system resources. To take advantage of TimeSync, all simulators present in the simulated environment use this software component by referring to its time instead of the one provided by the operating system. Fig. 6 shows an example of how two threads are scheduled in the real environment and in the simulated one by using the normal speed mode and full speed mode of TimeSync. In particular, in the simulation the tasks are not executed in parallel, rather the simulated clock is not advanced until all tasks scheduled for a certain point in time have been executed. In this way, the applications will behave as if the execution happened in parallel.

The use of the clock can be done in two different ways: using sleep functions or polling the current time. The main difference between them is that the former is a blocking action, whereas the latter is not. When a blocking function is called, a new target time is calculated by adding the sleep time to the target time. After the update of the time, it is work of the scheduler to compare the target times and perform the task with the lowest target time. Furthermore, before the task is executed a check against the system clock is done to decide if some idle time is required or if the task has to start immediately. This clock has the special benefit to operate in two different modes: normal speed and full speed. The former sets its tick pace as the one of the system; instead, the latter sets and changes continuously its tick pace in accordance to the availability of system resources. This means that if the system has free resources, TimeSync speeds up its tick pace with the aim to perform a faster simulation, whereas it slows down the tick pace if the system has limited resources. In this way it is possible to guarantee that the performance of the simulation and the corresponding test results are not affected by system slowdowns.

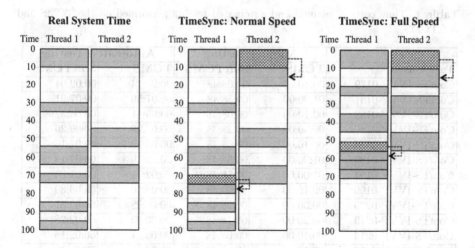

Fig. 6. Example of thread scheduling in the real and simulated environments

When automatic testing is performed in a simulated environment, there is no need for extra delays where no task is executing. So, the full speed mode is very useful to accelerate the testing by skipping the idle times and directly performing the next pending tasks. As a consequence, tasks that only need to check that a certain amount of time has elapsed, such as delays, can be realized as non-blocking functions. Another useful feature disclosed by TimeSync is the possibility to break and resume the simulation by stopping and resuming the clock and then providing a predictable behaviour when test applications measure the time. This feature allows developers and testers to break the execution of the simulation for debugging the code and then restart it without facing time-out issues. To summarize, TimeSync not only allows to speed-up testing and debugging phases by effectively exploiting resources available for the simulated environment, but also permits to perform actions that would not be possible in a real environment, notably stopping and resuming a testing procedure.

6   Performance Analysis

This section presents the results of a comparison done by performing selected test cases defined for a real train project. Each test can be decomposed in the following main phases: instrumentation, initialization, execution, and result storage. In Table 1 are shown testing times[4] devoted to manual testing and automated testing, both in the real (TCMS) and simulated environment (SoftTCMS). Each row represents a test case (the excerpt shown in Sect. 4.3 is ComTS-IVVP-0181 in the table) while the corresponding columns illustrate the time required to execute each test case both manually and automatically, and in both real and

---

[4] For the sake of space only the total testing time is shown, that is the time elapsed from instrumentation to result storage.

Table 1. Time costs of manual and automated testing performed on the TCMS and SoftTCMS

	Manual Testing		Automated Testing	
Test Cases	TCMS	SoftTCMS	TCMS	SoftTCMS
ComTS-IVVP-0179	00:10:00	00:08:48	00:03:14	00:02:04
ComTS-IVVP-0181	01:00:00	00:58:48	00:07:59	00:07:01
ComTS-IVVP-0183	00:10:00	00:08:48	00:05:41	00:04:32
ComTS-IVVP-0186	00:30:00	00:28:48	00:07:29	00:06:26
ComTS-IVVP-0188	00:10:00	00:08:48	00:03:19	00:02:16
ComTS-IVVP-0189	01:00:00	00:58:48	00:08:19	00:07:19
ComTS-IVVP-0194	01:00:00	00:58:48	00:02:11	00:01:05
ComTS-IVVP-0199	00:10:00	00:08:48	00:05:00	00:03:39
ComTS-IVVP-0205	00:30:00	00:28:48	00:06:08	00:02:57
ComTS-IVVP-0213	00:20:00	00:18:48	00:03:33	00:02:26
ComTS-IVVP-0214	00:10:00	00:08:48	00:03:21	00:02:15
ComTS-IVVP-0216	00:10:00	00:08:48	00:03:19	00:02:19
ComTS-IVVP-0225	00:05:00	00:03:48	00:02:21	00:01:11
Total	05:25:00	05:09:24	01:01:54	00:45:23

simulated environments. The times shown in the table, which are referred to the automated testing, are performed setting the TimeSync to normal speed.

By looking deeper at table data it is noticeable the significant difference between manual and automated testing, as well as between the operation on TCMS or SoftTCMS (see the row "Total"). In particular, in this case study the improvement achieved by using the automated testing is over 500%, which means that by following this approach the company is able to use less than 5 times the personnel involved in testing, or to quintuple the testing. Therefore, only by changing the testing process and keeping the same human resources, the software quality is expected to increase. Notably, in the current practice regression testing is a feasible activity that is performed each time changes are operated on the train application. The same practice could be hardly adopted without automated testing support since each re-testing would have required a couple of days to be completed. As a matter of fact, a quite widespread practice was to test changes only locally (e.g. the function subject to modifications) with the relevant risk of having a multitude of bugs appearing at system integration time.

Going down in detail and comparing TCMS versus SoftTCMS results, it is possible to notice that the difference between them is minimal, since they only differ for the re-initialization time that is typically faster when done virtually rather than on real hardware. Concretely, it takes about 1 minute and 52 seconds in the former case and only 45 seconds in the latter. Differently from manual testing, in automated testing some tests performed on the TMCS are twice slower than those performed on the SoftTCMS, even by setting normal speed for the TimeSync component (see Section 5.2) as in this case. This is due to the fact that the combination of automated testing and simulated environment tends to speed-up the testing, for example by shortening instrumentation phases.

Therefore, setting the TimeSync in full speed could have further improved test performances by a 200% factor, that is both manual testing and automated testing in the SoftTCMS would have taken half the time.

Finally, it is essential to remark that the comparison provided in the table above is only related to the time spent for a single test station. The benefits in terms of time and cost savings to reach the same coverage level are not taken into consideration at all. In fact, as aforementioned in this paper, the combination of the test system with SoftTCMS can be entirely executed on a computer, whereas the combination between the test system and TCMS needs a computer for running the test system and train hardware for running the TCMS. In this respect, Bombardier Transportation already equipped its testing laboratories with a dozen of simulation workstations, pursuing a drastic cut of testing costs.

7   Conclusions and Future Directions

Automated testing and simulated environments have been often considered premature for being used in industrial areas, especially when dealing with safety critical applications. However, nowadays' market expectations made their usage a way to pursue in order to reduce costs and time-to-market while still preserving (if not enhancing) the delivered products quality. As illustrated in this paper, automated testing and simulation environments are two orthogonal strategies that can support companies in matching market demands. However, they require a (possibly) long process in order to deeply analyse the domain and derive optimal automation and simulation solutions. In other words, the benefits granted by simulation and automation are the rewards gathered after a significant initial investment. On the other hand, when finally established those techniques allow companies to dramatically improve their testing performances, and as a consequence, their efficiency and efficacy in the application development. As a matter of fact, test automation permits companies to save relevant amounts of human resources that can be exploited in creating test cases and increasing the test coverage, for instance.

As future enhancements, Bombardier Trasportation and MAXIMATECC are investigating the extension of testing support to non-functional properties. Notably, they are working on the realization of fault injection [7] features to be added both in the automation testing and simulation tools in order to test fault-tolerance of system communications and applications. Moreover, in a long term view they envision the complete integration of Model-, Software-, and Hardware-in-the-Loop techniques to maximize the benefits of distributed development [8].

References

1. Kolawa, A., Huizinga, D.: Automated Defect Prevention: Best Practices in Software Management. Computer Society Press (January 2007) ISBN 0-470-04212-5
2. Jin, W., Orso, A., Xie, T.: Automated Behavioural Regression Testing. In: 3rd International Conference on Software Testing, Verification and Validation (2010)

3. Nguyen, H.Q., Hackett, M., Whitlock, B.K.: Global Software Test Automation: A Discussion of Software Testing for Executives. Happy About (July 2006) ISBN 1-60005-012-3
4. Rafi, D.M., Moses, K.R.K., Petersen, K., Mäntylä, M.V.: Benefits and Limitations of Automated Software Testing: Systematic Literature Review and Practitioner Survey. 10th International Workshop on Automation of Software Test (June 2012)
5. Bombardier Transportation, Train Control and Management System (July 2013), http://www.bombardier.com/en/transportation/products-services/propulsion-controls/products/train-control-and-management-system.html
6. MAXIMATECC, SimTecc Tutorial (2013)
7. Carreira, J.V., Costa, D., Silva, J.G.: Fault Injection Spot-Checks Computer System Dependability. IEEE Spectrum, 50–55 (August 1999)
8. Opal-Rt Technologies, About Hardware in the Loop and Hardware in the loop Simulation (July 2013), http://www.opal-rt.com/about-hardware-in-the-loop-and-hardware-in-the-loop-simulation
9. International Electrotechnical Commission, Programmable Controllers - Part 3: Programming Languages. IEC 61131-3, (February 2013)
10. Wong, B., Verner, J., Chulani, S., Boehm, B.: Third Workshop on Software Quality, ICSE 2005, pp. 688–689 (May 2005) ISBN 1-58113-963-2
11. Bombardier, About Us (November 2013), http://www.bombardier.com/en/about-us.html#1361982849731
12. Bombardier, MITRAC Game-Changing Electronics (November 2013), http://www.bombardier.com/content/dam/Websites/bombardiercom/supportingdocuments/BT/Bombardier-Transportation-MITRAC-Game-changing-Electronics.pdf
13. MAXIMATECC, About (November 2013), http://www.maximatecc.com/en-US/About.aspx
14. Neil, G.: On Board Train Control and Monitoring Systems. Electric Traction Systems, 211–241 (November 2006) ISBN 9780863417522
15. Zhu, F., Rayadurgam, S., Tsai, W.-T.: Automating regression testing for real-time software in a distributed environment. Object-Oriented Real-time Distributed Computing, 373–382 (April 1998) ISBN 0-8186-8430-5
16. Alegroth, E., Feldt, R., Olsson, H.H.: Transitioning Manual System Test Suites to Automated Testing: An Industrial Case Study. In: Software Testing, Verification and Validation (ICST), pp. 978–971 (March 2013) ISBN 978-1-4673-5961-0
17. SmartBear Why Automated Testing? (June 2014), http://support.smartbear.com/articles/testcomplete/manager-overview/

Testing Robotized Paint System Using Constraint Programming: An Industrial Case Study

Morten Mossige[1,3], Arnaud Gotlieb[2], and Hein Meling[3]

[1] ABB Robotics, Norway
morten.mossige@no.abb.com
[2] Simula Research Laboratory, Norway
arnaud@simula.no
[3] University of Stavanger, Norway
hein.meling@uis.no

Abstract. Advanced industrial robots are composed of several independent control systems. Particularly, robots that perform process-intensive tasks such as painting, gluing, and sealing have dedicated *process control systems* that are more or less loosely coupled with the motion control system. Validating software for such robotic systems is challenging. A major reason for this is that testing the software for such systems requires access to physical systems to test many of their characteristics.

In this paper, we present a method, developed at ABB Robotics in collaboration with SIMULA, for automated testing of such process control systems. Our approach draws on previous work from continuous integration and the use of well-established constraint-based testing and optimization techniques. We present a constraint-based model for automatically generating test sequences where we both *generate* and *execute* the tests as part of a continuous integration process. We also present results from a pilot installation at ABB Robotic where ABB's Integrated Process Control system has been tested. The results show that the model is both able to discover completely new errors and to detect old reintroduced errors. From this experience, we report on lessons learned from implementing an automatic test generation and execution process for a distributed control system for industrial robots.

1   Introduction

Developing reliable software for Complex Industrial Robots (CIRs) is a complex task, because typical robots are comprised of numerous components, including computers, field-programmable gate arrays (FPGAs), and sensor devices. These components typically interact through a range of different interconnection technologies, e.g. Ethernet and dual port RAM, depending on delay and latency requirements on their communication. As the complexity of robot control systems continuous to grow, developing and validating software for CIRs is becoming increasingly difficult. For robots performing process-intensive tasks

M.G. Merayo and E. Montes de Oca (Eds.): ICTSS 2014, LNCS 8763, pp. 145–160, 2014.

such as painting, gluing, or sealing, the problem is even worse as their dedicated process control systems is loosely coupled with the robot motion control system. A key feature of robotized painting is the ability to perform precise activation of the process equipment along a robot's programmed path. At ABB Robotics, Norway, they develop and validate Integrated Painting control Systems (IPS) for CIRs and are constantly improving the processes to deliver products that are more reliable to their customers.

Current practices for validating the IPS software involve designing and executing manual test scenarios. In order to reduce the testing costs and to improve quality assurance, there is a growing trend to automate the generation of test scenarios and multiplying them in the context of continuous testing. To facilitate this automation, we abandon the use of physical robots and instead run our tests on the IPS controllers with outputs connected to actuators. We monitor these outputs and compare with the expected results for the different tests.

In this paper, we report on our work using Constraint Programming (CP) over finite domains to *generate* automatically timed-event sequences (i.e., test scenarios) for the IPS and *execute* them within a Continuous Integration (CI) process [1]. Building on initial ideas sketched in a poster [2] one year ago, we have developed a constrained optimization model in SICStus Prolog `clpfd` [3] to help test the IPS under operational conditions. Due to online configurability of the IPS, test scenarios must be reproduced every day, meaning that indispensable trade-offs between optimality and efficiency must be found, to increase the capabilities of the CI process to reveal software defects as early as possible. While using CP to generate model-based test scenarios is not a completely new idea [4,5], it is to our knowledge, the first time that a CP model and its solving process been integrated into a CI environment for testing complex distributed systems.

Organization. The rest of the paper is organized as follows: Section 2 presents some background on robotized painting, with an example serving as a basis for describing the mathematical relations involved ; Section 3 describes ABB Robotics' current testing practices of the IPS and the rationale behind our validation choices ; Section 4 presents test objectives and scenarios ; Section 5 explains how the model is implemented and how it is integrated in in the CI process ; Section 6 discuss the errors found using the new model and compare our new approach with existing testing methods. Finally, Section 7 present the lessons learned from using the new testing approach and outlines ideas for further work, before we conclude the paper.

Notation. Throughout this paper the following notations is used: A symbol prefixed with a *, as in *$SeqLen$, is to be regarded as a constant integer value given as *input* to the CP-model. An underlined symbol, as D^+, is to be regarded as an integer *generated* by the CP-model, i.e. a result of the solving process.

2   Robotized Painting

This section briefly introduces robotized painting. A robot system dedicated to painting typically consists of two main parts: the robot controller, responsible for moving the mechanical arm, and the IPS, responsible for controlling the paint process. That is, to control the activation and deactivation of several physical processes such as paint pumps, air flows, air pressures, and to synchronize these with the motion of the robot arm.

A *spray pattern* is defined as the combination of the different physical processes. Typically, the physical processes involved in a spray pattern will have different response times. For instance, a pump may have a response time in the range 40-50 ms, while the airflow response time is in the range 100-150 ms. The IPS can adjust for these differences using sophisticated algorithms that have been analyzed and tuned over the years to serve different needs. In this paper, we focus on validating the timing aspects of the IPS.

2.1   Example of Robotized Painting

We now give a concrete example of how a robot controller communicates with the IPS in order to generate a spray pattern along the robot's path. A schematic overview of the example is shown in Figure 1, where the node marked *robot controller* is the CPU interpreting a user program and controlling the servo motors of the robot in order to move it. The example is realistic, but simplified, in order to keep the explanations as simple as possible.

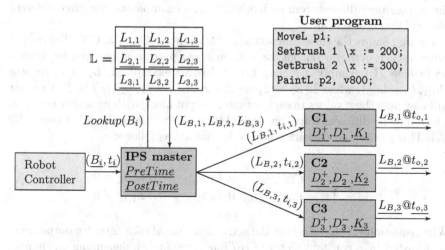

Fig. 1. Logical overview of a robot controller and the IPS

The program listing of Figure 1 shows an example of a user program. The first instruction MoveL p1 moves the robot to the Cartesian point p1. The next two SetBrush instructions tells the robot to apply spray pattern number 1 when the robot reaches $x = 200$ on the x-plane, and to apply spray pattern number 2 when it reaches $x = 300$. Both SetBrush instructions tell the IPS to apply a specific behavior when the physical robot arm is at a given position. The last instruction (PaintL) starts the movement of the robot from the current position p1 to p2. The v800 argument of PaintL gives the speed of the movement (i.e., 800 mm/s).

We now assume that the path from p1 to p2 results in a movement from $x = 0$ to $x = 500$. The robot controller interprets the user program ahead of the actual physical movement of the robot, and can therefore estimate *when* the robot will be at a specific position. Assuming that the movement starts at time $t = 0$, the robot can compute based on speed and length of path that the two SetBrush activations should be triggered at $t_1 = 250$ ms and $t_2 = 375$ ms.

The robot controller now sends the following messages (a.k.a. *events*) to the IPS master: $(B_1 = 1, t_1 = 250), (B_2 = 2, t_2 = 375)$, which means apply spray pattern 1 at 250 ms, and spray pattern 2 at 375 ms. The messages are sent around 200 ms before the actual activation time, or at ≈ 50 ms for spray pattern 1, and at ≈ 175 ms for spray pattern 2. These messages simply converts position into an absolute global activation time. Note also that the IPS receives the second message before the first spray pattern is bound for execution, which means that the IPS must handle a queue of scheduled spray patterns.

IPS master: When the IPS receives a message from the robot controller, it first determines the physical outputs associated with the logical spray pattern number. Many different spray patterns can be generated based on factors like paint type or equipment in use. In the IPS, each spray pattern is translated into 3 to 6 different physical actuator outputs that must be activated at appropriate times, possibly different from each other. In this example, we use three different physical actuator outputs.

Figure 1 shows the three different actuator outputs (**C1, C2, C3**). The output value of each actuator output for a given spray pattern is resolved by using a *brush table* ($\mathbb{L}$) (simply a lookup table). In this example, $\mathbb{L}(B_1 = 1)$ returns $(L_{1,1}, L_{1,2}, L_{1,3})$, while $\mathbb{L}(B_2 = 2)$ results in $(L_{2,1}, L_{2,2}, L_{2,3})$. The IPS master will now pass these values to each actuator output along with its activation time, which may be different from the original time received from the robot controller (t_i). This possible modification can be formalized as follows:

$$t_i' = \begin{cases} t_i - \underline{PreTime} & \text{if } L_{1,B_{i-1}} = 0 \wedge L_{1,B_i} \neq 0 \\ t_i - \underline{PostTime} & \text{if } L_{1,B_{i-1}} \neq 0 \wedge L_{1,B_i} = 0 \end{cases} \qquad (1)$$

What equation (1) shows is that the activation time of each actuator output may be adjusted by a constant factor ($\underline{PreTime}$, $\underline{PostTime}$), depending on changes from other actuator outputs. This is done because small adjustments may be necessary when there is a direct link between the timing of different actuator outputs. In our example, the timing on **C2** is influenced by changes on **C1**. A practical example of such compensation is to change the timing on an air actuator output when a paint-pump is turned on or off.

Activation of actuator outputs: By still referring to Figure 1, we now present how a message sent from the IPS master to a single actuator output is handled. Let us assume that message (L, t_i) is sent, and that the current actuator output is L'. Since painting involves many slow physical processes, the actuator output compensates for this by computing an adjusted activation time t_o, that accounts for the time it takes the physical process to apply the change.

The IPS can adopt two different strategies to compute this time compensation. The first consists of adjusting the time with a *constant* factor: D^+ for positive change, and D^- for negative change. The second one consists in using a *linear* timing function to adjust the time *linear* to the change of the physical output.

Equation (2) combines these strategies into a single compensation function, where $^*Min$ (resp. $^*Max$) is the physical minimum (resp. maximum) value possibly handled[1] by some actuator output.

$$t_o = t_i - \begin{cases} D^- \cdot (\frac{L-L'}{^*Max - ^*Min})^{\underline{K}} & \text{if } L' < L \\ D^+ \cdot (\frac{L'-L}{^*Max - ^*Min})^{\underline{K}} & \text{if } L' > L \\ 0 & \text{otherwise} \end{cases} \quad (2)$$

Physical layout of the IPS: Figure 1 only shows the logical connections in a possible IPS configuration. In real applications, each component (**IPS master, C1, C2, C3**) may be located on different embedded controllers, interconnected through an industrial-grade network. As such, the different components may be located at different physical locations on the robot, depending on which of physical process it is responsible for.

3   Testing IPS

In this section, we summarize some of the testing approaches that have been used to test the IPS, focusing on validating the accuracy of time-based activation. We discuss the benefits and drawbacks of these legacy-testing approaches, before we introduce our automated testing approach.

A major challenge that we are confronted with, when testing a robot system, is that it involves a physically moving part (the robot arm), which must be accurately synchronized with several external process systems. This quickly turns into labor-intensive procedures to set up the tests and execute them. Moreover, strict regulations with regard to safety must also be followed due to moving machinery and use of hazardous fluids like paint.

3.1   Painting on Paper

To simulate a realistic application of spray painting with a robot, we can configure a paint system to spray paint on a piece of paper. An example of this is shown in Figure 2[2]. This test includes both realistic movement of the robot while running a complete and realistic setup on the IPS. However, there are many drawbacks to using this method, where one is high cost of much manual

---

[1] These values are determined by the physical equipment involved in the paint process (pumps, valves, air, etc.).

[2] This video http://youtu.be/oq524vuO5N8 also shows painting on paper.

labor to set up, and hazardous environment due paint fluid exposure. It is also more or less impossible to automate this test, even after the initial setup is done.

A typical test execution will be to perform a single paint-stroke as shown in Figure 2, followed by manual inspection of the result. This inspection will typically require both a software engineer and a paint process engineer to interpret the results. Because of this manual inspection that need to be done between each paint-stroke, the possibility of automating this test method is limited. Such a test is typically performed during the final verification phase for a new product running the IPS software, such as the air controller of a paint controller. The test is also executed as part of major revisions of the IPS. Based on our experience at ABB Robotics, it is extremely rare that errors related to timing are found when running such a test.

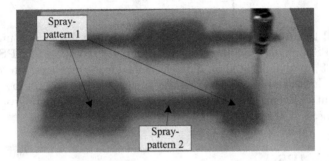

Fig. 2. Painting on paper

3.2   Activation Testing with an Oscilloscope

By reducing the IPS setup to include only a single digital actuator output, without any fluid or air, it is possible to perform some of the basic synchronization tests on the IPS. This can be done by connecting the digital output to an input channel on an oscilloscope, and the output from a proximity sensor to another input channel. The robot is then programmed to perform a linear movement passing over a proximity sensor, with the paint program set up to do an activation at exactly that point. Thus generating a signal which should be in sync with the signal from the proximity sensor. By comparing the signal from the digital output with the signal from proximity sensor, it is possible to test much of the timing behaviors of the IPS[3].

At ABB Robotics, this is one of the most frequently executed tests aimed at uncovering synchronization problems. However, also this test require manual labor to set up and to execute the test runs, and since it also involves physical movement of the robot arm, a hazard zone must be established for this test. However, different from the test described in Section 3.1, it can be executed without supervision, and the test results can be inspected after test completion.

---

[3] Two videos showing activation testing using a proximity sensor and oscilloscope: http://youtu.be/I1Ce37_SUwc and http://youtu.be/LgxXd_DN2Kg.

3.3   Running in a Simulated Environment

The IPS is designed to be portable to many microprocessor platforms and operating systems. It is even possible to run the IPS on a desktop system such as Windows. This has the advantage that much of the functional testing can be performed in a simulated environment. This has reduced some of the need for time consuming manual testing on actual hardware. However, testing against performance requirements is impossible in a simulated environment, due to lack of real-time behavior in the simulator.

3.4   Summary of Existing Test Methods

There are several drawbacks with the test methods described above. The methods that use real robots gives very realistic results, but require costly and slow manual labor to set up the test, and to interpret the results. For the method described in Section 3.3 it is clearly possible to automate both setup and result analysis. However, it cannot be used to execute tests related to real-time and synchronization between several embedded controllers.

3.5   A New Test Strategy

In the following, we outline some of the requirements for our new test strategy. The rationale behind the new requirements are mainly to reduce manual labor, and to be able to detect errors earlier in the development process: *1)* Automated: It should be possible to set up the test, execute the test, and analyze the results without human intervention. *2)* Systematic: Tests should be generated automatically by a model, rather than being contrived by a test engineer. *3)* Adaptive: Generated tests should automatically adapt to changes in the software and/or configurations, and should not require any manual updates to the testing framework. This implies that tests should be generated immediately prior to their execution, using as input, information obtained from the system under test.

4   Constraints and Scenario

With the mathematical relations described in Section 2 as background, we now describe the constraints used to generate test sequences. The constraints can be divided into two main categories. The first category expresses how a complete IPS behaves in a normal situation. That is, the IPS is not forced into any erroneous state, or other corner cases. The second category represents constraints where the model generates specially selected error scenarios, where the IPS is either pushed into an erroneous state, or where performance limitations are being tested. These constraints are summarized in Figure 3, and discussed in detail in the following sections.

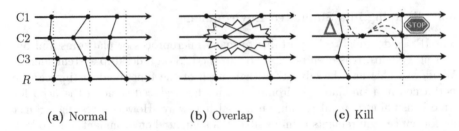

(a) Normal   (b) Overlap   (c) Kill

Fig. 3. Test scenarios considered as test objectives. The horizontal axis represent time, and the black dots correspond to output activations. A specific *spray pattern* is a collection of output activations, and is visualized by a line connecting the black dots.

4.1   Normal Scenario

During normal, non-erroneous behavior, the robot controller sends commands to the IPS according to the constraint given in (3), and the IPS generates output activations according to (4). These two constraints correspond to Figure 3a.

Input sequence:

$$\forall i \in 1\ldots{}^{*}SeqLen, \tag{3}$$
$$t_i - t_{i-1} \geq {}^{*}MinBrushSep,$$
$$t_i > t_{i-1}, \quad t_i \geq 0,$$
$$B_i \neq B_{i-1}, \quad B_i \in 0\ldots{}^{*}BTabSize$$

Each single actuator output:

$$\forall j \in 1\ldots{}^{*}C, \forall i \in 1\ldots{}^{*}SeqLen \tag{4}$$
$$t_{j,i} - t_{j,i-1} \geq {}^{*}MinTrigSep,$$
$$t_{j,i} > t_{j,i-1}, \quad t_{j,i} \geq 0$$

Where ${}^{*}C$ refers to the number of actuator output in the setup.

4.2   The Overlap Scenario

Figure 3b shows two overlapping event activations. This overlap can be generated using the constraint in (5). This scenario is used to test how well the IPS is able to handle that an activation time for one actuator output gets out of order with respect to time. For real robot applications, there are many possible sources for this particular problem scenario. The most common one being that a user increase the robot's speed by changing the speed parameter in a `PaintL` instruction. For the IPS, this behavior should be reported as an error message to the user, and resolve any conflicts with the actuator output.

$$t_{c,e} - t_{c,e+1} \geq {}^{*}MinOverlapTime,$$
$$t_{c,e+1} - t_{c,e-1} \geq {}^{*}MinTrigSep, \tag{5}$$
$$t_{c,e+2} - t_{c,e} \geq {}^{*}MinOverlapTime$$

Above, $t_{c,e}$ represents the activation time for a specific actuator output c and e indicates where in the sequence the overlap should be enforced.

4.3   The Illegal Value Scenario

The illegal value constraint is important for checking that the IPS is able to shut down safely in case of an error. By forcing one of the output channels to fail, the internal structure of the IPS should initiate a controlled shutdown. This shutdown procedure must be performed in a special sequence, taking care to avoid pressure build up in hoses, which could otherwise lead to rapturing hoses. This constraint is visualized in Figure 3c, and specified in Equation (6).

$$P_{c,e} = {}^*IllegalVal \tag{6}$$

Where $P_{c,e}$ is the output value of actuator output c for the $e'th$ event.

5   Implementation

This section explains how the model is implemented and used in ABB's production grade test facility. We will also discuss some of the design choices that we made during the deployment of the model.

5.1   Continuous Integration

CI [1] is a software engineering practice aimed at uncovering software errors at an early stage of development, to avoid problems during integration testing. One of the key ideas in CI is to build, integrate, and test the software frequently. For developers working in a CI environment, this means that even small source code changes should be submitted to the source-control system server frequently, rather than submitting large sets of changes occasionally. Typically, a CI infrastructure includes tools for source control system, automated build servers, and testing engines.

5.2   Testing in a CI Environment

Our goal in this work has been to develop an automated testing framework for the IPS as an integrated part of a CI environment. Compared to traditional software testing, a test running in a CI environment will have some additional requirements. In particular, Fowler [1] points out that the total *round-trip time* is crucial for a successful CI deployment. Here, round-trip time refers to the time it takes from a developer submits a change to the source repository, until feedback from the build and test processes can be collected. Thus, to keep the round-trip time to a minimum, we have identified a few areas that we have given special attention to in our design.

Test complexity: Testing based on CI will never replace all other kinds of testing. In CI, a less accurate but faster test will always be preferred over a slow but accurate test. In practice, a test must satisfy the *good enough* criteria, frequently used in industry.

Solving time: Many constraint-based optimization problems are time consuming to solve, especially if an optimal solution is sought. For our purposes, an optimal solution is unnecessary. Simply finding a good solution after running the solver for a limited period is considered good enough for our purpose.

Execution time: The most important factor for controlling the execution time for a generated test sequence is to control the length of the test sequence. By balancing the length of the test sequence between a reasonable, realistic enough but still small enough, the execution time of the test is kept under control. Clearly, it will require some experience, to determine what is *good enough*.

5.3   Model Implementation

We choose to use *Constraint Programming* (CP) over finite domains to solve the model. CP is a well-known paradigm introduced twenty years ago to solve combinatorial problems in an efficient and flexible way [6]. Typically, a CP model is composed of a set of variables V, a set of domains D, and a set of constraints C. The goal of constraint resolution is to find a solution, i.e., an assignment of variables to values that belong to the domains and that satisfy all the constraints. Finding solutions is the role of the underlying constraint solver, which applies several filtering techniques to prune the search space formed by all the possible combinations. In practice, the constraint models that are developed to solve concrete and realistic testing problems usually contain complex control conditions (conditionals, disjunctions, recursions) and integrate dedicated and optimized search procedures [7].

We have chosen to implement the constraint model using the finite domains library in Sicstus Prolog [3], and have thus written the actual model in Prolog. To integrate the model with ABB's existing testing framework, we have also built a front-end layer in Python. This front-end layer can be used by test engineers with no prior knowledge of CP or Prolog, and allows us to integrate with our existing build and test servers based on Microsoft Team Foundation Server. A schematic overview of the architecture is shown in Figure 4.

While referring to Figure 1, we now assume that the number of actuator outputs is a constant input parameter $^*C$, instead of 3. The variables for our problem can be divided into three groups: the input sequence $((\underline{B_1}, \underline{t_1}), \ldots, (\underline{B_N}, \underline{t_N}))$, where $N = {^*SeqLen}$ (the length of the test sequence). The configuration variables: $(\underline{PreTime}, \underline{PostTime}, \underline{D_1^+}, \underline{D_1^-}, \underline{K_1}, \ldots, \underline{D_{*C}^+}, \underline{D_{*C}^-}, \underline{K_{*C}})$, and the variables in the brush table $(\underline{L_{1,1}}, \ldots, \underline{L_{*BTabSize,*C}})$ where $^*BTabSize$ is the size of the brush table. By selecting one of the previously mentioned scenarios, a solution to the CP model is constructed by an instantiation of these variables. Thus, the expected output on each actuator output along with its activation time, represents the *test oracle*.

5.4   Test Setup

An overview of our test setup is shown in Figure 4. With reference to the numbers in Figure 4 a test sequence execution is typically triggered by a build server upon a successful build of the IPS software, (1). Building the software is scheduled to run every night, but can also be triggered manually by a developer. The first task the test server does is to upgrade all connected embedded controllers with the newly built software, (2). Then the IPS is configured with test specifications retrieved from the source control repository, (3). This is followed by executing a set of basic *smoke tests*, before the constraint model is launched for test cases generation. By feeding the constraint model with data retrieved from the new configuration and properties from the IPS (4), we ensure that the generated tests are synchronized with the current software and configuration. Further details on just-in-time test generation (JITTG) is discussed in Section 5.5. Finally, the actual test is executed by applying the generated test sequence, and comparing the actuator outputs with the model generated oracle, (5).

In the production test facility at ABB, each generated test sequence is executed on a total of 11 different configurations. The different configurations include execution on different hardware and software generations of the IPS, and execution on both VxWorks and Linux as the base operating system for the IPS. The test framework is written in Python and supports parallel execution of tests when there are no shared resources. Thus, the time to run the test sequence on many different configuration is very low, compared to running them in a sequence, one at a time.

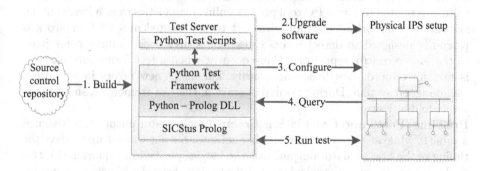

Fig. 4. Integration of CP-model with physical setup

5.5   Just-in-Time Test Generation

As shown earlier in this paper, there are many parameters in the model that must be specified before the model can be solved. Some of these parameters come from configuration files used to configure the IPS, and some of the parameters can be extracted by querying a newly built IPS. Common for both sets of parameters is that the resulting model will be different if the parameters have changed. This means that the model is closely linked to what is fetched from the source control system. Because of this, we decided to generate and solve the model at testing time, as opposite to solving the model once, and adding the resulting model to source control. There are several advantages to using JITTG, but there are also some drawbacks. The most important advantage of using JITTG is that there is a lower probability of falsely reporting an error due to mismatch between the generated model and the running system. The main drawback is that the time needed for solving the model becomes an important factor. If the model is solved once and used many times, a solving time of several hours is reasonable. However, with JITTG the solving time becomes a crucial. The models that we have solved so far have had a solving time of less than a few minutes.

6 Evaluation

This section presents the errors that were found after having used the new model in ABB Robotics production test facility for about four months. We also compare our new model-based testing approach with some of the other testing practices.

6.1 New Errors Found

This section describes the errors found immediately after we introduced the new model. We found three previously unknown errors in the IPS. These errors have been in the IPS for some time, and were only found through the use of the new model. Two of the errors was directly related to the behavior of the IPS, while the third was related to how a PC tool present online diagnostics from a live, running system. It is important to emphasize that tests executed in a CI framework is primarily designed to detect errors caused by source code changes committed to the source control repository. Consequently, when a test framework like this is first introduced, it will not necessarily find many new errors in a mature, well-designed system. During normal operation, the test framework should only rarely find any errors.

PreTime/PostTime Calculation Error: If an actuator output was assigned a value 0, while at the same time another actuator output was set up to slave the timing of the first actuator output, using the logic specified in Equation (1), this could lead to an erroneous calculation of the timing of the slaved actuator output. This error was found by running the *normal behavior* scenario as described in Section 4.1.

Event Queuing Blocks Shutdown: If a shutdown of the IPS occurred at the same time as a queue of actuator output events was scheduled for execution, the shutdown could be delayed. This could happen because the shutdown message was treated with the same priority as a normal output message, when placed in the scheduling queue.

Shift in Clock: There exist several online monitoring tools like RobView and Robot Studio. These tools can be used for online monitoring of the process data from the IPS. To be able to present very accurate timing on the presented signals, the clock on the PC running the tool, and the clock on the IPS is synchronized through a proprietary light weight version of the IEEE 1588 clock synchronization protocol. Our test framework found an error in this synchronization protocol, which could cause the reported time of a signal change to

Table 1. Historical data on old bugs that were reintroduced

Bug#[1]	Time in system[2]	Time to solve[3]	Time to validate[4]	Detected by model
44432	5-10 years	1-2 hours	1 day	Yes
44835	5-10 years	2-4 days	1 day	Yes
27675	6-12 months	1-2 months	1-2 weeks	Yes
28859	6-12 months	2-3 months	2-3 weeks	Yes
28638	4-6 months	1-2 weeks	2-3 weeks	Yes

[1] Refer to bug-number in ABB's bug tracking system.
[2] How long the bug was present in the IPS before it was discovered.
[3] How long it took from the bug was discovered until the bug was fixed.
[4] How long it took to validate that the bug had actually been fixed. For many
   bugs, this involved testing time spent at customer facilities.

deviate by as much as 10 ms compared to the actual time of the change. The
error could even cause changes in the causal ordering of events.

6.2   Detection of Old Errors

To further validate the robustness of the model, a collection of old, previously
detected errors were reintroduced into source control repository with the inten-
tion to verify that the model was able to detect the errors. The selected errors
were chosen by searching in ABB's bug tracking system, by interviewing ABB's
test engineers, and through discussions with the main architect of the IPS. Most
of the errors were originally discovered at customer sites during staging of a
production line, or after the production line was set into production. The chosen
errors are mainly related to timing errors of painting events, and several of the
errors can be classified as errors that appear when the IPS is put into a large
configuration with many components.

The chosen errors are summarized in Table 1. The table shows historical data
on how long it original took to detect the error, how long it took to fix the error,
and how long it took to validate that the error had in fact been fixed. Finally, the
table shows if our new model was able to detect the re-injected bug. Note that
some of these numbers cannot be accurately specified; they represent reasonable
estimates. Especially errors related to *how* long a bug has been in the system is
difficult to estimate. However, by interviewing the main architect of the IPS and
the lead test engineer, we feel that the numbers presented has high confidence.

6.3   Comparison of Test Methods

While our new model-based test strategy cannot entirely replace the current
testing methods, it represents an excellent supplement to identify bugs at a much
earlier stage in the development process. Nonetheless, we can still compare the

different methods quantitatively. Table 2 gives the results of our comparison. As we can see from this table, our new test strategy gives a huge improvement in number of activations that can be tested within a reasonable timeframe, which is not possible with existing testing methods. If we also include the automation in all aspects of testing, our strategy performs much better than our current test methods. However, it is important to note that our new method does not involve a mechanical robot, and this must be regarded as a weakness.

Table 2. Comparison of test methods

	Activation w/oscilloscope	Paint on paper	Constraint-based test
Setup time[1]	1-2 hours[5]	3-4 hours[5]	1-2 min[6]
Activations per test[2]	1	5-10	>100
Repetition time[3]	5 sec	10 min	< 1 sec
Interpretation time[4]	< 1 min[5]	2-4 min[5]	< 1 sec[6]
Synch. with mechanical robot	Yes	Yes	No
Run stand alone after initial setup	Yes	No	Yes

[1] Time to upgrade software, configure IPS, and loading test.
[2] The number of physical outputs that are verified with respect to time in one test.
[3] Time needed to repeat two identical tests.
[4] Time needed to inspect and interpret the result.
[5] Manual task performed by a test engineer.
[6] Automated task performed by a computer.

7   Conclusion

This section concludes the paper by presenting some lessons learned from our experience at ABB Robotics of introducing CP in our CI process. We also outline some ideas for further work.

7.1   Lessons Learned

Based on experience from about one year of live production in ABB Robotics software development environment, we report on lessons learned. The lessons learned presented here are based on experience gathered through development and deployment of the test framework, and on discussion with test engineers. We summarize lessons learned in the following:

Higher confidence when changing critical parts: Based on feedback from developers, there are now less 'fear' of applying changes in critical parts of the code. Previously such changes involved significant planning efforts and had to be synchronized with test engineers responsible for executing tests. With the new testing framework in place, it is easy to apply a change, deploy a new build with the corresponding execution of tests and inspect the result. If the change has caused unwanted side effects, the change is rolled back to keep the build 'green'.

Simple front-end, complex back-end: By using Python [8] as the front-end interface to the constraint solver and keeping the interface that a test engineer is exposed to as simple as possible, we are able to utilize personnel with minimal computer science background. It has been recognized by both [9] and [10] that CP has a high threshold for usage. By limiting the training to introduction of the famous classical problems like 'SEND+MORE=MONEY' and the N-Queens problem [11], the test engineers have received enough training to use the constraint solver from Python without major problems.

Less focus on legacy, manual tests: A positive side effect of introducing model-based testing is that the focus in the organization has shifted from lots of manual testing towards more automatic testing. Even for products beyond the scope of this paper, the introduction of a fully automatic test suite has inspired other departments to focus more on automatic testing.

Putting everything in source control repository: In our work, we never perform any installation on any build server. After a build server is installed with its CI software, absolutely everything is extracted from the source control repository. This is also a clear recommendation in CI [1]. By being 100 % strict to this philosophy, it is possible to utilize big farms of build servers without any prior installation of special build tools. This is also the case for the new CP based tool presented in this paper. We consider that the effort taken to do a 100 % integration of the tools is quite demanding, but in the long run very efficient.

Keeping tests in sync with source code and hardware: The combination of adding 'everything' to the source control repository and JITTG is that we experience less problems with tests generating false errors due to a mismatch. We still have other test suites where we do not have this tight integration, and thus these tests may occasionally produce false errors.

7.2 Further Work

The very promising results we got from use of the model inside the CI environment, has inspired us to also make use of the model outside the CI environment. This will enable us to use the model to generate tests where there is a focus on tests with longer duration. When using the model inside the CI environment, the focus is always on short duration tests, where each test never exceeds 3 minutes.

7.3 Conclusions

This paper introduced a new testing strategy for validating timing aspects of complex distributed control systems for robotics systems. A constraint-based mathematical model was introduced to automatically generate test cases through constraint solving and continuous integration techniques. The model, designed through a collaboration with SIMULA, has been implemented and a pilot installation has been set up at ABB Robotics. Using the model, both previously discovered bugs, as well as new bugs were found in a period that has been dramatically reduced with respect to other current testing practices.

Acknowledgements This work is funded by the Norwegian Research Council under the frame of the Industrial PhD program, the Certus SFI grant and ABB Robotics.

References

1. Fowler, M., Foemmel, M.: Continuous integration (2006) (accessed August 13, 2013)
2. Mossige, M., Gotlieb, A., Meling, H.: Poster: Test generation for robotized paint systems using constraint programming in a continuous integration environment. In: 2013 IEEE Sixth International Conference on Software Testing, Verification and Validation (ICST), pp. 489–490 (2013)
3. Carlsson, M., Ottosson, G., Carlson, B.: An open-ended finite domain constraint solver. In: Hartel, P.H., Kuchen, H. (eds.) PLILP 1997. LNCS, vol. 1292, pp. 191–206. Springer, Heidelberg (1997)
4. Di Alesio, S., Nejati, S., Briand, L., Gotlieb, A.: Stress testing of task deadlines: A constraint programming approach. In: 2013 IEEE 24th International Symposium on Software Reliability Engineering (ISSRE), pp. 158–167. IEEE (2013)
5. Balck, K., Pearson, J., Grinchtein, O.: Model-based protocol log generation for testing a telecommunication test harness using clp. In: Proceedings of DATE 2014, the 3rd International Conference on Design, Automation, & Test in Europe. IEEE Computer Society (2014)
6. Van Hentenryck, P.: Constraint Satisfaction in Logic Programming. MIT Press (1989)
7. Gotlieb, A.: TCAS Software Verification using Constraint Programming. The Knowledge Engineering Review 27(3), 343–360 (2012)
8. Rossum, G.: Python reference manual. Technical report, Amsterdam, The Netherlands, The Netherlands (1995)
9. Francis, K., Brand, S., Stuckey, P.J.: Optimisation modelling for software developers. In: Milano, M. (ed.) CP 2012. LNCS, vol. 7514, pp. 274–289. Springer, Heidelberg (2012)
10. de la Banda, M.G., Stuckey, P.J., Van Hentenryck, P., Wallace, M.: The future of optimization technology. Constraints, 1–13 (2013)
11. Marriott, K., Stuckey, P.J.: Programming with constraints: an introduction. MIT press (1998)

What Characterizes a Good Software Tester? – A Survey in Four Norwegian Companies

Anca Deak

Department of Computer Science,
Norwegian University of Science and Technology (NTNU),
Trondheim, Norway
deak@idi.ntnu.no

Abstract. The aim of this paper is to identify the most favourable perceived characteristics of software testers and contrast them with the group of existing software engineers' characteristics provided by prior research. We conducted a qualitative survey among four software development companies using interviews as a main method for data collection and the thematic-analysis approach for analyzing the data. Our findings describe the characteristics which are perceived as most valuable for a tester based on the working experience accumulated by the participant testers and testing managers. The study findings suggest that there are differences between the characteristics of a software engineer and a software tester, with communication and possessing an IT background being cited as the most frequently favoured characteristics for ensuring a high performing tester.

Keywords: software testers, software testing, software engineers, characteristics, human factors.

1 Introduction

Successful software projects outcomes are highly dependent on the skills and commitment of the testers involved. Having good testers will significantly improve the odds of project success and the delivery of high quality products. Since testing projects often occur under tight deadlines, budget constraints and organizational challenges, the success of a project can be highly dependent on the employee's characteristics.

There are not many studies focusing on the testers or on testing teams, although it is acknowledged that some of the problems associated with software testing in the industry are not technical, but originate from other sources, such as the socio-technical environment and organizational structure of the company as presented in Rooksby, Rouncefield and Sommerville study [1]. Although there is extensive work on characteristics of software engineers, to our knowledge there is a lack of research focusing specifically on the characteristics of software testers. The goal of this study is to empirically determine specific traits for software testers and contrast them with software engineers' characteristics provided by prior research. A better understanding

M.G. Merayo and E. Montes de Oca (Eds.): ICTSS 2014, LNCS 8763, pp. 161–172, 2014.

of these traits could assist in the identification of individuals with potential to be high performing testers and help the software companies within their recruiting process.

The remainder of this article is structured as follows. A literature background on characteristics of software engineers and software testers is presented in Section 2. We describe the research questions and design of the survey in Section 3. In Section 4, we present the survey's results. Section 5 discusses the lessons learned while Section 6 summarizes the findings and suggest areas for further research.

2   Characteristics of Software Engineers and Software Testers

2.1   Research on Characteristics of Software Engineers

Software Engineers characteristics was the scope of a systematic literature review conducted by Beecham et al. [2], in which 92 papers published between 1980 and June 2006 were analyzed. The result of this study provided 16 characteristics of the software engineer together with a group of motivators and de-motivators which were identified in the literature. The study conducted by Beecham et al. [2] indicates that several factors have influence on a software engineers' motivation. One of these factors is related to the personal characteristics of the software engineer. The most cited characteristics of software engineers were: Growth orientation, Need for independence and Low need for social interaction which is associated with introverts.

These characteristics have two set of determinants: the control factors and the moderators. The control factors group relate to individual's personality, their career paths and their competencies. The second group, the moderators, are considered external factors that can influence the characteristics, such as: career stage and culture which are most often cited, followed by the type of job and the type of organisation which have less influence. A subsequent study by Franca et al. [3] extended and updated this research by analyzing 53 papers published between March 2006 to August 2010. As a result, another three characteristics were identified: Competent in Management, Flexible and Have fear of punishment. Most of the studies involved in these two literature reviews were quantitative survey studies and they provided important insights into characterizing the factors and results related to motivation. One limitation of the two literature reviews, is that the majority of the studies are referring to the job itself as being the main motivational factor.

Since the position of software engineer can contain multiple roles and responsibilities which can vary from one position to another, more information about the characteristics which influence the motivation of software engineer is required. Our studies focus on software testers, who are often considered as software engineers in job title terminology, but may have different responsibilities than their fellow developers.

Lack of motivation has been seen as an important factor for failure in software development projects [4] and a recent study of a vendor organization's testing show that the quality of testing is affected by the motivation of the testers [5]. Previous studies observing the testing activities examined how the organization and the relationships between the members of a software development team are impacting the testing process and implicitly the quality of the product [6]. We wanted to build on this research by determining the characteristics which influence the motivation of different types of testers'.

2.2   Research on Software Testers' Characteristics

Testing literature written by practitioners proposed skills and characteristics which they considered most important for software testers. Pettichord provides a list of twelve desired traits which he compares between testers and developers [7]. Good testers are expected to have broad knowledge of many domains, learn new things quickly, focus on user needs and behaviour, think empirically, tolerate tedium, be sceptical, concentrate on reporting problems and be comfortable with conflicts. Black [8] suggests concrete desired skills, such as the ability to interpret the product requirements and other types of available material as well as the ability to write good defect reports. The skills are also described in Pol [9] study, but they are not so strongly emphasized. Both studies acknowledged the need for strong knowledge both of software development and application domain of the product.

An ethnographical study of a small start-up software product company conducted by Martin, Rooksby et al. [10] studied how testing is performed in an environments with extremely volatile requirements. Their study focused on integration and acceptance testing done in the company. The results showed that testers working in contexts where requirements where not defined in detailed and without any strict processes, needed understanding of the business and experience in the domain and techniques that were used to test the product. Testers were also required to possess good skills in test automation.

The importance of experience in testing was also studied by Beer and Ramler [11] trough a multiple-case study, which covered three industrial software projects. The results of the study identified two kinds of experience: experience in testing and experience with the domain of the product. Experience in testing was used in general management of the testing and especially in automation of the testing. Testers who have accumulated experience in the business domain and have strong business knowledge and expertise proved valuable when performing test case design, regression test case selection, or facing incomplete or evasive requirements and specifications.

A case study on high performing testers reported by [12], was conducted in three Finnish software product companies. The aim of the study was to identify the characteristics which were considered important for testers with high performance. Among the findings were that experience, reflection, motivation and personal characteristics had the highest importance. The results also strengthen the findings of the previous studies by stating that domain knowledge and specialized technical skills were considered more relevant that test case design and test planning skills.

Taipale and Smolander conducted a qualitative study [13], which explored the software-testing practices and suggested improvements in this process based on the knowledge acquired during their study. Their improvement proposition include adjusting testing according to the business orientation of the company, enhanced testability of software components, efficient communication, early involvement of testers and increased interaction between developers and testers. The same group of authors conducted another study, focusing on the conditions that influence software testing as an online service, looked among other at the skills required for software testing [14]. The results of the study showed that in order to assure a successful execution of an online testing process, both technical and soft skills are required. An ability to adjust to different working methods, increased understanding of customer's business needs and requirements, communication, project management, technical skills alongside with a flexibility to learn and adapt to evolving technologies were considered the required testing skills.

An empirical study of a vendor organization's testing team conducted by Shah, Harrold and Sinha [5], studied the perceptions the participants had about testing. The testers showed enthusiasm about their job and they have a positive attitude toward testing, which is the opposite of the common attitude towards testing, as being not so high valued as a software development job. A desire for innovation and a high values among the testers were also observed in the same study. In addition, the study shows that the quality of testing is affected by the motivation of the testers and emphasizes the need for appreciating testers' efforts.

3   Research Questions and Method

The aim of this paper is to study the characteristics of software testers (**RQ1**), and to contrast the group of characteristics derived from our study with the group of existing characteristics for software engineers provided by two previous systematic literature reviews of motivation in software engineering, [2] and [3], (**RQ2**). Thus, we investigated the following two research questions:

- *RQ1 What are the characteristics perceived as important of software testers?*
- *RQ2 Are there specific characteristics that separates software testers from a software engineer?*

The target population for our study is represented by software testing professionals. In the testers' category we will consider all software engineers who have software testing as their main job responsibility. A total of 14 participants from four companies were interviewed, with seven interviews being performed in agile working teams from two companies, while the other seven interviews were done in two companies following the traditional development methodology. The participants included testers and testing managers who face the daily problems of software testing activities. The companies and interviewees are described in Table 1.

During the interviews we used semi-structured questions in order to encourage the respondents to provide us with their own reflections and use their own terms. During the interviews the respondents were encouraged to freely express their opinions, by guaranteeing their anonymity and assuring them that the records will be accessible only to the researchers involved in this study. The interview guideline included both closed questions, for which responses will be easier to analyze and compare, and open questions which will allow the participants to point out issues that were not mentioned in the closed-form questions. The open questions were theme based and concerned problems of testing, collaboration within their team, relationships with fellow colleagues, plus positive and negative aspects of their daily activities. In addition, we enquired about their working environment, schedules and the influence of the business domain. The same set of questions will enable us to see if there is a difference between the characteristics of a tester and those of the more general category of software engineers.

Table 1. Companies and interviewees

Business	Size	Methodology	Testing	Interviewees
Company A				
Software producer and service provider	medium international	Agile, TDD	Functional	Testing manager Tester (3)
Company B				
Software producer and testing provider	medium national	Agile, Scrum	Non functional	Testing manager Tester (2)
Company C				
Software producer	medium national	Traditional	Functional	Testing manager Tester (2)
Company D				
Software producer	large international	Traditional	Functional	Testing manager (2) Tester (2)

The interviews varied between half an hour and one hour and a half, and were performed on the company premises, in quiet meeting rooms. Each participant was interviewed individually. During the interviews the respondents were encouraged to express their opinions freely and as recommended by Myers and Newman [15], we used a mirroring technique in questions and answers in order to encourage the respondents to share their stories. During the interviews we asked the participants to talk about both current events and to reflect retrospectively on previous scenarios. All interviews were recorded and transcribed, and the transcriptions were sent to each participant for final checking and approval. Notes were also taken with the leading issues for each interview. The transcribed interviews were coded in several rounds.

Starting the process of analyzing the research data available, we first identified the segments of text relevant to the two research questions and discarded those bearing no relation to it. The transcripts were reexamined several times, and the coding process was performed in repeated rounds and the results were peer reviewed and discussed. Afterwards, we proceeded with the coding phase and labelled each segment by means of one or more easily recognizable terms or categories, using a software tool designed for qualitative analysis (NVivo 10) in which we imported all the transcripts. Afterwards the codes were analyzed and similar codes were aggregated into more general codes in order to reduce the number of codes utilized and retrieve the emerging categories. We derived the categories using the framework provided in the studies by Beecham et al. [2] as a model for constructing a list of characteristics for software testers. Each category and code can be linked to quotations from the interviews and these are used to strengthen and enhance the results. The list combining characteristics from both studies [2] and [3] and our proposal is available in Appendix A.

4   Results

In this section we present and describe the characteristics of software testers derived from the study during the qualitative analyze process. Table 2 shows the characteristics sorted in quantitative descendent order starting from the characteristics mentioned by the higher number of participants:

Table 2. Characteristics of software testers

Most wanted tester characteristics	Rank	Most wanted tester characteristics	Rank
Communication skills	7	Diplomacy	3
IT background	6	Need for challenge	3
Need for variety	6	Domain knowledge	3
Details oriented	5	Courage	3
Curious	4	Creative	2
Passion for quality	4	Proactive	2
Patient	4	Structured	2
Testing experience	4	Team player	2
Achievement orientated	3	Mind set to find bugs	2

Communication

Good communication skills is the most cited characteristic. Participants mentioned that during the communication process the testers must be able to know how to provide the right information and how to communicate it properly to the parties involved. *"The communication characteristic, both oral and by writing is very important in a team because we often give some bad news (defects or problems) and it must be communicated in a way that do not blame anyone for it."* (Tester Manager, Company C

A tester is required to communicate with different project team members, managers, sometimes clients, to report defects, discuss and follow them up with the developers: *"The tester needs communication skills in order to communicate with the project manager, developers and the users, and he has to make them understandable to each other"* (Tester, Company C)

IT Background

Possessing an IT background refers to having an education and/or knowledge within computer science fields. Interviewees in this study held programming knowledge and experience, as valuable assets due to the expertise accumulated which can help in certain testing activities. *"A development experience can help a lot. All the knowledge I gain while working as a developer, helped me in my testing work."* (Tester, Company A)

An IT background was considered an important characteristic for a tester by our interviewees. The IT background proved valuable when communicating with the developers.*"In order to speak to a developer and understand what they are talking about, an IT background is a very good thing"*. (Tester, Company B)

Need for Variety

In all participant companies the **Need for variety** characteristic was often cited as a positive trait due to the varying nature of tasks in which a tester could be involved. A testers who is enjoys having a variety of tasks could adapt better to the different nature responsibilities alongside a project lifecycle starting from the design phase until the maintenance stage. *"The biggest factor for me is that you do different things, it's very varied and you get to see the whole picture. You can participate from the start of a project to the end doing various things, that's the biggest thing for me, the different things I can do."* (Tester Manager, Company B).

Details Oriented

Being a details oriented person was considered an advantageous skill for a tester among the study participants. *"You have to have an eye for details... you cannot just check the normally expected results. You cannot just test the happy path scenarios".* (Tester Manager, Company B)

Curious

Some of the participant considered that being curious was an incentive for continuously improving the understanding of the product and for pursuing several testing scenarios. Curiosity was also advantageous for coming up with unusual testing scenarios. *"You don't have to be afraid to click on new things and that you are going to break something. That is part of being curious."* (Tester Manager, Company D) *"Curiosity. You should want to learn new things because you will get new software, new projects, new teams all the time"* (Tester, Company B)

Passion for Quality

Some of the participants have expressed their desire to improve the quality in the products they are working on and taking pride in participating in the delivery of a high quality product. They talked about their joy in investigating and finding defects which will lead to a better product. *"I do have a passion for improving the quality and finding defects... I'm happy when I find bugs. Of course, I'm also happy when things are working."* (Tester, Company A)

Patient

Patience was mentioned is being an important requirement for software testers. The testers may need to work outside of regular office with little warning in advance. *"you say: <<today I'll leave at 4>>, but at 3:45 they say <<you have to do this testing before you leave today>>, and you have to work 2 or 3 hours more. That's a part of it"* (Tester Manager, Company D)

Patience was considered critical in situations where often and recurrently the planned scheduled was discarded and new plans were proposed. *"I think you have to be patient, because usually you are at the end of the cycle and your plans and timetables are going to change, a lot."* (Tester, Company A)

Testing Experience
The interviewees thought that testing experience and testing knowledge could improve the design skills such as writing Test Cases: *"Defining the TC's is very important and you find all kind of situations where you need quite a lot of fantasy, since you have to go further than the developers go. And that has a lot to do with experience"* (Tester Manager, Company A)

Experience with requirements engineering was also valued among the interviewed testing participants: *"I would like them to have some competency in requirements, how should requirements be, because often they will be asked to review requirements and provide feedback."* (Tester Manager, Company D)

5   Discussion

The answer to RQ1, *"What are the characteristics perceived as important of software testers?"* can be constructed by starting from the information provided in Table 2. Communication skills are seen as a valuable characteristic both from the participants of this study and from the research literature. During the **communication** process the testers must be able to know how to provide the right information and how to communicate it properly to the parties involved. For example, management may not be interested in the details of every defect that has been located. They are interested in the overall quality of a release and if the release can go in production. Testers have to be able to write clear defects reports and they also must be able to describe a problem while taking into consideration the type of interlocutors: *"The communication characteristic, both oral and by writing is very important in a team because we often give some bad news (defects or problems) and it must be communicated in a way that do not blame anyone for it."* (Tester Manager, Company C).

One contrasting results with [2] and [3] is that the three most rated characteristics, growth orientation, need for independence and low need for social interaction associated with introverts did not score high with our participants. The characteristic of being Introverted was not mentioned at all in our interviews. This seems to be one of the strong difference between a tester and a developer. If you are introverted, then spending most of your workday behind a computer screen alone, as a developer, is a good choice, but not necessarily for a tester. Testers often have to report problems and they have to be comfortable with conflict [7], which lead to a vast amount of communication on daily basis. They have to learn a new product or feature in short time and posses or develop an ability, so a certain need for variety and curiosity might prove the right incentive. A note of caution should be taken for this characteristic, the **need of variety** is a useful trait in a domain where you might often need to acquire new knowledge of a new topic, but a strong need for variety may clash with the possible monotonous nature of some testing activities and desired characteristics such as patience and tolerance to tedium which corroborate the findings of Pettichord [7].

If we compare our results with the characteristics derived from studies for Software Engineers [2] and [3], we notice that communication is not mentioned among the study's result, which leads us to the conclusion that communication skills is a specific valuable trait for a tester, hence proving an answer for our second research question: *"Are there specific characteristics that separates software testers from a software engineer?"*.

Other characteristics which were not present in [2] and [3] are patience and curiosity. Patience is a virtue, especially among testers. They might invest a lot of effort in testing a new release and it may turn out that an incorrect version was deployed, so all their test results are worthless. During the testing process, testers might encounter opposition, aggression or debating situations which require patience. A tester might need to listen to the comments, criticism and deal with frustrated colleagues or managers on a daily basis. Software Testing can and should be seen as a journey for discovering and exploring freshly delivered software. A curious and inquisitive mind will be important to understand the why and how of products, their interactions and dependencies.

In most of the existing studies on testing domain knowledge and testing experience are ranked highly, but our participant emphasised the need for an IT background. This type of background can provide knowledge and language which will improve the testers ability to write technical reports, relate and discuss with developers.

One company valued the domain knowledge above the technical ones due to the sensitivity and complexity for the of business they were involved in. One possible explanation is that in some of the participant organizations, parts of testing are done by non-specialized software testers alongside their other activities, or as a temporary task according to the projects' needs. In these cases, the people performing the testing usually lack testing skills, experience, and training which can lead to difficulties when communicating with more technical member of the team and when reporting defects. This situation was also described in Pol's study [9], and one of the consequences is that testing is seen as a job anyone can do.

As explained by Black [8], we have to remind ourselves and be aware that different levels of testing requires different skills. Unit testing requires programming and software development skills, while specialized tester are doing functional testing. When the process reach the level of acceptance or beta testing the most fitted testers are the one with best user knowledge such as people from customer support or business analysts. One negative aspect of this practice will be to rely too much on borrowing people from support group for testing, since they might not have sufficient knowledge for testing at earlier stages.

Limitations and Threats to Validity

In order to avoid threats to validity presented by Robson [16] in this kind of research, we ensured observer triangulation by having the data analyzed by three researchers, while the collected data and the results of this study were compared with our earlier quantitative study [17], which allowed us to apply data and method triangulation.

We are aware that the low number of participants is a limitation and given the high number of variables playing an important role in the survey, the results of this study should be considered as preliminary. However, since the focus was on depth rather than breadth we still think that the participants provided a typical sample giving us a lot of input and perspectives. Since increasing the number of participants could reveal more details and strengthen the conclusion of this study, our plan is to further expand our research by inviting new companies and increase the total number of interviewees. In addition, we will enhance our target population by inviting developers and project managers to take part our study. This augmentation could provide us with valuable information on the desirable characteristics for testers as seen from the developers perspective and from a higher managerial angle.

In addition to the small sample research, other factors such as the organizational mode or the type of product might influence the characteristics which were most valued or encountered in the participant companies. Nevertheless, our qualitative analysis spanned across four companies with mixed sizes and methodologies, involved in national and international business, handling data with medium or high risk. The participants were involved in performing functional and non-functional testing, and were coming from a mixed background with some having good technical skills and an IT background, while other were poses more strength in the domain business knowledge. All the mentioned factors could give better generalizability of findings than performing interviews in just one company [15].

6   Conclusion

In this paper we present the results of a qualitative survey among four Norwegian companies and the characteristics which were perceived as most valuable for a software tester. We contrasted our results with exiting work on software engineers' characteristics and noticed that the most frequent cited characteristics for software engineers were not applicable to software testers. A strong emphasis was laid on communication skills and on IT background which implied programming knowledge and certain technical capabilities. Testing knowledge and domain knowledge were also valued but not as strongly as found in previous research conducted Beer and Ramler [11]. Testing experience was considered to be an advantage especially for the testers involved in domains with volatile requirements which seems to be in line with Martin, Rooksby et al. [10] earlier study.

The list of characteristics provided by our study should not be seen as exhaustive or definitive but rather as a starting point and each company should consider the type of knowledge they value at hiring and the ability to provide internal training for testing or domain knowledge for their relevant business.

Acknowledgment. We are very grateful to the companies and their employees for their contribution to this project. Also, we would like to thank to Torgeir Dingsøyr at the Norwegian University of Science and Technology, for comments of versions of this article.

References

1. Rooksby, J., Rouncefield, M., Sommerville, I.: Testing in the Wild: The Social and Organisational Dimensions of Real World Practice. Comput. Support. Coop. Work. 18, 559–580 (2009)
2. Beecham, S., Baddoo, N., Hall, T., Robinson, H., Sharp, H.: Motivation in Software Engineering: A systematic literature review. Inf. Softw. Technol. 50, 860–878 (2008)
3. Franca, A.C.C., Gouveia, T.B., Santos, P.C.F., Santana, C.A., da Silva, F.Q.B.: Motivation in software engineering: a systematic review update. In: 15th Annual Conference on Evaluation & Assessment in Software Engineering (EASE 2011), pp. 154–163. IET (2011)
4. DeMarco, T., Lister, T.: Peopleware: Productive Projects and Teams. Dorset House (1999)
5. Shah, H., Harrold, M.J., Sinha, S.: Global software testing under deadline pressure: Vendor-side experiences. Inf. Softw. Technol. 56, 6–19 (2014)
6. Cohen, C.F., Birkin, S.J., Garfield, M.J., Webb, H.W.: Managing conflict in software testing. Commun. ACM. 47, 76–81 (2004)
7. Pettichord, B.: Testers and developers think differently: Understanding and utilizing the diverse traits of key players on your team. Softw. Test. Qual. Eng. 2, 42–45 (2000)
8. Black, R.: Managing the Testing Process – Practical Tools and Techniques for Managing Hardware and Software Testing. Wiley Publishing Inc., New York (2002)
9. Pol, M., Teunissen, R., Veenendaal, E., van, S.T.: A Guide to the TMap Approach. Pearson Education (2002)
10. Martin, D., Rooksby, J., Rouncefield, M., Sommerville, I.: "Good" Organisational Reasons for "Bad" Software Testing: An Ethnographic Study of Testing in a Small Software Company. In: 29th International Conference on Software Engineering (ICSE 2007), pp. 602–611. IEEE (2007)
11. Beer, A., Ramler, R.: The Role of Experience in Software Testing Practice. In: 2008 34th Euromicro Conference Software Engineering and Advanced Applications. pp. 258–265. IEEE (2008)
12. Iivonen, J., Mantyla, M., Itkonen, J.: Characteristics of High Performing Testers – A Case Study. In: Proceedings of the 2010 ACM-IEEE International Symposium on Empirical Software Engineering and Measurement, p. 1. ACM (2010)
13. Taipale, O., Smolander, K.: Improving software testing by observing practice. In: Proc. 2006 ACM/IEEE Int. Symp. Int. Symp. Empir. Softw. Eng. - ISESE 2006, p. 262 (2006)
14. Riungu, L.M., Taipale, O., Smolander, K.: Software Testing as an Online Service: Observations from Practice. In: 2010 Third Int. Conf. Softw. Testing, Verif. Valid. Work, pp. 418–423 (2010)
15. Myers, M.D., Newman, M.: The qualitative interview in IS research: Examining the craft. Inf. Organ. 17, 2–26 (2007)
16. Robson, C.: Real World Research, 2nd. Edn. Blackwell Publ., Malden (2002)
17. Deak, A., Stalhane, T.: Organization of Testing Activities in Norwegian Software Companies. In: 2013 IEEE Sixth International Conference on Software Testing, Verification and Validation Workshops. pp. 102–107. IEEE (2013)

7   Appendix

Characteristics for software engineers

Proposing study	Software Engineer characteristics	Frequency
Beecham 01	Growth orientated	9
	Introverted	7
	Autonomous	7
	Need for stability	5
	Technically competent	5
	Need to be sociable	5
	Achievement orientated	4
	Need for competent supervising	4
	Need for variety	4
	Need for challenge	4
	Need to make a contribution	3
	Need for feedback	2
	Marketable	2
	Creative	2
	Need for involvement in personal goal setting	1
	Need for Geographic stability	1
França01	Competent in Management	2
	Flexible / Team worker (easy to work with)	2
	Have fear of punishment	1
Our study	**Communication**	

A Customizable Monitoring Infrastructure for Hardware/Software Embedded Systems

Martial Chabot and Laurence Pierre

TIMA Lab. (CNRS-INPG-UJF),
46 Av. Félix Viallet, 38031 Grenoble, France

Abstract. The design of today's embedded systems requires a complex verification process. In particular, due to the strong hardware/software interdependence, debugging the embedded software is a demanding task. We have previously reported our results about the development of a framework that enables the Assertion-Based Verification (ABV) of temporal requirements for high-level reference models of such systems. In this paper, we describe conceptual and practical improvements of this monitoring infrastructure to give the user the possibility to customize and to optimize the verification process. Experimental results on industrial case studies illustrate the benefits of the approach.

1 Introduction

With the increasing complexity of systems on chips (SoC) and time-to-market pressure, rising the abstraction level to *ESL* (Electronic System Level) modeling is becoming indispensable. *Platform-based design* emerges as a new paradigm for the design and analysis of embedded systems [1]. In that context, SystemC TLM (*Transaction Level Modeling*) [2] is gaining acceptance, in particular because the simulation of TLM models is several orders of magnitude faster, thus considerably improving productivity in SoC design [3]. SystemC [4] is in fact a C++ library; a SystemC model is made of modules that have I/O ports and can run processes. They are interconnected using *channels*. A SoC model includes modules that are models of microprocessors (ISS, Instruction Set Simulator) which execute embedded software, busses, memories, hardware coprocessors like DSP (Digital Signal Processor), DMAs (Direct Memory Access, components that perform memory transfers),... In a transaction-level model (TLM), the details of communication among components are separated from the details of computation [5]. Transaction requests take place by calling interface functions of the channel models.

The challenge addressed here is Assertion-Based Verification (ABV) for complex SoCs modeled at the System level in SystemC TLM. Requirements to be verified at this level of abstraction express *temporal constraints* on the interactions (between hardware and software components) in the SoC. They can be formalized with a language such as the FL (Foundation Language) class of the IEEE standard PSL [6], which essentially represent linear temporal logic (LTL).

M.G. Merayo and E. Montes de Oca (Eds.): ICTSS 2014, LNCS 8763, pp. 173–179, 2014.

In [7] we have presented a methodology that enables the runtime verification of PSL assertions for TLM specifications: *assertion checkers* (monitors) are automatically generated from PSL properties, and the design is instrumented with these monitors using an ad hoc observation mechanism. Then, the SystemC simulation is run as usual, and the assertion checkers dynamically report property violations, if any. In that context, simulation traces must be sampled according to *communication actions* involved in the assertions, hence the observation mechanism detects the communication functions calls and triggers the monitors accordingly. A prototype tool called ISIS has been developed; experimental results on industrial case studies have been reported in [8], [9].

However, this original version of the tool offers few flexibility to the user. It is only possible to select, at the SystemC compile time, the assertions/monitors to be attached to the design. We present here conceptual extensions of the underlying observation model, and their implementation, that enable the designers - in particular the software developers - to customize and optimize the verification process and to get concise and easily analyzable verification results.

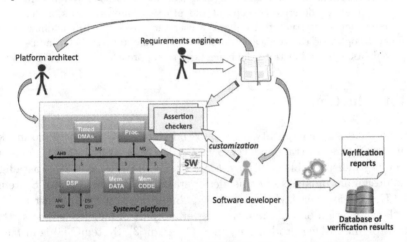

Fig. 1. Customizable Assertion-Based Verification infrastructure

2   A Customizable ABV Infrastructure

While acknowledging the tangible benefits of this verification environment, industrial partners noticed some matters of improvement. The ABV infrastructure pictured by Figure 1 targets the following characteristics:

- the SystemC platform is used by the software designer to develop the application, but he usually does not wish to recompile the platform (or even has it only under executable form). Hence selecting the assertions to be attached to the design should be feasible *at runtime*, not at the SystemC compile time,
- more essentially, it should be possible to configure the instrumented simulation to take into account relationships between assertions to dynamically disable/enable monitors, thus *clarifying and optimizing the verification*,

– it should also be possible to store concise information about assertions activations, satisfactions, violations, and to *easily analyze verification results.*

2.1 Configuration without Platform Recompilation

The assertion checkers generated from the PSL expression of the requirements,
and the observation mechanism, are SystemC modules that instrument the SystemC platform. ISIS takes as input the platform source files and an XML configuration file that specifies the selected assertions, and produces this instrumented
design. With the original version of the tool, the user must execute again this
procedure, and recompile the resulting platform, every time he wants to choose
other requirements to be checked. The tool has been improved to generate an
instrumented source code that import all the assertion checkers but enables their
optional runtime instantiation, according to choices given in a configuration file.

2.2 Monitors Enabling/Disabling

The observation mechanism is based on a model, inspired from the observer
pattern, that allows to observe the transactional actions in the system and to
trigger the monitors when needed [7]. Each monitor is enclosed in a wrapper
that *observes* the channels and/or signals involved in the property associated
with this monitor; the channels/signals are *observable* objects (or *Subjects*).

Originally, the assertion checkers remain active all along the simulation. However, requirements are usually *correlated* (not by purely *logical* relations, that
could be identified by subsumption detection [10], but by *conceptual* relations,
determined by the designer). The tool has been enhanced to *enable/disable monitors* according to these relations. The model has been extended with a *Verification Manager* component, as described by the class diagram of Figure 2.

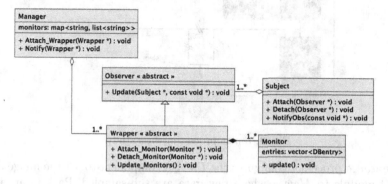

Fig. 2. Extended model - Verification manager

A Manager can include a collection of wrappers, and takes care of the associated monitors. By means of a configuration file, the user specifies relations of
the form $A_i \; \mathcal{R} \; A_j$ which express that, if assertion A_i experiences violations, then

checking assertion A_j becomes worthless. The Manager can be configured such that, when it detects that the monitor of A_i reports violations, either it only disables A_i immediately (Level 1), or it also disables the monitor of A_j (Level 2). As illustrated in section 3, this has two main advantages: simulation traces *only include the most relevant information* provided by the checkers, thus simplifying the interpretation of the verification results; the CPU time overhead induced by the checkers *may be minimized*, thus optimizing the verification process.

2.3   Database with Verification Results

To ease the analysis of the verification results, in addition to the textual verification reports, verification results are now stored in a database. To achieve this, the *Monitor* class has been extended with a member which is a vector of database entries (see Fig. 2). During a simulation, the monitor stores here the information about every assertion activation: start time, end time, status (pass or fail). This information is ultimately committed to the database. A post-processing tool extracts a concise and easily analyzable tabular representation of the results. Other post-processing tools e.g., for statistical analysis, are under development.

3   Experimental Results

3.1   Space High Resolution Image Processing

This case study (from Astrium) is an image processing platform that performs spectral compression, see Figure 3. It mainly includes two processors, *leon_a* and *leon_b*, two DMA components, memories, a FFT coprocessor, and an IO module.

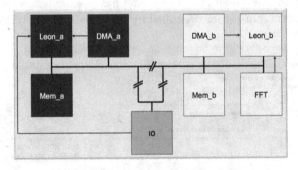

Fig. 3. Image processing case study

The *leon_a* processor configures the *DMA_a* component to get the image from the *IO* module to *Mem_a* where raw data are sub-sampled. Packets are then transferred to *Mem_b* and a 2D-FFT is applied to obtain the corresponding spectrum. The resulting packets are then compressed by the *leon_b* processor which configures *DMA_b* to send the output packets back to the *IO* module. Process synchronization is ensured by software. A set of requirements has been defined for this platform, some of them are presented below:

- A_1: *DMA_a must not be reconfigured before the end of a transfer.*
- A_2: *The FFT must not be reconfigured before the end of a computation.*
- A_3 (no loss of input data): *Every input data packet must be transferred by DMA_a to Mem_a before the IO module generates a new interrupt.*
- A_4 (software not too slow): *Every data packet stored in Mem_a must be processed by leon_a before being overwritten* (note: Mem_a is 32 MB large)
- A_5 (no loss of processed data): *Each incoming data packet* (read by DMA_a from the IO module) *must have a corresponding output packet* (written by DMA_b to the IO module), *before 3 new incoming data packets are processed.*

There are conceptual dependencies between these requirements. For example, if A_3 is violated (meaning that input data are lost), the results of A_5 become irrelevant because paying attention to the loss of output data is useless, the bug revealed by A_3 must first be fixed. Property A_2 however might still be enabled, to continue checking the interactions between *leon_b* and its FFT coprocessor. Table 1 summarizes results for processing 10000 images, with configurations that can induce data loss: CPU times, total number of checkers activations (notifications on function calls), and of checkers actual triggerings. Column 1 is for the raw simulations, column 2 gives the full monitoring results (Level 0), column 3 corresponds to Level 1 of the Manager, columns 4 and 5 correspond to Level 2, with the management of one or several assertion correlations. Assertion A_4 is the most time-consuming one (it may require several thousands of concurrent monitor instances), configurations in which it may be disabled are optimum.

3.2 Avionics Flight Control Remote Module

This case study (from Airbus) is an avionics module dedicated to processing data from sensors and controlling actuators according to predefined flight laws. Certification issues and specific safety requirements must be taken into account. Properties are associated with the joint behaviour of the software and the DSP coprocessor (see Figure 4). This component stores and uses data that represent digital filter coefficients and analog input (ANI) calibration coefficients. Data integrity must be checked, to protect the device against SEU (Single Event Upset, change of state caused by energetic particles). Among the requirements:

- A'_1 : *Checksum computation must be performed every CHECKSUM_PERIOD ms* (the corresponding result is stored in the register STATUS of the DSP).
- A'_2 (ensures detection of potential checksum errors): *The software must read the content of STATUS every CHECK_PERIOD ms.*
- A'_3 : *When a checksum error is detected (wrong value in STATUS), the DSP function must be deactivated (within LIMIT ms).*

Those properties are clearly intercorrelated. Table 1 summarizes some results, for the processing of 25000 analog data coming from the ANI port, with configurations that can induce missed deadlines. Here full monitoring is not really time-consuming (about 2% CPU time overhead), therefore the benefit rather comes from the fact that the number of assertions triggerings significantly decreases, hence making the results more conveniently analyzable because avoiding

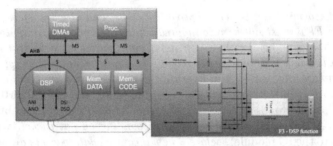

Fig. 4. Flight control case study

Table 1. Comparative results for various manager configurations

	Raw simulation	Full monitoring	Violation detect. (Level 1)	Level 2, 1 correlation	Several correlations
Image proc.	71.10 s	211.2 s $1311\ 10^6$ activ. $2.13\ 10^6$ trigerrings	219 s $1310\ 10^6$ activ. $2.11\ 10^6$ trig.	$A_3\ \mathcal{R}\ A_5$ 213.84 s $1310\ 10^6$ activ. $2.1\ 10^6$ trig.	$\forall j, A_3\ \mathcal{R}\ A_j$ 72.68 s 461340 activ. 632 trig.
Flight control	52.41 s	53.5 s $1.2\ 10^6$ activ. 67 trigerrings	52.84 s 860000 activ. 58 trigerrings	$A_1'\ \mathcal{R}\ A_2'$ 52.57 s 500000 activ. 8 trigerrings	$\forall j, A_1'\ \mathcal{R}\ A_j'$ 52.52 s 135000 activ. 7 trigerrings

irrelevant trigerrings means that only the most useful information appears in the simulation trace.

4 Conclusion

The results show that this version of the ABV tool can significantly improve the efficiency of the instrumented simulations (e.g., fifth column of the first row), and can produce more easily analyzable results, which is crucial to facilitate debug. On-going work includes the identification of correlations between monitoring results and specific patterns in the simulation traces.

References

1. Carloni, L., De Bernardinis, F., Pinello, C., Sangiovanni-Vincentelli, A., Sgroi, M.: Platform-Based Design for Embedded Systems,
   http://citeseerx.ist.psu.edu/viewdoc/summary?doi=10.1.1.66.7365
2. Grötker, T., Liao, S., Martin, G., Swan, S.: System Design with SystemC. Kluwer Academic Pub. (2002)
3. Klingauf, W., Burton, M., Günzel, R., Golze, U.: Why We Need Standards for Transaction-Level Modeling. SOC Central (2007)
4. IEEE Std 1666-2005, IEEE Standard SystemC Language Ref. Manual (2005)

5. Cai, L., Gajski, D.: Transaction Level Modeling: An Overview. In: Proc. International Conference CODES+ISSS 2003 (2003)
6. IEEE Std 1850-2005, Standard for Property Specification Language, PSL (2005)
7. Pierre, L., Ferro, L.: A Tractable and Fast Method for Monitoring SystemC TLM Specifications. IEEE Transactions on Computers 57 (2008)
8. Ferro, L., Pierre, L., Bel Hadj Amor, Z., Lachaize, J., Lefftz, V.: Runtime Verification of Typical Requirements for a Space Critical SoC Platform. In: Salaün, G., Schätz, B. (eds.) FMICS 2011. LNCS, vol. 6959, pp. 21–36. Springer, Heidelberg (2011)
9. Pierre, L., Ferro, L., Bel Hadj Amor, Z., Bourgon, P., Quévremont, J.: Integrating PSL Properties into SystemC Transactional Modeling - Application to the Verification of a Modem SoC. In: Proc. IEEE SIES 2012 (2012)
10. Biere, A.: Resolve and expand. In: Hoos, H.H., Mitchell, D.G. (eds.) SAT 2004. LNCS, vol. 3542, pp. 59–70. Springer, Heidelberg (2005)

Towards Testing
Self-organizing, Adaptive Systems

Benedikt Eberhardinger, Hella Seebach, Alexander Knapp, and Wolfgang Reif

Institute for Software & Software Engineering, University of Augsburg, Germany
{benedikt.eberhardinger,seebach,knapp,reif}@informatik.uni-augsburg.de

Abstract. The characteristics of self-adaptive, self-organizing systems lead to a significant higher flexibility and robustness against a changing environment. This flexibility makes it hard to test these systems adequately. To assure their quality, however, it is inevitable to do so. We introduce a new approach for systematically testing these self-* systems based on a feedback control-oriented system architecture called Corridor Enforcing Infrastructure (CEI). Thus, it is possible to examine particular situations, where the system is forced to reorganize or adapt to new situations. This is where the self-* mechanisms come into play and can be tested separately.

Keywords: Self-Organizing Systems, Adaptive Systems, Software Engineering, Software Testing, Multi-Agent Systems, Quality Assurance.

1 Introduction

For many years, nature has been a source of inspiration for the design of information systems, e.g., in the research areas of artificial intelligence, multi-agent systems, and self-organizing systems. The core idea is to develop systems by using the so called self-* properties (self-healing, self-configuring, and self-optimizing), which correspond to biological mechanisms. The foundation of many of the self-* properties is self-organization (SO). SO enables a restructuring of the system and its components in order to conform to its environment to fulfill its goals. This new flexibility leads to challenges in engineering these systems. For example, the behavior can not be specified fully at design-time and adaptation decisions are moved to run-time. This makes it hard to assure that those systems fulfill their requirements, but even more necessary to take appropriate measures. In this connection testing plays a decisive role. The pivotal question is how to handle the state space of a self-organizing, adaptive systems (SOAS) which is developing in an evolutionary fashion during the execution of the system.

Our approach for testing is based on the *Corridor Enforcing Infrastructure (CEI)*, an architectural pattern for SOAS. The CEI uses the concepts of feedback-loops to continuously observe and control the system if necessary. On that account monitoring is used to achieve situational awareness which is prerequisite to organize the system in a way to fulfill its requirements. The bulk of concepts and techniques used in the CEI for controlling and organizing the system is triggered

M.G. Merayo and E. Montes de Oca (Eds.): ICTSS 2014, LNCS 8763, pp. 180–185, 2014.

by the violation of constraints. An error-free CEI will consequently guarantee a system that fulfills its requirements at every time. On this account, we claim that testing SOAS can be achieved by testing the CEI. Here we benefit from specific characteristics: we are able to reduce the relevant state space of the system to be tested tremendously and to gain a clear distinction between correct and incorrect behavior out of the concepts of the CEI—essential for evaluating the tests. SOAS are highly distributed systems—making them hard to test—and are interacting locally to solve problems. This locality is exploited in our approach, because many test cases focus on single agents or small agent groups of which the system is composed; this focus make it easier to execute and evaluate them.

In the following sections we will discuss related work and describe our approach for testing SOAS, which is based on concepts of the CEI that are introduced in Sec. 3 and concepts to reveal failures out of the CEI in Sec. 4.

2   Related Work

The necessity of testing adaptive systems has been recognized in the testing community [8,9,12] as well as in the community of adaptive systems [5,11]. Both run-time and design-time approaches have considered indeterminism and the emergent behavior as main challenges for testing adaptive systems.

Run-time approaches for testing take up the paradigm of run-time verification [3,7,4]. They shift testing into run-time to be able to observe and test, i.a., the adaption to new situations. Camara et al. [1] are using these concepts to consider fully integrated systems. The authors simulate the environment of the system to investigate its adaptive capabilities, and to collect data about how the system reacts. The sampled data is then combined with a probabilistic model of the system and used as input for a model checker in order to evaluate given system properties. Similar approaches are taken by Ramirez et al. [10]. They use the sampled data from a simulation to calculate a distance to expected values derived from the goal specification of the system.

Overall the run-time approaches are limited to test the fully integrated system and are only sampling, but not evaluating, data at run-time. We extend this simulation testing of a fully integrated system by a bottom-up testing strategy, starting from single agents, in order to cover testing in the whole software development life cycle. Furthermore, we are able to evaluate the runs online without complex model checking on the system level with the usage of the CEI.

Design-time approaches for testing adaptive systems [8,9,12] are focusing on specific subsets, e.g., the implementation of single agents. Zhang et al. [12] are focusing on testing the execution of plans of single agents and groups of agents. This focal point does not allow to evaluate adaptive or even self-organizing characteristics of the system, contrary to our approach.

In conclusion, testing adaptive systems is in focus of some research groups. However, none of them is extending the techniques to self-organizing systems which are able to form emergent behavior. We aim to deal with SO in all its facets and therefore combine run- and design-time testing techniques.

3   The Corridor Enforcing Infrastructure: Enabler for Systematic, Automatic Testing of SOAS

The CEI is an architectural pattern for SOAS, based on decentralized feedback-loops used to monitor and control single agents or small groups of agents in order to enforce that all system requirements are fulfilled at all times. The decentralization follows from a modular system structure where the system requirements are addressed to single or small groups of autonomous agents. An error-free CEI makes it unnecessary to test concrete system states, because the CEI guarantees that all states fulfill the system requirements. Consequently, only the CEI and its mechanisms must be tested instead of the whole SOAS en bloc, this significantly reduces the test effort.

The CEI is based on the concept of the corridor of correct behavior (CCB) which is formally introduced by Güdemann et al. [6]. The corridor is formed by all requirements, realized as constraints, of the considered system. An exemplary corridor is shown in Fig. 1. If all constraints are fulfilled, the system is inside the corridor. Otherwise, the system leaves the corridor, indicated by a flash in Fig. 1, this demands that the system is transitioned into a safe-mode. Furthermore, the system has to be reorganized to return to a state within the corridor; this is shown through the check mark in Fig. 1. An error would occur if a transition outside of the corridor is taken, indicated by a cross in Fig. 1. The CEI implementation

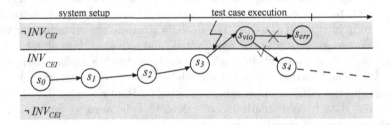

Fig. 1. Schematical state-based view of the corridor of correct behavior and the different phases of testing SOAS. INV_{CEI} is the conjunction of all constraints of the system controlled by the CEI.

of the CCB is based on a monitoring and controlling infrastructure. The monitoring infrastructure observes the system and detects a violation of the corridor; in some cases it can be (semi-)automatically generated from the requirement documents of the system, as shown by Eberhardinger et al. [2]. The controlling infrastructure ensures that the system is transitioned into a safe mode when the constraints are violated and reorganizes the system that all requirements are fulfilled again.

The CEI and its mechanisms will be tested in order to validate that the SOAS fulfills all requirements at all times. Several failures can occur independently due to the SO mechanisms used in the controlling infrastructure, e.g., genetic algorithms or constraint solving. Our SOAS testing approach examines special situations where the system is confronted with environmental situations in which SO or adaptation is required and the CEI stressed. In the next section we will outline how to cope with this in our testing concepts in more detail.

4   Environmental Variation Scenarios: Forcing the CEI to Reveal Failures

To force the CEI to reveal failures we use test scenarios which stress this infrastructure. We apply a compositional test strategy which is geared to the classic testing strategies unit testing, integration testing, and system testing. Thus, we are able to form a test process for the whole development cycle.

The nature of the mechanisms within the CEI are on adapting and reorganizing the system to react to its changing environment. Thus, we aim to automatically generate so called environmental variation scenarios (EVS) for testing the mechanisms of the CEI. For a *single agent*, this means in fact we want to validate that changes in the environment are detected via sensors used by the monitoring infrastructure and the agent adapts accordingly to fulfill its goals. The input for the agent can be simulated by mocking in the test system without setting up complex initial states. We automatically extract the EVS from the specification of the agents and use them for testing. For this purpose we have to take a closer look at the behavioral model (e.g., state machines) of the agents to derive a model of their interactions with the environment. To build the EVS from these models we use model checking techniques that find sequences in which the interaction between the agent and its environment leads to a violation of the CCB, illustrated by a flash in Fig. 1. Such a violation has to be detected by checking the system state according to the CCB through the monitoring-infrastructure. It must be pointed out that such violations are no failures of the CEI, but the CEI has to detect them and take the adequate actions.

The EVS are, as introduced, based on single agent situations. This means a fine-grained level of decomposition which also reflects the way the constraints of the CCB are defined and consequently the concepts of the CEI. To be able to test scenarios where several agents are interacting, we need to extend the EVS. Interactions are essential in testing, especially to cover SO mechanisms, since the results of these mechanisms mainly depend on interactions of the participating agents, which lead to restructuring and adaptation of these participating agents. This characteristic has to be reflected in the test scenarios for groups of agents on the *agent interaction level*. Interactions between agents in SOAS use different mechanisms, e.g., stigmergy or simple message passing. These interdependencies have to be taken into account to derive a scenario for a group of agents as well as for a fully integrated system under test. The interactions can be culled from the communication protocols of the system. The scenarios for single agents can now be connected via the possible interactions between agents. The result will be an interaction model for selected scenarios. Because of evolutionarily changing system structures, it is hard to predict which communication scenarios will be executed. But by focusing on the EVS for derivation of test cases, the resulting interaction scenarios are just small subsets of the overall system communication and therefore much more manageable in testing. In contrast to the tests for single and separated agents, the execution of EVS for groups of interacting agents can, in general, not be executed without a setup phase, because the mocked up environment is increasingly replaced by real, interacting agents. The needed structures or parameter settings of the mechanisms have to be initialized in a setup phase. This reflects the fact that the SO mechanisms are sometimes based on evolutionary algorithms, e.g., genetic algorithms can be used for calculating new interaction structures in an agent group and therefore the needed edge weights have to be trained initially before the execution of a test case.

Subsequent to single agent and agent interaction the next step is—analogously to classical system testing—to test the *fully integrated system*. All mocked-up components will be replaced by real agents. To minimize the overhead for setup we combine test cases so that they can be executed in sequence. In order to connect the scenarios it is necessary that the system state of a completed test case matches with the needed system state a next test case. We use search-based techniques to retrieve the matching scenarios. Furthermore, it is of interest to test interleaving scenarios in the fully integrated system to evaluate interdependencies of the self-* mechanisms within the CEI. To form these scenarios we combine agents with the following specifics: agents which know each other, agents which are able to communicate with each other, and agents which cooperate.

Besides developing test strategies we aim at establishing a set of coverage metrics which are focused on the coverage of the CEI. These metrics are reflecting our approach on testing SOAS by using the CEI. Standard coverage metrics make statements on code fragments, logical elements in the code, or on control/program flow coverage. For our testing approach the significance of classical coverage metrics is no longer sufficient. Based on the concepts of input space partitioning we describe the expressiveness characteristics for the input domain. The metrics based on partitioning consequently give evidence on the coverage of each region separated by the defined characteristics. As already stated above the most important characteristics for the mechanisms in the CEI are based on changing environmental situations and interactions between agents. Consequently, we will use these features to partition the input space. Based on this partitioning different kinds of combinatorial metrics can be retrieved and used for SOAS. The resulting metrics are able to cope with indeterministic, evolutionary structures of SOAS by benefiting from the CEI concepts.

5   Conclusion and Outlook

We outlined an approach to cope with the complexity which arises from the flexibility of SOAS. For this purpose, we briefly introduced the architectural pattern called CEI that enables systematic, (semi-)automatic testing of SOAS. The concept of the CCB is used to form EVS. We generate these scenarios to accelerate the system to adapt and reorganize to new situations in order to investigate the CEI. To make a statement about the adequacy of the performed tests and to select concrete test cases, we introduced metrics in the context of the CEI. Overall, this constitutes a research agenda towards testing self-organizing, adaptive systems.

References

1. Camara, J., Lemos, R.D.: Evaluation of resilience in self-adaptive systems using probabilistic model-checking. In: Proc. 2012 ICSE Wsh. Software Engineering for Adaptive and Self-Managing Systems (SEAMS 2012), pp. 53–62 (2012)
2. Eberhardinger, B., Steghöfer, J.-P., Nafz, F., Reif, W.: Model-driven synthesis of monitoring infrastructure for reliable adaptive multi-agent systems. In: Proc. 24th IEEE Int. Symp. Software Reliability Engineering (ISSRE 2013), pp. 21–30. IEEE (2013)
3. Falcone, Y., Jaber, M., Nguyen, T.-H., Bozga, M., Bensalem, S.: Runtime verification of component-based systems. In: Barthe, G., Pardo, A., Schneider, G. (eds.) SEFM 2011. LNCS, vol. 7041, pp. 204–220. Springer, Heidelberg (2011)
4. Filieri, A., Ghezzi, C., Tamburrelli, G.: A formal approach to adaptive software: Continuous assurance of non-functional requirements. Formal Asp. Comp. 24(2), 163–186 (2012)
5. Fredericks, E.M., Ramirez, A.J., Cheng, B.H.C.: Towards run-time testing of dynamic adaptive systems. In: Proc. 8th Int. Symp. Software Engineering for Adaptive and Self-Managing Systems (SEAMS 2013), pp. 169–174. IEEE (2013)
6. Güdemann, M., Nafz, F., Ortmeier, F., Seebach, H., Reif, W.: A specification and construction paradigm for organic computing systems. In: Proc. 2nd IEEE Int. Conf. Self-Adaptive and Self-Organizing Systems, pp. 233–242. IEEE Computer Society (2008)
7. Leucker, M., Schallhart, C.: A brief account of runtime verification. J. Log. Algebr. Program. 78(5), 293–303 (2009)
8. Nguyen, C.D.: Testing Techniques for Software Agents. Ph.D. thesis, Università di Trento (2009)
9. Padgham, L., Thangarajah, J., Zhang, Z., Miller, T.: Model-based test oracle generation for automated unit testing of agent systems. IEEE Trans. Softw. Eng. 39(9), 1230–1244 (2013)
10. Ramirez, A.J., Jensen, A.C., Cheng, B.H.C., Knoester, D.B.: Automatically exploring how uncertainty impacts behavior of dynamically adaptive systems. In: Alexander, P., et al. (eds.) Proc. 26th IEEE/ACM Int. Conf. Automated Software Engineering (ASE 2011), pp. 568–571. IEEE (2011)
11. Wotawa, F.: Adaptive autonomous systems – from the system's architecture to testing. In: Hähnle, R., Knoop, J., Margaria, T., Schreiner, D., Steffen, B. (eds.) ISoLA 2011 Workshops 2011. CCIS, vol. 336, pp. 76–90. Springer, Heidelberg (2012)
12. Zhang, Z., Thangarajah, J., Padgham, L.: Model based testing for agent systems. In: Decker, et al. (eds.) Proc. 8th Int. Conf. on Autonomous Agents and Multiagent Systems (AAMAS 2009), pp. 1333–1334. IFAAMAS (2009)

Design of Prioritized N-Wise Testing

Eun-Hye Choi, Takashi Kitamura, Cyrille Artho, and Yutaka Oiwa

Nat. Inst. of Advanced Industrial Science and Technology, Amagasaki, Japan
{e.choi,t.kitamura,c.artho,y.oiwa}@aist.go.jp

Abstract. N-wise testing is a widely used technique for combinatorial interaction testing. Prioritizing testing reorders test cases by relevance, testing important aspects more thoroughly. We propose a novel technique for N-wise test case generation to satisfy the three distinct prioritization criteria of interaction coverage, weight coverage, and KL divergence. The proposed technique generates small N-wise test cases, where high-priority test cases appear early and frequently. Our early evaluation confirms that the proposed technique improves on existing techniques based on the three prioritization criteria.

Keywords: Combinatorial testing, N-wise testing, prioritized testing.

1 Introduction

N-wise testing ($N = 1, 2, ...$), e. g., *pairwise testing* when $N = 2$, is a widely used technique for combinatorial interaction testing. It is based on a coverage criterion called *interaction coverage*, which stipulates to test all N-tuples of parameter values at least once, given a system under test (SUT) model as sets of parameters, parameter values, and constraints to express parameter interactions.

Recently, techniques for *prioritized N-wise testing*, which covers prioritized test aspects earlier and more thoroughly, have been proposed. This is motivated by practical demand, as resources for testing are often limited in real-world software development. Previous work on prioritized N-wise testing mainly falls into two categories: (1) reordering of test cases based on coverage criteria such as code coverage [2, 8], and (2) generating prioritized test cases given SUT models with user-defined priorities assigned to parameters or values [1, 3, 5, 6]. (We call such models *weighted SUT models*.)

In this paper, we propose a novel approach to prioritizing N-wise testing, along the line of category (2). Our technique for prioritized N-wise test case generation, given weighted SUT models, satisfies the following criteria:

- CO: Higher-priority test cases should appear earlier.
- CF: Higher-priority parameter values should appear more frequently.
- CS: The number of test cases should be as small as possible.

Our proposed technique provides a strategy to achieve a good balance between the three criteria. By considering CO, CF, and CS together, our strategy obtains important test cases early and frequently in a small test suite.

M.G. Merayo and E. Montes de Oca (Eds.): ICTSS 2014, LNCS 8763, pp. 186–191, 2014.

Table 1. An example SUT model with value pairs and weights

(a) An example SUT model. $N=2$.

Parameter:	Value(Weight)
CPU:	AMD(2), Intel(6)
OS:	Mac(1), Ubuntu(1), Win(2)
Browser:	IE(3), Firefox(3), Chrome(3), Safari(3), Opera(3)

(b) All value pairs and weights.

CO	W
AM	3
AU	3
AW	4
IM	7
IU	7
IW	8

CB	W	CB	W
AI	5	II	9
AF	5	IF	9
AC	5	IC	9
AS	5	IS	9
AO	5	IO	9

OB	W	OB	W
MI	4	US	4
MF	4	UO	4
MC	4	WI	5
MS	4	WF	5
MO	4	WC	5
U I	4	WS	5
UF	4	WO	5
UC	4		

The next section describes the state-of-the-art techniques for prioritized N-wise test case generation. It shows that existing techniques only consider some of the criteria. In Section 3, we explain the proposed technique in detail, together with a comparison of our technique with the state-of-the-art techniques using sample data. The last section concludes this paper and proposes future work.

2   Related Work

Our running example, the weighted SUT model shown in Tab. 1-(a), has three parameters: *(OS, CPU, Browser)*. Each parameter has two, three, and five values, respectively. Weights are assigned to values, as specified in parentheses, e. g., value *Win* has weight 2. (For brevity, we do not consider constraints; N-wise constraints can be managed in the initial enumeration phase of our algorithm.) The weight of a value pair is the sum of the weights of its values. Tab. 1-(b) shows all the value pairs and their weights, W, in the model. A test case is a set of value assignments for all parameters. A pairwise (N-wise) test suite is a set of test cases that covers all pairs (N-tuples) of values in the model.

For prioritized N-wise test generation given a weighted SUT model, several techniques have been proposed [1,3,5,6]. Some techniques use priority for *ordering* test cases [1,6], while others use it for balancing the occurrences *(frequency)* of test cases [3,5,7]. Tab. 2(c)−(f) show the test suites generated by these techniques. They all generate test cases one at a time, until all value pairs are covered. We briefly introduce the difference among these methods here. Prioritization criteria are considered when selecting a new test case as follows.

Order-focused prioritization: CTE-XL [6] aims to obtain test cases ordered by weight. It focuses on the weight of values assigned to a new test case. On the other hand, Bryce's technique [1] aims to obtain test cases with better *weight coverage*, as defined in Fig. 1. To this aim, it provides an approximate algorithm to maximize the weight of newly-covered pairs in a new test case.

Both techniques share the advantage that important test cases appear at an earlier stage of a test suite, satisfying criterion CO. The disadvantage is that they do not consider the frequency aspect (CF) at all (see Tab. 2). Furthermore, CTE-XL generates a test suite that is larger than necessary for interaction coverage; this is because it focuses on ordering test cases, rather than improving interaction coverage. Actually, the size of CTE-XL's test suite (18 test cases) is larger than Bryce's (15 test cases), which suffices for satisfying pairwise coverage.

Table 2. Generated test suites by the proposed and previous methods

(a) A1. (CS>CO>CF)

	COB	n	w	p-cov	w-cov	D
1	IWI	3	22	0.097	0.132	2.590
2	IMF	3	20	0.194	0.251	1.551
3	IUC	3	20	0.290	0.371	0.855
4	AWF	3	14	0.387	0.455	0.570
5	AUS	3	12	0.484	0.527	0.385
6	AMI	3	12	0.581	0.599	0.480
7	IWS	2	14	0.645	0.683	0.194
8	IWO	2	14	0.710	0.766	0.088
9	AWC	2	10	0.774	0.826	0.124
10	AMO	2	9	0.839	0.880	0.154
11	IUI	1	4	0.871	0.904	0.117
12	IMC	1	4	0.903	0.928	0.107
13	IUF	1	4	0.935	0.952	0.089
14	IMS	1	4	0.968	0.976	0.085
15	IUO	1	4	1	1	0.074

(b) A2. (CO>CS>CF)

	COB	n	w	p-cov	w-cov	D
1	IWI	3	22	0.097	0.132	2.590
2	IMF	3	20	0.194	0.251	1.551
3	IUC	3	20	0.290	0.371	0.855
4	AWF	3	14	0.387	0.455	0.570
5	IWS	2	14	0.452	0.539	0.304
6	IWO	2	14	0.516	0.623	0.126
7	AMI	3	12	0.613	0.695	0.097
8	AUS	3	12	0.710	0.766	0.088
9	AWC	2	10	0.774	0.826	0.124
10	AMO	2	9	0.839	0.880	0.154
11	IUI	1	4	0.871	0.904	0.117
12	IMC	1	4	0.903	0.928	0.107
13	IUF	1	4	0.935	0.952	0.089
14	IMS	1	4	0.968	0.976	0.085
15	IUO	1	4	1	1	0.074

(c) Bryce's.

	COB	n	w	p-cov	w-cov	D
1	IWI	3	22	0.097	0.132	2.590
2	IMF	3	20	0.194	0.251	1.551
3	AWC	3	14	0.290	0.335	0.816
4	IWS	2	14	0.355	0.419	0.527
5	IWO	2	14	0.419	0.503	0.338
6	IUC	3	20	0.516	0.623	0.126
7	AWF	2	10	0.581	0.683	0.158
8	AMI	3	12	0.677	0.754	0.141
9	AUS	3	12	0.774	0.826	0.124
10	AMO	2	9	0.839	0.880	0.154
11	AUI	1	4	0.871	0.904	0.217
12	AUF	1	4	0.903	0.928	0.290
13	AMC	1	4	0.935	0.952	0.343
14	AMS	1	4	0.968	0.976	0.399
15	AUO	1	4	1	1	0.440

(d) CTE XL.

	COB	n	w	p-cov	w-cov	D
1	IWI	3	22	0.097	0.132	2.590
2	IMF	3	20	0.194	0.251	1.551
3	AWI	2	9	0.258	0.305	1.278
4	AMF	2	8	0.333	0.353	1.407
5	AUC	3	12	0.419	0.425	0.882
6	AMS	2	9	0.484	0.479	0.807
7	AMO	2	9	0.548	0.533	0.766
8	IUC	2	16	0.613	0.629	0.536
9	IUS	2	13	0.677	0.707	0.411
10	IUO	2	13	0.742	0.784	0.337
11	AMI	1	4	0.774	0.808	0.437
12	AMC	1	4	0.806	0.832	0.529
13	AUI	1	4	0.839	0.856	0.609
14	AUF	1	4	0.871	0.880	0.661
15	AWF	1	5	0.903	0.910	0.622
16	AWC	1	5	0.935	0.940	0.603
17	AWS	1	5	0.968	0.970	0.575
18	AWO	1	5	1	1	0.556

(e) PictMaster.

	COB	n	w	p-cov	w-cov	D
1	IWF	3	22	0.097	0.132	2.590
2	IWC	2	14	0.161	0.216	1.897
3	IUC	2	11	0.226	0.281	1.548
4	IWS	2	14	0.290	0.365	1.161
5	IMC	2	11	0.355	0.431	0.967
6	IMO	2	13	0.419	0.509	0.683
7	IUS	1	4	0.452	0.533	0.630
8	IUF	1	4	0.484	0.557	0.620
9	AWC	2	9	0.548	0.611	0.415
10	AWS	1	5	0.581	0.641	0.347
11	IMI	2	13	0.645	0.719	0.159
12	IMS	1	4	0.677	0.743	0.204
13	AUF	2	8	0.742	0.790	0.179
14	IWO	1	5	0.774	0.820	0.111
15	IUO	1	4	0.806	0.844	0.111
16	IWI	1	5	0.839	0.874	0.051
17	AUI	2	9	0.903	0.928	0.038
18	IMF	1	4	0.935	0.952	0.039
19	AMF	1	3	0.968	0.970	0.055
20	AWI	0	0	0.968	0.970	0.039
21	AMC	0	0	0.968	0.970	0.064
22	IUI	0	0	0.968	0.970	0.067
23	AMS	0	0	0.968	0.970	0.089
24	AWO	1	5	1	1	0.075
25	AUC	0	0	1	1	0.102
26	AWF	0	0	1	1	0.109
27	AMI	0	0	1	1	0.136
28	AMO	0	0	1	1	0.156

(f) PICT+Fujimoto's.

	COB	n	w	p-cov	w-cov	D
1	AWC	3	14	0.097	0.084	3.689
2	AMI	3	12	0.194	0.156	2.649
3	IMF	3	20	0.290	0.275	1.413
4	IWI	3	22	0.387	0.407	1.060
5	IUI	2	11	0.452	0.473	0.767
6	IMC	2	13	0.516	0.551	0.759
7	AUC	2	7	0.581	0.593	0.790
8	AUO	2	9	0.645	0.647	0.629
9	IWO	2	14	0.710	0.731	0.444
10	IMO	1	4	0.742	0.754	0.439
11	AUF	2	9	0.806	0.808	0.442
12	AWF	1	5	0.839	0.838	0.424
13	AUS	2	9	0.903	0.892	0.328
14	IWS	2	14	0.968	0.976	0.200
15	AMS	1	4	1	1	0.239
16	IWI	0	0	1	1	0.183
17	IWF	0	0	1	1	0.139
18	IWC	0	0	1	1	0.105
19	IWS	0	0	1	1	0.077
20	IWO	0	0	1	1	0.054
21	IMI	0	0	1	1	0.049
22	IUF	0	0	1	1	0.042
23	IWC	0	0	1	1	0.030
24	IWS	0	0	1	1	0.021
25	IMO	0	0	1	1	0.015
26	IUI	0	0	1	1	0.014
27	IWF	0	0	1	1	0.010
28	IWC	0	0	1	1	0.007

n: Number of new value pairs
w: Weight of new value pairs
p-cov: Pairwise coverage
w-cov: Weight coverage
D: KL Divergence

Frequency-focused prioritization: PICT [3], PictMaster [7], and Fujimoto's method [5] obtain higher-priority values more frequently; in our example, for parameter *OS*, value *Win* with weight 2 should appear twice as frequently as values *Mac* and *Ubuntu* with weight 1. In PICT, given weights are considered only if two value choices are identical, and thus the frequency is reflected only approximately. To improve this, PictMaster constructs a test suite to redundantly cover pairs according to their weights, and thus the size is unnecessary large as shown in Tab. 2-(e). On the other hand, Fujimoto developed a method to add test cases to an existing test suite that more accurately reflect given weights for value frequency. The test suite generated by Fujimoto's method in Tab. 2 shows that *Win* appears 14 times, twice as frequently as *Mac* (7 times), but the test suites by PICT and PictMaster contains the same numbers of *Win* and *Mac*.

In the example, PictMaster generates 28 test cases, while Fujimoto's method uses 15 test cases by PICT plus 13 optional test cases (to more accurately reflect given weights for value frequency); see Tab. 2-(e),(f). The strength of these approaches is that more important values appear more frequently; however, the order of important test cases is completely disregarded.

Algorithm 1. Prioritized N-wise test generation.

Input: A weighted SUT model, Combinatorial strength N.
Output: A N-wise test suite.
1) For each parameter, order all parameter values by weight.
2) Enumerate all N-tuples of parameter values and their weights.
3) Set a set of uncovered combinations, UC, as the set of all the value N-tuples.
while $UC \neq \emptyset$ **do**
    4) List test case candidates to cover the max. number of combinations in UC. [CS]
    4-1) If there is one candidate, choose it as t.
    4-2) If there are several candidates, list candidates with the max. weight of new combinations. [CO]

    4-2-1) If there is one candidate, choose it as t.
    4-2-2) If there are several candidates, choose any candidate with min. KL divergence as t. [CF]

    5) Set t as the next test case and add it to the test suite.
    6) Remove the value N-tuples covered by t from UC.
end while

---

3 Proposed Approach to Prioritized Test Generation

We propose a novel approach to prioritized N-wise test generation, which integrates the three prioritization criteria of *order,* CO, *frequency,* CF, and *size,* CS. For CS, we select a new test case to cover as many uncovered value N-tuples as possible. For CO, we select a new test case to cover value N-tuples with the highest weight. For CF, a new test case is selected according to the occurrence ratio of values in a test suite. To rigorously consider CF, we employ the notion of *KL Divergence* used in [5]. KL divergence, $D_{KL}(P||Q)$ defined in Fig. 1, expresses the distance between the current value occurrence distribution, P, and an ideal distribution, Q, according to given weights. In the ideal distribution, for each value, the number of occurrences is proportional to its weight. By integrating the three criteria CO, CF, and CS, our approach obtains small test suites where high-priority test cases appear early and frequently.

Algorithm 1 shows the pseudo code of the algorithm with priority order CS>CO>CF. Given a weighted SUT model, the algorithm generates test cases one by one until all N-tuples of parameter values are covered. For a new test case, we choose the best one w.r.t. CS, i.e., the test case that covers the most new N-tuples of parameter values (step 4). If there are several candidates, choose the best one for CO, i.e., the test case that covers the new N-tuples of parameter values with the highest weight (step 4-2). If there are still several candidates, choose the best one for CF; i.e., the test case with min. KL divergence (step 4-2-2) to ensure that the value frequency distribution is closest to the ideal state.

Tab. 2-(a) shows the pairwise test suite generated from the example model in Tab. 1-(a), by Algorithm 1 (A1). For the first test case, all the test cases in which the number of newly-covered value pairs (n) is 3 become candidates, since this is the max. number at this stage. Among them, (*Intel, Win,* $-$[1]) is selected as it has the max. value of w, 22. For the 11th test case, test cases 11–15 have the same n and w. In the first ten test cases, *AMD* and *Intel* are assigned equally often to parameter *CPU*, even though the weight of *Intel* is twice of that

---

[1] The symbol $-$ can take any value for *Browser* as all values have the same weight.

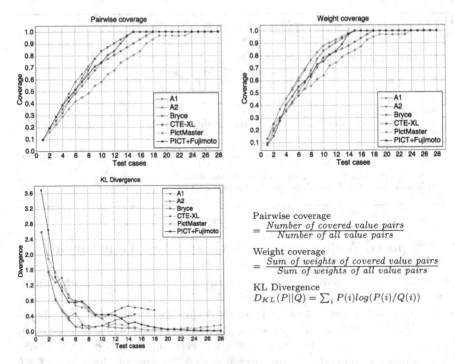

Fig. 1. Comparison of the evaluation metrics

of *AMD*. Furthermore, *Ubuntu* occurs less often than *Mac* despite their weights being the same. Thus, *Intel* and *Ubuntu* are assigned to the 11th test case to achieve a better KL divergence.

We can construct variants of the algorithm with different orders of prioritization criteria CO, CF, and CS, by swapping the conditions in steps 4, 4-2, and 4-2-2 in Algorithm 1. For example, we can construct another algorithm A2 with CO>CS>CF. Tab. 2-(b) shows the pairwise test suite generated by A2. Note that test cases by A1 (resp., A2) are ordered by n (w), since CO (CW) is the first priority criterion. Test cases with the same value of n (resp., w) are ordered by w (n) for A1 (A2), since CW (CO) is the second priority criterion. Furthermore, the test suites generated by A1 and A2 require only 15 test cases, which is fewer than those computed by most previous methods.

We compared our method with the previous methods from the three metrics of interaction coverage, weight coverage, and KL divergence, using several examples of weighted SUT models. As a result, we confirmed that our proposed method can improve on all the metrics.[2] Fig. 1 shows the evaluation result on our example in Tab. 1-(a).[3] The proposed algorithms are superior to the previous methods according to the three metrics. A1 and A2, respectively, provide the

---

[2] To search locally optimal test cases, our algorithm can incur a high computing cost with a high quality for large models. The cost will be evaluated in our next paper.

[3] See http://staff.aist.go.jp/e.choi/evaluationGraphs.html for larger sized graphs.

best results for pairwise coverage and weight coverage, and thus we can obtain a high coverage of higher-priority test cases even when only a small number of test cases is selected. When considering KL divergence, A2 (resp., A1) provides the best result when the number of test cases is higher than 4 (7). Our method provides a good balance of value occurrences, even in a small test suite.

4 Conclusion and Future Work

We have proposed a novel technique for prioritized N-wise test generation, which integrates the three prioritization criteria of order, CO, frequency, CF, and size, CS. Our technique is designed to generate small N-wise test suites, where high-priority test cases appear early and frequently. Our early evaluation has shown that the technique can outperform the state-of-the-art techniques on all the three metrics. The technique is currently under implementation, and will be evaluated including computing cost on practical-sized SUT models. We are also considering to develop approximate algorithms with a lower computing cost, in case our technique is not scalable for practical sized SUT models. Future work also includes handling weights attached to both of parameters and values, and to structured SUT models [4].

Acknowledgements. The authors would like to thank Goro Hatayama and Tatsuhiro Tsuchiya for their helpful comments. This work is supported by JST ASTEP grant (No. AS2524001H).

References

1. Bryce, R., Colbourn, C.: Prioritized interaction testing for pair-wise coverage with seeding and constraints. Information & Software Technology 48(10), 960–970 (2006)
2. Bryce, R., Sampath, S., Pedersen, J., Manchester, S.: Test suite prioritization by cost-based combinatorial interaction coverage. Int. J. Systems Assurance Engineering and Management 2(2), 126–134 (2011)
3. Czerwonka, J.: Pairwise testing in the real world: Practical extensions to test case generators. In: Microsoft Corporation, Software Testing Technical Articles (2008)
4. Do, N., Kitamura, T., Tang, N., Hatayama, G., Sakuragi, S., Ohsaki, H.: Constructing test cases for N-wise testing from tree-based test models. In: Proc. of SoICT 2013. ACM ICPS (2013)
5. Fujimoto, S., Kojima, H., Tsuchiya, T.: A value weighting method for pair-wise testing. In: Proc. of APSEC 2013, pp. 99–105 (2013)
6. Kruse, P., Luniak, M.: Automated test case generation using classification trees. In: Software Quality Professional, pp. 4–12 (2010)
7. PictMaster, http://sourceforge.jp/projects/pictmaster/
8. Xiao, Q., Cohen, M., Woolf, K.: Combinatorial interaction regression testing: A study of test case generation and prioritization. In: Proc. ICSM 2007, pp. 255–264. IEEE (2007)

Change Detection System for the Maintenance of Automated Testing

Miroslav Bures

Department of Computer Science, Faculty of Electrical Engineering,
Czech Technical University in Prague,
Prague, Czech Republic
buresm3@fel.cvut.cz

Abstract. Maintenance of automated test scripts is one of the important factors leading to success and return of investment of the test automation projects. As the key prerequisite to maintain the scripts correctly, we need to be informed about all relevant changes in the project scope, specification or system under test to be able to reflect them in updates of the test scripts. In this paper we introduce a concept on how to track these changes in semi-automated way with acceptable additional effort. The proposed solution is based on automated detection of changes in test management and requirement management tools, combined with optional manual inputs and automated scanning of changes in system under test user interface.

Keywords: Test Automation, Automated Detection of Change, Maintenance of Test Scripts, Better Efficiency, Traceability, Change Management.

1 Introduction

Automated testing represents a promising concept, how to organize the software testing more efficiently. By automation of repetitive, manual (and often intellectually uninteresting) tests, we can invest human effort better in testing of advanced combinations, risk-based testing or error-guessing techniques to generally increase the confidence, the system is tested well. Why the potential of automated testing is used only partially today?

One of the major issues is expensive and inaccurate maintenance of the created test scripts, when the system under test (let us use abbreviation SUT further on) is changing. This is a frequently reported issue, for example [1] or [2].

Also a recent survey we have performed in the Czech Republic among 28 professionals in test automation (currently going to be published), confirms, that the maintenance of the automated test scripts is the most important issue influencing the return of investment (let us use abbreviation ROI further on).

This issue deserves our attention. By enhancing and optimizing of test automation methods, we make the ROI of this technology more probable and earlier. Process of maintenance of the automated test scripts starts with the identification of the scripts, which have to be updated, when the SUT changes. A simplified view on this process is outlined in Fig.1.

M.G. Merayo and E. Montes de Oca (Eds.): ICTSS 2014, LNCS 8763, pp. 192–197, 2014.
© IFIP International Federation for Information Processing 2014

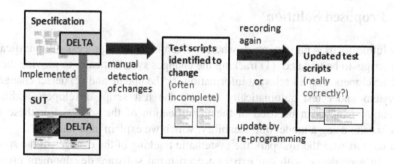

Fig. 1. Simplified process of identification of automated test scripts to update

When prepared manually with insufficient documentation of the changes in source specification or system under test, the set of test scripts identified to update can be incomplete. It can also contain scripts, which are not needed to be updated. This results in overhead and possible wrong update of the scripts.

2   Related Work

Maintenance of the test scripts has been addressed in literature by various approaches, in which we can basically identify two major streams. The first principal approach is based on a modelling work, where a system organizing automated tests to particular structure or taxonomy is presented, for instance [3].

Although well structured organization of the test scripts can increase the efficiency, a general problem of the proposed models is that they are often not sufficiently flexible to fully adapt to real projects. Various states of test scripts organization and also technological limits on various diverse projects are often challenging the pure modelling-based proposals.

The second approach is based on a traceability often combined with a structuring framework. The idea of traceability is essential here. Generally the maintenance is easier, when we capture and maintain the links connecting the requirements, parts of design documentation, features of the implemented SUT and mainly the respective test scripts. Further in the text, we will be referring to this traceability system. For our purpose we have adopted and extended a generally accepted standard BDTM (Business Driven Test Management) [4] from TMap Next methodology [5]. In the previous work we can find also examples of traceability focused on structuring of the test scripts, for example [6].

The topic of change management has been also a subject of many studies, for instance [7], nevertheless a combination of change management and detection system with a system for the maintenance of test scripts is a topic not sufficiently covered in literature. We approach this key area as suitable subject of our research.

3   Proposed Solution

Our solution focuses on two areas, where we can enhance a process of identification of the scripts to be updated: (1) tracking the changes systematically to provide the test script developers with all relevant information for the update and (2) detect changes in the system under test automatically to give the test script developers additional information which can be used in the identification of the scripts. For these both tracks, we are using a model of traceability, which we explain later on.

Let us start with the first part, the systematic tracking of the changes in the specification. In accordance with our experience on usual software development projects, testing sub-team preparing the test scripts is not usually systematically informed about all relevant changes in the scope by a design team or by the project manager. For this reason, we propose a system to help all involved parts to reduce an overhead with collecting the relevant information and increase its accuracy.

The second part, automated detection of changes in the user interface, combines with the previous part. The aim is to have another source of reliable information on what has been changed in the SUT. In this stage, we limit our proposal to automated testing based on the simulation of user's actions in the front-end part of the SUT. With this focus, changes of SUT front-end bring essential information we need for update of the automated test scripts (which are using location of front-end elements to exercise test steps by them). Further on in this paper let us elaborate the first part, the systematic tracking of changes. The second part is currently in a stage of the conceptual design with aim to employ already existing solutions, if any of them will suit our purpose.

4   Model of Change Traceability

As we have introduced the idea of our enhancement, let us explain the basis on which the solution is based on. The first part of the model (Fig. 2) depicts mutual relations between specification, its changes, a part of changes that is known to test designers, the system under test, test scripts and their coverage and regression caused by changes (defects introduced to the other part of the system by implementing the changes).

By DELTA we mean the change to be implemented. If the project organizes its change management properly, all DELTAs should be exactly specified by formal change requests. Nevertheless, the situation on many projects differs from this ideal and we have to find a solution which can deal with such a situation efficiently.

In our proposal we further focus on the following parts of the model: A set Complete delta (**CD**) represents all changes in the specification (formalized or existing in the minds of the software development team) which arises on the project in a current iteration. A common situation is, that the test design (or test maintenance) team has information only about the part of these changes, a set **KD** in the model. The aim of our proposal is to make the sets **CD** and **KD** equal (or much more the same) with a minimal effort.

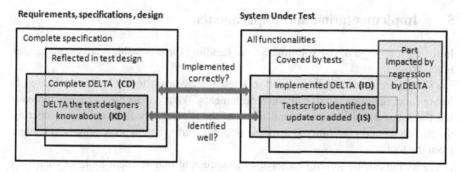

Fig. 2. Basic components of the conceptual model of the change traceability

Then, the changes should be propagated to the System under test by the development sub-team (a set **ID**) and also to the updated automated test scripts by the test design team (a set **IS**). The reduction of the difference between **CD** and **KD** then significantly contributes to the accuracy of update of the **IS**. And together with this, we need to support the update process also from another line: a traceability of the changes to automated test scripts.

As we have mentioned already, for the test management purposes, it is generally very productive to organize the information on the project to be able to track, which requirements are designed by which part of design documentation, implemented by which features of the system under test and, mainly, covered by which test scripts. We have adopted this general concept, described for instance in BDTM [4] further for change identification and propagating the changes to automated test scripts. The principle is depicted in the Fig. 3.

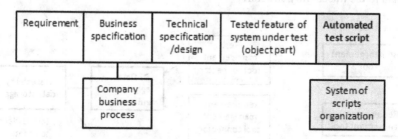

Fig. 3. The model of the change traceability: tracking metadata part

In addition to the BDTM, we emphasize more explicitly links to company business processes, which help us to work with this source of changes and allows us to align more clearly and exactly with the business part of the organization. Moreover, we have added the system of script organization, which represents taxonomy, name conventions, and physical organization of the automated test scripts, including optional organization of the test scripts by their reusable parts.

5   Implementation and Experiments

In the current stage of our solution, we are handling three possible sources of changes in the project:

(1) Requirements possibly stored in a test management tool. Current tools are offering functionalities for storing the requirements. We are detecting a change by loading the set of requirements several times as the project proceeds and are comparing them. The second possibility is a simple import of information on requirement change from the tool.

(2) Requirements stored in a separate requirement management tool, varying from a simple issue tracking tools, which can be used to capture and formalize the requirements, for example Redmine, to a specialized modelling tools, for example Sparx Enterprise Architect. Here, a process of change detection and import is the same as in the previous case.

(3) Changes detected directly by members of the test automation team. This is an important source of information, which has to be processed. The test designers can add and update this information in the traceability tree by a special front-end application.

An overview of the architecture is introduced in Fig. 4. The system is based on a shared repository, the Traceability data storage, whose core is the traceability tree, the model described in the previous chapter.

For the variants (1) and (2), we gather the data by specialized connectors, which are adapted to the particular tools. A side effect of the solution is a possible consistency check between the various systems storing the requirements, if there are more of them co-existing on the project. Then, the data aggregator and analyzer transform the data to the traceability structure.

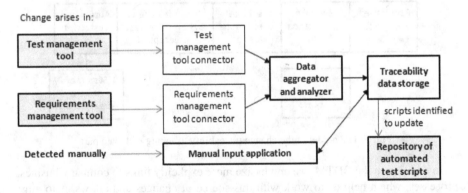

Fig. 4. Conceptual schema of the solution

Currently, the system is in detailed design and implementation. The conceptual parts have been verified by simulation on real data in a SW development company, where a sufficient set of automated test scripts is available. We have compared a time needed to identify the changes to update the automated test scripts manually and its possible accuracy with a thorough detailed simulation, testing how this overhead and accuracy would be changed, when using the proposed concept. In this particular case, taking all initial overhead in account, time to identification would be reduced by 40% one year after roll-out of the proposed solution (in the situation that the test designers are really detecting the changes, not simply ignoring them). Then, changes not reflected in test design by lack of information or human mistake would be reduced by 85% in the same period, which is significant. This result encourages us to continue with implementation to get feedback from more experiments, despite the fact that in productive run we expect this result being lower due to overhead which can arise.

6   Conclusions and Future Work

Our proposal aims to increase efficiency of automated testing by focusing on its key issue negatively influencing it: maintenance of the automated test scripts, particularly on its sub-problem, detection of change which we need to propagate in automated test scripts maintenance.

Our approach is based on automated detection of changes form design or test management tools, where the relevant information is stored, in combination with the support for test scripts maintenance team to propagate other information they acquire during the project meetings or communication on general. The main idea behind this concept is to aggregate possible all sources of information available and perform that with minimal effort and overhead.

The results of the first simulation on real data and also an initial feedback from various test managers and engineers in the Czech Republic leads to the conclusion that the proposed concept deserves further evolution and application on the several test automation project to refine and optimize the proposal in the upcoming period.

References

1. Rafi, D.M., et al.: Benefits and limitations of automated software testing: Systematic literature review and practitioner survey. In: 7th International Workshop on Automation of Software Test (AST), Zurich, Switzerland, pp. 36–42 (2012)
2. Dustin, E., Garrett, T., Gauf, B.: Implementing Automated Software Testing, pp. 24–26. Addison-Wesley, Boston (2009)
3. Xie, Q., Memon, A.M.: Using a Pilot Study to Derive a GUI Model for Automated Testing. ACM Transactions on Computational Logic 18(2) (November 2008)
4. Van der Alast, L., et al.: TMap Next: Business Driven Test Management. UTN Publishers, Nederlands (2008)
5. Koomen, T., et al.: TMap Next for result-driven testing. UTN Publishers, Nederlands (2006)
6. Haswell, J.J., Young, R.J., Schramm, K.: System, method, and article of manufacture for test maintenance in an automated scripting framework, US Patent 6 701 514 B1 (March 2, 2004)
7. Ibbs, C., Wong, C., Kwak, Y.: Project Change Management System. Journal of Management in Engineering 17(3) (July 2001)

On Code Coverage of Extended FSM Based Test Suites: An Initial Assessment

Khaled El-Fakih[1], Tariq Salameh[1], and Nina Yevtushenko[2]

[1] American University of Sharjah, Sharjah, UAE
{Kelfakih,b00046306}@aus.edu
[2] Tomsk State University, Tomsk, Russia
ninayevtushenko@yahoo.com

Abstract. In this paper, we present an assessment of the fault coverage of several Extended FSM (EFSM) based test suites. More precisely, EFSM specifications and their corresponding Java implementations are considered. Mutants of these implementations are derived using the standard arithmetic, conditional, and relational mutation operators. The fault coverage of test suites derived by different EFSM based strategies are evaluated and obtained results are summarized.

Keywords: Extended FSM test suites, test coverage, case study.

1 Introduction and Summary

Extended Finite State Machines (EFSMs) provide a rigorous approach for the development of functional tests for reactive systems, protocols and software. As an EFSM specification expresses both the data-flow and the control-flow behavior of a system, test derivation from an EFSM can be done using traditional software test selection criteria, such as the well-known All-Uses criterion, or using other criteria such as the derivation of test suites (TSs) that cover all EFSM mutants with single transfer faults, called STF TS, or a test suite, with one test case, called Transition Tour (TT), that traverses each transition of the specification, or a test suite, called DSTS, with tests that for each transition of the specification, the test suite includes input sequences that traverse the transition appended with a set of input sequences that distinguish the ending state of the transition from all other states of the machine. Another possibility for test derivation is to randomly derive a test suite with one test case of a particular length, for example, a test case with the same length as an All-Uses test suite [1], called Random All-Uses, or as investigated in this paper, the derivation of a test case of the same length as a DSTS test suite, called Random DSTS. In [1] it is shown that a test suite that covers All-Uses may not detect all STF mutants of the EFSM specification and a test suite that covers all STF mutants of the specification may not satisfy the All-Uses criterion of the specification, etc. Thus, an empirical study is needed to assess the coverage of these test suites.

For evaluating the code fault coverage, in this paper, four known EFSM specifications and corresponding Java code implementations are considered. Then All-Uses,

M.G. Merayo and E. Montes de Oca (Eds.): ICTSS 2014, LNCS 8763, pp. 198–204, 2014.

STF, TT, DSTS test suites are derived and the coverage of these test suites is calculated using mutants of the Java implementations where code mutants are derived using the traditional arithmetic, logical, and conditional operators [4].

Major contributions of the conducted experiments can be summarized as follows:

- All-Uses, STF, and TT test suites provide comparable (fault) coverage.
- DSTSs outperform all other considered test suites.
- Random-All-Uses and All-Uses test suites provide comparable coverage where DSTS test suites slightly outperform Random-DSTSs.
- Test suites coverage of conditional faults is significantly higher than their coverage of mutants with arithmetic, logical, or relational faults.
- Test suites coverage of mutants with relational faults is much less than that of the coverage of mutants with arithmetic, conditional or logical faults.
- All-Uses and TT test suites both achieve comparable coverage of mutants with arithmetic faults; however, STF test suites have significantly lower coverage of arithmetic faults than All-Uses and TT test suites.
- All considered test suites provide comparable coverage of conditional faults, also all test suites provide comparable coverage of logical (or relational) faults.

Empirical assessment studies related to code based data-flow, control-flow, mutation testing, and some specification based test selection criteria are studied in many papers which are mostly summarized in [3] and [5]. For specifications modeled as EFSMs, a preliminary assessment of STF, TT, All-Uses, All-Predicates, double transfer faults and some random test suites has been recently presented in [1]. The assessment is done based on the coverage of the test suites of EFSM mutants of the specification with single and double transfer faults. In this paper, unlike [1], the considered test suites are assessed in terms of their coverage of code mutants of implementations of these specifications. Thus, the work allows us to compare the coverage of considered test suites w.r.t. known code based types of mutants. Further, in this paper, DSTS test suites are also considered in the assessment and the results show that such test suites outperform all other considered test suites. Finally, it is worth stating that the results obtained here are rather different than those in [1]. For example, in [1] it is found that All-Uses, TT, and STF test suites do not provide comparable coverage of EFSM mutants with single or double transfer faults while in this paper these test suites achieve comparable coverage of code mutants.

2   Preliminaries

The EFSM Model. Let X and Y be finite sets of inputs and outputs, R and V be finite disjoint sets of parameters and context variables, respectively. For $x \in X$, $R_x \subseteq R$ denotes the set of input parameters and D_{Rx} denotes the set of valuations of the parameters over the set R_x. Similarly, for $y \in Y$, $R_y \subseteq R$ denotes the set of output parameters and D_{Ry} denotes the set of valuations of the parameters over the set R_y. The set D_V denotes the set of context variable valuations.

An EFSM [6] M over X, Y, R, V with the associated valuation domains is a pair (S, T) where S is a finite non-empty set of states and T is the set of transitions between states in S, such that each transition $t \in T$ is a tuple (s, x, P, op, y, up, s'), where, s and s' are the *start* and *final* states of the transition t, $x \in X$ is the *input* of transition t, $y \in Y$ is the *output* of transition t, P and up, op are functions defined over context variables V and input parameters as follows: $P: D_{Rx} \times D_V \rightarrow \{True, False\}$ is the *predicate* of the transition t; $up : D_{Rx} \times D_V \rightarrow D_V$ is the *context update* function of transition t; $op : D_{Rx} \times D_V \rightarrow D_{Ry}$ is the *output parameter update* function of transition t. A context variable valuation $\mathbf{v} \in D_V$ is called a *context* of M. A *configuration* of M is a tuple $(s, \mathbf{v})$ where s is a state and $\mathbf{v}$ is a context. Given input x and the input parameter valuations, a *(parameterized) input* is a tuple $(x, \mathbf{p}_x)$, where $\mathbf{p}_x \in D_{Rx}$. A sequence of inputs is also called *an input sequence*. An *output sequence* can be defined in a similar way. In this paper, hereafter, we consider deterministic complete EFSM specifications, i.e. for each input sequence there exists exactly one corresponding output sequence. If an EFSM is partial then a complete version of the machine is obtained by appropriately augmenting the machine will transitions with the null output.

Assume that EFSM M is at a current configuration $(s, \mathbf{v})$ and the machine receives an input $(x, \mathbf{p}_x)$ such that $(\mathbf{v}, \mathbf{p}_x)$ satisfies the guard P of an outgoing transition $t = (s, x, P, op, y, up, s')$. Then when receiving the input $(x, \mathbf{p}_x)$, the machine executes the update statements of t; produces the (parameterized) output where parameter values are provided by the output parameter function op, and moves to configuration $(s', \mathbf{v}')$, where $\mathbf{v}' = up(\mathbf{p}_x, \mathbf{v})$. Thus, such an execution of transition t can be represented as $(s, \mathbf{v}) - (x, \mathbf{p}_x)/(y, \mathbf{p}_y) \rightarrow (s', \mathbf{v}')$, where $op(\mathbf{p}_x, \mathbf{v}) = \mathbf{p}_y$. Such a transition can also be written as $((s, \mathbf{v}), (x, \mathbf{p}_x), (y, \mathbf{p}_y), (s', \mathbf{v}'))$.

It is well known that not each transition with the start state s is executable at any configuration $(s, \mathbf{v})$. A *path* is a sequence of consecutive transitions $(s_1, x_1, P_1, op_1, y_1, up_1, s_2)\dots (s_l, x_l, P_l, op_l, y_l, up_l, s_l)$. A path is *feasible* or *executable* if there is a sequence of (executable) transitions $(s_1, \mathbf{v}_1) - (x_1, \mathbf{p}_{x1})/(y_1, \mathbf{p}_{y1}) -- (x_l, \mathbf{p}_{xl})/ (y_l, \mathbf{p}_{yl}) \rightarrow (s_l, \mathbf{v}_l)$ in EFSM M starting from configuration $(s_1, \mathbf{v}_1)$. The *input/output projection* of such an executable path is the *sequence of input/output pairs* $(x_1, \mathbf{p}_{x1})/(y_1, \mathbf{p}_{y1}) .. (x_l, \mathbf{p}_{xl})/ (y_l, \mathbf{p}_{yl})$ and is called a *trace* of M starting from configuration $(s_1, \mathbf{v}_1)$.

A test case is a (parameterized) input sequence of the EFSM specification. A *test suite (TS)* is a finite set of test cases. The length of a test suite TS is the total length of its corresponding test cases.

EFSM Based Test Suites:

Single Transfer Faults (STF) Test Suites. Given an EFSM M, a transition $t = (s, x, P, op, y, up, s')$ of an EFSM IUT M' has a *transfer fault* if its final state is different from that specified by M, i.e., M' has a transition $(s, x, P, op, y, up, s'')$, $s'' \neq s'$, $s'' \in S$. Such M' is a *mutant of M with a transfer fault*. EFSMs M and M' are distinguishable if their initial configurations are distinguishable by an input sequence (or a test case) α. In this case, we say that α *kills* M'. A test suite, called a STF test suite, covers single transfer faults of M, if for each mutant of M with a single transfer fault that is distinguishable from M, the test suite has at least one test case that kills such a mutant.

Transition Tour (TT) Test Suites: A TT test suite of M is an input sequence that starts at the initial configuration of M and traverses each transition of M.

EFSM Flow-Graph Based All-Uses Test Suites: All-Uses test suite is a set of test cases of EFSM M that cover the All-Uses of each context variable and every parameterized input of M. Such a test suite can be derived directly from M as illustrated in [2] or from a flow-graph representation of M as illustrated in [7].

Distinguishing Set Test Suites (DSTS): An input sequence α_{ij} is a *distinguishing sequence* for states s_i and s_j of M if α_{ij} distinguishes each pair of configurations $(s_i, \mathbf{v})$ and $(s_j, \mathbf{v}')$, $\mathbf{v}, \mathbf{v}' \in D_V$, of M. M is *state reduced* if each two different states of M are distinguishable. Given state $s_j \in S$ of a state reduced EFSM M with n states, a set W_j of input sequences is called a *distinguishing set* of state s_j, if for any other state s_i there exists a sequence $\alpha \in W_j$ that distinguishes states s_i and s_j. Given distinguishing sets $W = \{W_0, W_1, .., W_{n-1}\}$ of states of M, a Distinguishing Sets Test Suite (DSTS) is a set of test cases that satisfies the following property. For every transition $t = (s, x, P, op, y, up, s')$ of M and each $\alpha \in W_j$, the TS has the input sequence $\gamma .(x, \mathbf{p}_x).\alpha$, where γ is the input sequence that takes M from the initial configuration to a configuration $(s, \mathbf{v})$ such that $(\mathbf{v}, \mathbf{p}_x)$ satisfies P of t.

3   Assessment Methodology, Results, and Further Work

We consider four known EFSM specifications, namely, complete EFSM versions the Initiator and Responder of the INRES protocol, the SCP, and the Cruise Control. The method has three steps. In **Step 1**, for each considered EFSM specification, all EFSM mutants of M with STF faults are derived and a corresponding STF test suite (with optimal or near optimal length) is derived as illustrated in [1]. Moreover, for every specification, a corresponding flow-graph representation annotated with definitions and uses of variables is constructed and then a corresponding All-Uses test suite is derived from the obtained flow-graph as illustrated in [1] based on related work [7]. In **Step 2**, three corresponding Java code implementations are developed by three different software engineers, based on the EFSM specification and its textual description, under the following coding rules. State variables cannot be explicitly or implicitly introduced in an implementation, for example, no state variables and no flags indicating state variables can be used; moreover, no labels and no Go-to statements can be used. In addition, names of context variables, inputs and outputs with their parameters of the EFSM specification should be preserved in a code implementation. Each implementation should be implemented as one function that inputs a string separated by a delimiter "," representing an input sequence to the function and returns as an output a string representing the output response of the implementation to the input sequence. A Reader/Writer class is used in all implementations that handles reading/writing the input and the output strings in order to separate reading and writing outputs from the function that implements the specification and thus, code mutants are only derived from the function that implements the specification. We note that before deriving mutants, each Java implementation is thoroughly tested using all the considered test suites written in JUnit. In **Step 3**, 1-Order Java code mutants are derived using the Java arithmetic, relational, conditional, logical-shift, and assignment operators shown in List 1. As usual, 1-Order code mutants are considered to alleviate problems related to the coupling effect of using N-order mutants, when $N > 1$. Afterwards, the fault detection capabilities (*fault coverage*) of each considered test suite of a given EFSM specification is measured as $(J_{killed} / J_{Mutants}) \times 100$, where $J_{Mutants}$ denotes the number of derived mutants of the Java implementation and J_{killed} is the number of these mutants killed by the given test suite. MuClips [8], MuJava [4], and JUnit are used for the automatic derivation of mutants, execution of test suites, and for determining fault coverage.

List 1. Selected Mutation Operators [4]:

(AORB) Arithmetic Operator Replacement, (AORS) Arithmetic Operator Replacement– Shortcut, (AOIS) Arithmetic Operator Insertion – Shortcut, (AOIU) Arithmetic Operator Insertion – Unary, (COI) Conditional Operator Insertion, (COD) (Conditional Operator Deletion, (LOI) Logical Operator Insertion.

Results. This part contains the results of all conducted experiments. Fig. 1 includes the coverage of the All-Uses, STF, TT, and DSTS test suites. These results clearly show that the All-Uses and STF have almost the same coverage, TTs slightly outperforms (approximately by 2%) All-Uses and STF test suites. However, DSTSs outperform all other test suites by at least 5%. This pattern is almost the same for each considered example. These results clearly show the importance of using state identifiers based test suites in EFSM based test derivation.

Fig. 2 shows the coverage of all considered test suites using arithmetic, conditional, logical, and relational operators. According to these results, there is a significant difference between the coverage per mutation operator, for example, the coverage of conditional faults is 15.3, 23.5, and 32.5 percent higher than the coverage of mutants with arithmetic, logical, or relational faults. In addition, the coverage of relational faults is much less than the coverage of mutants with arithmetic, conditional and logical faults. Fig. 3 depicts the coverage of each test suite per each mutation operator. According to these results, it is clear that there is a huge difference, approximately by 16 percent, of the coverage of arithmetic faults by the STF test suites in comparison with the All-Uses and TT test suites. As expected, the All-Uses (data-flow based) test suites coverage of arithmetic faults is higher than that of STF (control-flow based) test suites; however, we were surprised that TT test suites provide comparable (even slightly higher) coverage of arithmetic faults as the All-Uses test suites. All considered test suites provide comparable coverage of conditional faults. Also, all test suites achieve comparable coverage of logical (or relational) faults.

Experiments with Random Test Suites: As All-Uses and TT and STF test suites provide comparable coverage and are all outperformed by the DSTS test suites, we were curious to determine if All-Uses and DSTS test suites would outperform random test suites derived as (executable) random paths of the EFSM transitions. To this end, for each considered example, we considered the All-Uses (DSTS) test suite and derive

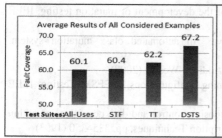

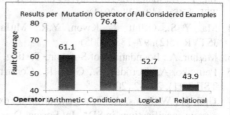

Fig. 1. Coverage of test suites   **Fig. 2.** Results per mutation operator

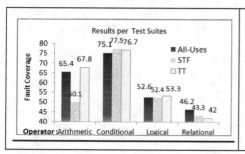

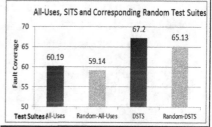

Fig. 3. Results per mutation operator of test suites   **Fig.4.** results with random test suites

three random test suites, called Random-All-Uses (Random-DSTS); each random test suite has one test case that has the same length as the corresponding All-Uses (DSTS) test suite. Obtained results, shown in Fig. 4, show that All-Uses and Random-All Uses provide comparable coverage; however, DSTSs slightly outperform (by 2%) Random DSTSs. These results clearly indicate the good performance of such random test suites and further experiments are needed to verify these important results.

Future Work. Though a clear pattern of the fault coverage of the considered test suites is indicated using the four conducted experiments, yet, experiments with more application examples would be useful to clearly confirm the obtained pattern. Assessing the coverage of more types of EFSM based, especially random, test suites would also be useful as future work on EFSM based testing. It would also be useful to consider length of obtained test suites and assess the relationship between length of a generated random test suite and its fault coverage.

References

1. El-Fakih, K., Simao, A., Jadoon, N., Maldonado, J.C.: On studying the effectiveness of ex-tended finite state machine based test selection criteria. In: IEEE ICST Workshops, Mutation 2014 (2014)
2. Bourhfir, C., Abdoulhamid, E., Khendek, F., Dssouli, R.: Test cases selection from SDL specifications. Computer Networks 35(6), 693–708 (2001)

3. Jia, Y., Harman, M.: An anaylsis an survey of the development of mutation testing. IEEE TSE 37(5), 649–678 (2011)
4. Ma, Y.-S., Offutt, J., Kwon, Y.R.: MuJava: An automated class mutation system. JSTVR 15(2), 97–133 (2005)
5. Mathur, A.: Foundations of Software Testing, Addison-Wesley (2008)
6. Petrenko, A., Boroday, S., Groz, R.: Confirming configurations in EFSM Testing. IEEE TSE 30(1), 29–42 (2004)
7. Ural, H., Williams, A.: Test generation by exposing control and data dependencies within system specifications in SDL. In: Formal Description Techniques, pp. 335–350 (1993)
8. MuClipse Team, MuClipse - Mutation Testing tool for Eclipse (September 2011), http://muclipse.sourceforge.net/

Search-Based Testing for Embedded Telecom Software with Complex Input Structures

Kivanc Doganay[1,2], Sigrid Eldh[3,4], Wasif Afzal[2], and Markus Bohlin[1,2]

[1] SICS Swedish ICT AB, Kista, Sweden
[2] Mälardalen University, Västerås, Sweden
[3] Ericsson AB, Kista, Sweden
[4] Karlstad University, Karlstad, Sweden

Abstract. In this paper, we discuss the application of search-based software testing techniques for unit level testing of a real-world telecommunication middleware at Ericsson. Our current implementation analyzes the existing test cases to handle non-trivial variables such as uninitialized pointers, and to discover any setup code that needs to run before the actual test case, such as setting global system parameters. Hill climbing (HC) and (1+1) evolutionary algorithm (EA) metaheuristic search algorithms are used to generate input data for branch coverage. We compare HC, (1+1)EA, and random search with respect to effectiveness, measured as branch coverage, and efficiency, measured as number of executions needed. Difficulties arising from the specialized execution environment and the adaptations for handling these problems are also discussed.

1 Introduction

Embedded systems are prevalent in many industries such as avionics, railways and telecommunication systems. The use of specialized microprocessors such as digital signal processors (DSPs) and electronic control units have enabled more complex software in the embedded domain. As a consequence, quality control has become more time consuming and costly, similar to the non-embedded software domains.

It is well known that software testing is an expensive activity [6]. Thus considerable research has focused on automating different test activities, notably software test data generation. In recent years, the use of metaheuristic search algorithms have shown promise in automating parts of software testing efforts [3], including test data generation, which is commonly referred to as search-based software testing (SBST). SBST has received increasing attention in the academia. While random testing and fuzzing have gained reasonable visibility and acceptance, search-based approaches are not yet adopted in the industry. To gain wider acceptance, we believe that experiments of search-based techniques on real-world industrial software should be performed. With a family of such experiments, we would be in a better position to argue for the industrial uptake of SBST.

In this paper, we present a case study of applying search-based testing on a real-world telecommunication middleware at Ericsson. We use hill climbing

M.G. Merayo and E. Montes de Oca (Eds.): ICTSS 2014, LNCS 8763, pp. 205–210, 2014.
© IFIP International Federation for Information Processing 2014

(HC) and $(1+1)$ evolutionary algorithm (EA) metaheuristic search algorithms to generate unit level input data that exercise different branches in the control flow. The algorithms, along with random search as a baseline, are compared for effectiveness, measured in branch coverage, and efficiency, measured in number of executions. Existing test cases are automatically analyzed in order to handle complex data structures, pointers, and global system parameters. We also discuss difficulties arising from the specialized execution environment, and the adaptations for handling these problems. A further detailed account of the case study can be found in the corresponding technical report [1].

2 System Under Test

The system under test is written in the DSP-C programming language. DSP-C is an extension of the C language with additional types and memory quantifiers designed to allow programs to utilize hardware architectural features of DSPs [2]. Ericsson uses a proprietary compiler to compile DSP-C code for various DSP architectures, and a proprietary simulator to execute the resulting binaries on a normal Linux environment. The whole tool chain is connected via a test execution framework. Currently we do not integrate to the test framework, but we extract certain information from it.

2.1 Analysis and Instrumentation

We adapted `pycparser`[1], which produces the abstract syntax tree (AST) for the C language to the DSP-C language including Ericsson specific memory identifiers. Our tool analyzes the resulting AST to produce the control flow graph (CFG) of the function under test (FUT).

The `Assimilator` module (Fig. 1) instruments the FUT by inserting observation code at the branching points in the CFG. The code is instrumented without changing its functional behavior. For example, the statement `if(a>b && c)` is instrumented as `if(observe_gt(12,0,a,b) && observe(12,1,c))`, where 12 is the branch identifier in the CFG, while 0 and 1 are the clause identifiers in the given expression. Note that the variable c will not be read if the first condition `(a>b)` is false. This ensures that instrumentation do not change the functional behavior of the FUT.

Existing Test Cases. We analyze the existing test cases (developed by Ericsson engineers) for a given FUT to discover the input interface, and any *setup code* that needs to be executed before calling the FUT. Test cases may include some setup code, such as allocating memory, or setting a global variable. We replicate these setup code sections in the generated template test case. Then all assignments in the test code are parsed, and the discovered assignments are used to define the input space. Only the variables and fields of data structures which

---

[1] Available at `https://github.com/eliben/pycparser`

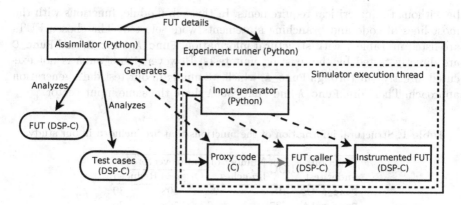

Fig. 1. Prototype's architecture and the execution environment

are set in at least one test function are used to construct the input space, as it is likely that variables and fields which are never set are uninteresting for testing purposes. In particular, this is true for variables which do not affect the execution of the FUT (e.g., output variables), or for variables which are initialized in the setup phase and should not be changed due to the logic of the system.

2.2 Execution Environment

The DSP simulator supports interacting with simulated code in a restricted manner, e.g., direct function calls are not possible. Therefore our implementation was heavily adapted to the simulator.

The **Input generator** (Fig. 1) implements the search algorithms using a vector representation of basic types, which is oblivious to the actual input structures. The **Proxy code** and **FUT caller** (automatically synthesized by the **Assimilator** module) packs the input vector into the input data structures, which is then passed to the simulated DSP-C environment. After each FUT execution observation data is read to calculate the fitness value of the last input vector. Then the execution cycle is repeated with the next input vector generated by the search algorithm.

3 Experimental Evaluation

In this section we compare the experimental results of hill climbing (HC), (1+1)EA, and random search (RS) algorithms for branch coverage on a set of four functions in a library sub-module of Ericsson's middleware code base. Both HC and (1+1)EA algorithms use the same popular fitness function for branch coverage that combines *approach level* and *branch distance* [5].

The particular sub-module was selected as it was considered suitable to be tested using the simulator, rather than the real hardware. In particular, suitable sub-modules should have no or minimal inter-module dependencies, and should be without timing critical requirements. In this sub-module, functions with the most lines of code and branching statements were selected. The chosen FUTs are listed in Table 1 with structural information. Func_A, Func_B, and Func_C are directly tested by the existing unit tests. However, Func_subA is not executed directly but through Func_A, which we mimic in our test data generation approach. Therefore, Func_A and Func_subA share the same input vector.

Table 1. Structural information of the functions that are included in our study.

Function under test	LOC	Number of branches	Input vector size Original	Reduced
Func_A	191	20	508	30
Func_subA	37	6	508	30
Func_B	352	20	143	28
Func_C	179	32	659	146

Experiments were run on Ericsson servers using the simulator. We use execution count (i.e., the number of calls to the FUT) for comparison, instead of the clock time, so that the efficiency of our implementation, interactions with the simulator, or the server load do not affect the results. For practical purposes we imposed a limit of 1000 executions (FUT calls) per targeted branch. In order to account for the stochastic nature of the search algorithms, we repeated each experiment 50 times per algorithm per FUT. The total time for executing all experiments was around 150 hours, or 6 days.

Statistical significance tests and effect size measurements are applied for pairwise comparison of algorithms, with respect to branch coverage and execution counts. We omit this analysis for the sake of brevity, which can be found in the technical report [1]. The minimum, maximum, mean, and median values for the achieved branch coverage by each algorithm are shown in Table 2. Branch coverage of the existing test cases are also listed for comparison. For Func_A and Func_subA all algorithms were able to reach full coverage at most of the runs, while some branches of Func_B were covered only by the HC algorithm.

Table 3 shows the number of executions needed per algorithm for each FUT. Again the minimum, mean, median, and maximum values among the 50 independent runs are reported in the table.

The results indicate that both HC, (1+1)EA, and RS were able to achieve high branch coverage most of the time (Table 2). At least one of the algorithms were able to achieve 100 % branch coverage in the case of three out of the four FUTs. For two of the FUTs (Func_subA and Func_B) the achieved branch coverage was higher than branch coverage of the existing test cases. Therefore, we were able to increase the branch coverage for the FUTs that are studied in our case study. However, search algorithms did not always reach the highest possible branch coverage (Func_C in Table 2).

We observed that RS was not much worse than other algorithms at branch coverage, except for Func_B where HC was the clear winner. This indicates that

Table 2. Branch coverage achieved by hill climbing, (1+1)EA, and random search algorithms, as well as the existing test cases

FUT	Exist.	Hill Climbing				(1+1)EA				Random Search			
		min	mean	med.	max	min	mean	med.	max	min	mean	med.	max
Func_A	1.0	0.95	0.996	1.0	1.0	1.0	1.0	1.0	1.0	1.0	1.0	1.0	1.0
Func_subA	0.83	0.5	0.99	1.0	1.0	0.5	0.983	1.0	1.0	0.5	0.947	1.0	1.0
Func_B	0.85	0.95	0.998	1.0	1.0	0.7	0.701	0.70	0.75	0.7	0.705	0.70	0.75
Func_C	1.0	0.656	0.746	0.75	0.812	0.75	0.812	0.812	0.875	0.75	0.824	0.812	0.906

Table 3. Number of executions (fitness evaluations or FUT calls) that each search algorithm needed before terminating

FUT	Hill Climbing				(1+1)EA				Random Search			
	min	mean	med.	max	min	mean	med.	max	min	mean	med.	max
Func_A	330	641	576	1555	288	551	506	1059	73	151	150	310
Func_subA	167	448	382	3234	110	493	408	3143	52	436	131	3034
Func_B	1853	2231	2194	2838	5650	6401	6364	6955	5382	5996	6042	6070
Func_C	10043	11722	11551	13763	7710	9396	9256	11970	5605	7353	7591	9686

many of the branches are relatively easy to cover. One such branch predicate that we found to be common in the code base is inequality comparison with a signed input value and a small constant, such as $(x \leq 10)$. For example, a signed 32-bit integer input x would mean that the probability of a random input leading to the false and true branches approximately equal $(P(false) \approx P(true) \approx 0.5)$. Similar situation can be observed if the variable being compared is unsigned type, but is defined as a bit field with, e.g., 4-bit length. In embedded software bit fields are commonly used, in order to reduce the memory usage as much as possible.

Furthermore, on average RS is faster (i.e., needs less number of FUT calls) to cover a branch, if it can, compared to other algorithms (Table 3). It is known in the literature that RS is typically faster at covering easy branches than more informed search algorithms.

3.1 Threats to Validity

Due to practical reasons (such as computational resources) we imposed arbitrary limits on the execution of the algorithms on each targeted branch. Different execution limits might have led to differing results.

We selected limited number of FUTs from one sub-module. FUTs were selected among the functions with more lines of code and number of branches. We do not know if many smaller FUTs, instead of few big ones, would give significantly different results. In the future, we plan to extend this work to more sub-modules and functions in the code base.

4   Discussion and Conclusion

In this paper, we discussed a case study on application of SBST techniques for an industrial embedded software. The implemented tool was heavily adapted to the simulated execution environment (Section 2). This can be seen as a special version of the *execution environment problem*, which usually refers to the concerns about interacting with the file system, the network, or a database in the context of non-embedded systems [4]. Moreover, we did not have enough detailed technical knowledge of the system under test to understand the input space. To overcome this problem, we used existing test cases to automatically craft a test case template (Section 2.1).

During the experiments we were able to increase the total branch coverage of existing test cases. So we can say that the employed SBST techniques indicate beneficial results. However, we observed that randomly generated inputs were as effective as more informed search algorithms in many (but not all) cases, which indicate that there are many branches that are easy to cover. A practitioner may prefer to start with random search to cover easy branches first, before using informed search algorithms to target other branches.

For future work, we would like to extend the case study to more FUTs in a similar code base. We plan to investigate alternative ways of interacting with the simulator to reduce the execution times, which was a practical bottleneck for the experiments. Another interesting idea is the use of hybrid search algorithms that can cover easy branches swiftly (e.g., by using random search) and then move to other branches.

Acknowledgments. This work was supported by VINNOVA grant 2011-01377, and the Knowledge Foundation (KKS), Sweden. We would like to thank Jonas Allander, Catrin Granbom, John Nilsson, and Andreas Ermedahl at Ericsson AB for their help in enabling the case study.

References

1. Doganay, K., Eldh, S., Afzal, W., Bohlin, M.: Search-based testing for embedded telecommunication software with complex input structures: An industrial case study. Tech. Rep. 5692, SICS Swedish ICT (July 2014)
2. Leary, K., Waddington, W.: DSP/C: a standard high level language for DSP and numeric processing. In: International Conference on Acoustics, Speech, and Signal Processing, ICASSP 1990, vol. 2, pp. 1065–1068 (1990)
3. McMinn, P.: Search-based software test data generation: A survey. Software Testing, Verification and Reliability 14(2), 105–156 (2004)
4. McMinn, P.: Search-based software testing: Past, present and future. In: Search-Based Software Testing: Past, Present and Future, ICSTW 2011, pp. 153–163. IEEE Computer Society, Washington, DC (2011)
5. Wegener, J., Baresel, A., Sthamer, H.: Evolutionary test environment for automatic structural testing. Information and Software Technology 43(14), 841–854 (2001)
6. Yang, B., Hu, H., Jia, L.: A study of uncertainty in software cost and its impact on optimal software release time. IEEE Transactions on Software Engineering 34(6), 813–825 (2008)

Author Index

Abdelmoula, Mariem   97
Acher, Mathieu   80
Afzal, Wasif   205
Ali, Shaukat   17
Artho, Cyrille   186
Auguin, Michel   97

Baudry, Benoit   80
Bogusch, Ralf   80
Bohlin, Markus   205
Bozic, Josip   48
Bures, Miroslav   192

Chabot, Martial   173
Choi, Eun-Hye   186
Cicchetti, Antonio   129

Deak, Anca   161
Doganay, Kivanc   205
Domínguez-Jiménez, Juan José   1
Dwarakanath, Anurag   63

Eberhardinger, Benedikt   180
Eldh, Sigrid   205
El-Fakih, Khaled   198
Estero-Botaro, Antonia   1

Gaffe, Daniel   97
García-Domínguez, Antonio   1
Gotlieb, Arnaud   145

Jankiti, Aruna   63

Kitamura, Takashi   186
Knapp, Alexander   180

Le Guen, Hélène   80

Medina-Bulo, Inmaculada   1
Meling, Hein   145
Mossige, Morten   145

Öberg, Anders   129
Oiwa, Yutaka   186

Palmieri, Manuel   129
Palomo-Lozano, Francisco   1
Pierre, Laurence   173

Reif, Wolfgang   180

Salameh, Tariq   198
Samih, Hamza   80
Schmidberger, Rainer   113
Seebach, Hella   180

Türker, Uraz Cengiz   32

Ünlüyurt, Tonguç   32

Wotawa, Franz   48

Yenigün, Hüsnü   32
Yevtushenko, Nina   198
Yue, Tao   17